Collins
EUROPE HA

C000214439

Contents

Published by Collins
An imprint of HarperCollins Publishers
Westerhill Road
Bishopbriggs
Glasgow G64 2QT
www.harpercollins.co.uk

First published 2009

Fifth edition 2017

© HarperCollins Publishers Ltd 2017
Maps © Collins Bartholomew Ltd 2017

Collins® is a registered trademark of HarperCollins Publishers Ltd

All rights reserved. No part of this publication may be reproduced, stored in a retrieval system, or transmitted, in any form or by any means, electronic, mechanical, photocopying, recording or otherwise, without the prior permission in writing of the publisher and copyright owners.

The contents of this publication are believed correct at the time of printing. Nevertheless the publisher can accept no responsibility for errors or omissions, changes in the detail given or for any expense or loss thereby caused.

HarperCollins does not warrant that any website mentioned in this title will be provided uninterrupted, that any website will be error free, that defects will be corrected, or that the website or the server that makes it available are free of viruses or bugs. For full terms and conditions please refer to the site terms provided on the website.

A catalogue record for this book is available from the British Library

ISBN 978-0-00-821418-0

10 9 8 7 6 5 4 3 2 1

Printed in China by RR Donnelley APS Co Ltd

All mapping in this atlas is generated from Collins Bartholomew digital databases.
Collins Bartholomew, the UK's leading independent geographical information supplier, can provide a digital, custom, and premium mapping service to a variety of markets.
For further information:
Tel: +44 (0)141 306 3752
e-mail: collinsbartholomew@harpercollins.co.uk
or visit our website at: www.collinsbartholomew.com

If you would like to comment on any aspect of this book, please contact us at the above address or online.
e-mail: collinsmaps@harpercollins.co.uk
facebook.com/collinsref   @collins_ref

Country Capital city Country identification National flag	Official language	Currency	Speed limits 🚗 Motorway 🚗 Dual carriageway 🚜 Rural 🏘 Town	Emergency numbers 👮 Police 🔥 Fire ✚ Ambulance	Motoring Organisations
Austria Wien (A)	German	Euro = 100 cents	🚗 130 km/h 🚜 100 km/h 🏘 50 km/h	👮 112 🔥 112 ✚ 112	**ÖAMTC** Österreichischer Automobil-, Motorrad- und Touring Club www.oeamtc.at **ARBÖ** Auto-, Motor- und Radfahrerbund Österreichs www.arboe.at/home
Albania Tiranë (AL)	Albanian	Lek = 100 qindarka	🚗 110 km/h 🚗 90 km/h 🚜 80 km/h 🏘 40 km/h	👮 19/129 🔥 18/128 ✚ 17/127	**ACA** Klubi i Automobilit te Shqipërisë aca.al
Andorra Andorra la Vella (AND)	Catalan	Euro = 100 cents	🚜 60-90 km/h 🏘 50 km/h	👮 110/112 🔥 118/112 ✚ 116/112	**ACA** Automòbil Club d'Andorra www.aca.ad
Belgium Brussel/Bruxelles (B)	French Dutch Flemish	Euro = 100 cents	🚗 120 km/h 🚗 120 km/h 🚜 90 km/h 🏘 50 km/h	👮 112 🔥 112 ✚ 112	**RACB** Royal Automobile Club of Belgium www.racb.com **TCB** Touring Club Belgium https://www.touring.be/nl/
Bulgaria Sofia (BG)	Bulgarian	Lev	🚗 140 km/h 🚗 120 km/h 🚜 90 km/h 🏘 50 km/h	👮 166/112 🔥 160/112 ✚ 150/112	**UAB** Union of Bulgarian Motorists www.uab.org/home-2/
Bosnia and Herzogovina Sarajevo (BIH)	Bosnian Serbian Croatian	Konvertibilna Marka = 100 pfennig	🚗 120/130 km/h 🚗 100 km/h 🚜 80 km/h 🏘 60 km/h	👮 122 🔥 123 ✚ 124	**BIHAMK** Bosanskohercegovački auto-moto klub bihamk.ba
Belarus Minsk (BY)	Belarusian Russian	Belarusian Rouble	🚗 100-120 km/h 🚗 110 km/h 🚜 90 km/h 🏘 60 km/h	👮 02 🔥 01 ✚ 03	**BKA** Belarusian Auto Moto Touring Club www.bka.by
Switzerland Bern (CH)	German French Italian	Swiss Franc = 100 rappen/ centimes	🚗 120 km/h 🚗 100 km/h 🚜 80 km/h 🏘 50 km/h	👮 117/112 🔥 118/112 ✚ 144/112	**TCS** Touring Club Suisse/Schweiz/Svizzero https://www.tcs.ch **ACS** Automobil Club der Schweiz/Automobil club de Suisse www.acs.ch/ch-de/index.asp
Cyprus Lefkosia (Nicosia) (CY)	Greek Turkish (North Cyprus)	Euro = 100 cents North Cyprus New Lira = 100 new kurus	🚗 65-100 km/h 🚗 65/80 km/h 🏘 50/65 km/h	👮 199/112 🔥 199/112 ✚ 199/112 👮 155/112 🔥 199/112 ✚ 112 (N Cyprus)	**CAA** Cyprus Automobile Association www.caa.com.cy
Czechia (Czech Rep.) Praha (CZ)	Czech	Koruna = 100 hellers	🚗 130 km/h 🚗 110 km/h 🚜 90 km/h 🏘 50 km/h	👮 158/112 🔥 150/112 ✚ 155/112	**ÚAMK** Ústřední automotoklub České republiky www.uamk.cz **ACCR** Autoklub České Republiky www.autoklub.cz
Germany Berlin (D)	German	Euro = 100 cents	🚗 130 km/h 🚜 100 km/h 🏘 50 km/h	👮 110/112 🔥 112 ✚ 110/112	**ADAC** Allgemeiner Deutscher Automobil Club https://www.adac.de **AVD** Automobilclub von Deutschland https://www.avd.de
Denmark København (DK)	Danish	Krone = 100 øre	🚗 90-130 km/h 🚜 80 km/h 🏘 50 km/h	👮 112 🔥 112 ✚ 112	**FDM** Forenede Danske Motorejere www.fdm.dk

Country Capital city Country identification National flag	Official language	Currency	Speed limits 🛣 Motorway 🛤 Dual carriageway 🚗 Rural 🏘 Town	Emergency numbers 👮 Police 🔥 Fire ✚ Ambulance	Motoring Organisations
Spain Madrid E	Spanish Catalan Galician Basque	Euro = 100 cents	🛣 120 km/h 🛤 120 km/h 🚗 90 km/h 🏘 50 km/h	👮 112 🔥 112 ✚ 112	**RACE** Real Automóvil Club de España www.race.es
Estonia Tallinn EST	Estonian	Euro = 100 cents	🛤 90/110 km/h 🚗 90 km/h 🏘 50 km/h	👮 112 🔥 112 ✚ 112	
France Paris F	French	Euro = 100 cents	🛣 110/130 km/h 🛤 110 km/h 🚗 90 km/h 🏘 50 km/h	👮 17/112 🔥 18/112 ✚ 15/112	**Automobile Club Association** Association Française des Automobilistes https://www.automobile-club.org
Finland Helsinki FIN	Finnish Swedish	Euro = 100 cents	🛣 100/120 km/h 🛤 80/100 km/h 🚗 80/100 km/h 🏘 50 km/h	👮 112 🔥 112 ✚ 112	**AL** Autoliitto https://www.autoliitto.fi
Liechtenstein Vaduz FL	German	Swiss Franc = 100 rappen	🚗 80 km/h 🏘 50 km/h	👮 112 🔥 112 ✚ 112	**ACFL** Automobil Club Fürstentum Liechtenstein www.acfl.li
United Kingdom London GB	English	Pound = 100 pence	🛣 70 mph 🛤 70 mph 🚗 60 mph 🏘 30 mph	👮 999/112 🔥 999/112 ✚ 999/112	**AA** Automobile Association www.theaa.com **RAC** Royal Automobile Club www2.rac.co.uk
Greece Athina GR	Greek	Euro = 100 cents	🛣 130 km/h 🚗 90/110 km/h 🏘 50 km/h	👮 1571/112 🔥 112 ✚ 112	**ELPA** Automobile and Touring Club of Greece www.elpa.gr
Hungary Budapest H	Hungarian	Forint = 100 fillér	🛣 130 km/h 🛤 110 km/h 🚗 90 km/h 🏘 50 km/h	👮 107 🔥 112 ✚ 104	**Magyar Autóklub** www.autoklub.hu
Croatia (Hrvatska) Zagreb HR	Croat	Kuna = 100 Lipa	🛣 130 km/h 🛤 110 km/h 🚗 90 km/h 🏘 50 km/h	👮 192/112 🔥 193/112 ✚ 194/112	**HAK** Hrvatski Autoklub www.hak.hr
Italy Roma I	Italian	Euro = 100 cents	🛣 130 km/h 🛤 110 km/h 🚗 90 km/h 🏘 50 km/h	👮 113/112 🔥 115/112 ✚ 118/112	**ACI** Automobile Club d'Italia www.aci.it
Ireland Dublin IRL	Irish English	Euro = 100 cents	🛣 120 km/h 🚗 80/100 km/h 🏘 50 km/h	👮 999/112 🔥 999/112 ✚ 999/112	**AA Ireland** The Automobile Association Ireland Limited www.theaa.ie
Iceland Rekyavik IS	Icelandic	Icelandic Króna	🚗 90 km/h (tarmac) 🚗 80 km/h (untarred) 🏘 50 km/h	👮 112 🔥 112 ✚ 112	**FIB** Félag íslenskra bifreiðaeigenda www.fib.is

Country Capital city Country identification National flag	Official language	Currency	Speed limits ⊞ Motorway ⊞ Dual carriageway ⊥ Rural ⊥ Town	Emergency numbers ⚲ Police ♦ Fire + Ambulance	Motoring Organisations
Luxembourg Luxembourg (L)	Luxembourgish French German	Euro = 100 cents	⊞ 130 km/h ⊥ 90 km/h ⊥ 50 km/h	⚲ 113 ♦ 112 + 112	**ACL** Automobile Club du Grand-Duché de Luxembourg www.acl.lu
Lithuania Vilnius (LT)	Lithuanian	Euro = 100 cents	⊞ 110/130 km/h ⊞ 100/120 km/h ⊥ 70/90 km/h ⊥ 50 km/h	⚲ 112 ♦ 112 + 112	**LAS** Lietuvos automobilininkų sąjunga wlas.lt
Latvia Rīga (LV)	Latvian	Euro = 100 cents	⊞ 100 km/h ⊥ 90 km/h ⊥ 50 km/h	⚲ 02/112 ♦ 01/112 + 03/112	**LAMB** Latvijas Automoto Biedrība www.lamb.lv
Malta Valletta (M)	Maltese English	Euro = 100 cents	⊥ 80 km/h ⊥ 50 km/h	⚲ 112 ♦ 112 + 112	**RMF** www.rmfmalta.com/en/home.htm
Monaco Monaco (MC)	French	Euro = 100 cents	⊞ 110/130 km/h ⊞ 110 km/h ⊥ 90 km/h ⊥ 50 km/h	⚲ 112 ♦ 112 + 112	**ACM** Automobile Club de Monaco acm.mc/en/
Moldova Chişinău (MD)	Romanian Ukranian	Moldovan Leu = 100 bani	⊞ 110 km/h ⊥ 80 km/h ⊥ 50 km/h	⚲ 902 ♦ 901 + 903	**ACM** Automobil Club din Moldova www.acm.md
Macedonia (F.Y.R.O.M.) Skopje (MK)	Macedonian Albanian	Macedonian Denar = 100 deni	⊞ 120 km/h ⊞ 100 km/h ⊥ 80 km/h ⊥ 50 km/h	⚲ 192 ♦ 193 + 194	**AMSM** Avto Moto Sojuz na Makedonija www.amsm.mk
Montenegro Podgorica (MNE)	Serbian (Montenegrin) Albanian	Euro = 100 cents	⊞ 100 km/h ⊥ 80 km/h ⊥ 50 km/h	⚲ 92 ♦ 93 + 94	
Norway Oslo (N)	Norwegian	Norwegian Krone = 100 øre	⊞ 90-110 km/h ⊥ 80-90 km/h ⊥ 50 km/h	⚲ 112 ♦ 110 + 113	**KNA** Kongelig Norsk Automobilklub kna.no
The Netherlands Amsterdam (NL)	Dutch	Euro = 100 cents	⊞ 120/130 km/h ⊞ 100 km/h ⊥ 80 km/h ⊥ 50 km/h	⚲ 112 ♦ 112 + 112	**ANWB** Koninklijke Nederlandse Toeristenbond ANWB www.anwb.nl **KNAC** Koninklijke Nederlandsche Automobiel Club www.knac.nl
Portugal Lisboa (P)	Portuguese	Euro = 100 cents	⊞ 120 km/h ⊞ 100 km/h ⊥ 90-100 km/h ⊥ 50 km/h	⚲ 112 ♦ 112 + 112	**ACP** Automóvel Club de Portugal www.acp.pt

Country Capital city Country identification National flag	Official language	Currency	Speed limits 🚗 Motorway 🚗 Dual carriageway 🚜 Rural 🏘 Town	Emergency numbers 👮 Police 🔥 Fire ✚ Ambulance	Motoring Organisations
Poland Warszawa (PL)	Polish	Złoty = 100 groszy	140 km/h 100/120 km/h 90 km/h 50/60 km/h	997/112 998/112 999/112	**PZM** Polski Związek Motorowy www.pzm.pl
Kosovo Prishtinë (RKS)	Albanian Serbian	Euro = 100 cents	110-130 km/h 100 km/h 80-100 km/h 50 km/h	92/112 93/112 94/112	
Romania Bucureşti (RO)	Romanian	Romanian Leu = 100 bani	130 km/h 100 km/h 90/100 km/h 50 km/h	112 112 112	**ACR** Automobil Clubul Roman www.acr.ro
San Marino San Marino (RSM)	Italian	Euro = 100 cents	130 km/h 110 km/h 90 km/h 50 km/h	113/112 115/887777 118	**ACS** Automobile Club San Marino www.automobileclub.sm
Russia Moskva (RUS)	Russian	Rouble = 100 kopeck	110 km/h 90 km/h 60 km/h	02 01 03	**VOA** All-Russian Society of Motorists www.voa.ru
Sweden Stockholm (S)	Swedish	Swedish Krona = 100 öre	90-120 km/h 70-100 km/h 70-100 km/h 30-70 km/h	112 112 112	**M** Motormännens Riksförbund https://www.motormannen.se
Slovakia Bratislava (SK)	Slovak	Euro = 100 cents	90/130 km/h 90/130 km/h 90 km/h 50 km/h	158/112 150/112 155/112	**SATC** Slovenský Autoturist Klub www.satc.sk
Slovenia Ljubljana (SLO)	Slovene	Euro = 100 cents	130 km/h 110 km/h 90 km/h 50 km/h	113 112 112	**AMZS** Avto-Moto Zveza Slovenije https://www.amzs.si/
Serbia Beograd (SRB)	Serbian Albanian Hungarian	Serbian Dinar = 100 paras Euro = 100 cents	120 km/h 100 km/h 80 km/h 40/50 km/h	92 93 94	**AMSS** Auto-moto savez Srbije www.amss.org.rs
Turkey Ankara (TR)	Turkish	Turkish Lira = 100 kuru	120 km/h 110 km/h 90 km/h 50 km/h	155 110 112	**TTOK** Türkiye Turing ve Otomobil Kurumu www.turing.org.tr
Ukraine Kyiv (UA)	Ukrainian	Hryvnya = 100 kopiyok	130 km/h 110 km/h 90/110 km/h 60 km/h	02 01 03	**FAU** Federation Automobile de l'Ukraine fau.ua

Country	Official website	Tourism website
Albania	www.kryeministria.al/en	www.albania.al
Andorra	www.govern.ad	http://visitandorra.com/en
Austria	www.bundeskanzleramt.at	www.austria.info/uk
Belarus	www.belarus.by/en	http://eng.belarustourism.by
Belgium	www.belgium.be	Flanders: www.visitflanders.com
		Wallonia: www.opt.be
		www.eastbelgium.com
Bosnia and Herzegovina	www.fbihvlada.gov.ba	www.bhtourism.ba
Bulgaria	www.government.bg	http://bulgariatravel.org
Croatia	https://vlada.gov.hr	www.croatia.hr
Cyprus	www.cyprus.gov.cy	www.visitcyprus.com
Czechia (Czech Republic)	www.czech.cz/en/Home-en	www.czechtourism.com/home/
	www.vlada.cz/en/	
Denmark	www.denmark.dk	www.visitdenmark.com
Estonia	https://valitsus.ee	www.visitestonia.com/en
Finland	http://valtioneuvosto.fi	www.visitfinland.com
France	www.gouvernement.fr	uk.france.fr
Germany	www.deutschland.de	www.germany.travel
Greece	www.primeminister.gr	www.visitgreece.gr
Hungary	https://magyarorszag.hu	http://gotohungary.com
Iceland	www.iceland.is	www.visiticeland.com
Ireland	www.gov.ie	www.discoverireland.ie
Italy	www.governo.it	www.italia.it
Kosovo	www.rks-gov.net/	www.kosovo-info.com
Latvia	www.saeima.lv	www.latvia.travel/en
Liechtenstein	www.liechtenstein.li	www.tourismus.li/en
Lithuania	www.lrv.lt	www.lithuania.travel
Luxembourg	www.gouvernement.lu	www.visitluxembourg.com/en
Macedonia (F.Y.R.O.M.)	www.vlada.mk	www.exploringmacedonia.com
Malta	www.gov.mt	www.visitmalta.com
Moldova	www.moldova.md	www.turism.gov.md
Monaco	www.gouv.mc	www.visitmonaco.com
Montenegro	www.gov.me	www.visit-montenegro.com
Netherlands	www.overheid.nl	www.holland.com
Norway	norway.org.uk	www.visitnorway.com
Poland	www.premier.gov.pl	www.poland.travel
Portugal	www.portugal.gov.pt	www.visitportugal.com/en
Romania	www.guv.ro	romaniatourism.com
Russia	www.gov.ru	www.russiatourism.ru
San Marino	www.consigliograndeegenerale.sm	www.visitsanmarino.com
Serbia	www.srbija.gov.rs	www.serbia.travel
Slovakia	www.government.gov.sk	http://slovakia.travel/en
Slovenia	www.gov.si/en	www.slovenia.info
Spain	www.lamoncloa.gob.es	www.spain.info
Sweden	https://sweden.se	www.visitsweden.com/sweden
Switzerland	www.eda.admin.ch/aboutswitzerland	www.myswitzerland.com
Turkey	www.mfa.gov.tr	www.hometurkey.com
Ukraine	www.kmu.gov.ua	www.traveltoukraine.org
United Kingdom	https://www.gov.uk	www.visitbritain.com/en/EN/
Vatican City	www.vaticanstate.va	www.vaticanstate.va

International country identification

A	Austria	Autriche	Österreich
AL	Albania	Albanie	Albanien
AND	Andorra	Andorre	Andorra
B	Belgium	Belgique	Belgien
BG	Bulgaria	Bulgarie	Bulgarien
BIH	Bosnia and Herzegovina	Bosnie-et-Herzégovine	Bosnien und Herzegowina
BY	Belarus	Bélarus	Belarus
CH	Switzerland	Suisse	Schweiz
CY	Cyprus	la Chypre	Zypern
CZ	Czechia (Czech Republic)	Tchéquie (République tchèque)	Tschechien (Tschechische Republik)
D	Germany	Allemagne	Deutschland
DK	Denmark	Danemark	Dänemark
DZ	Algeria	Algérie	Algerien
E	Spain	Espagne	Spanien
EST	Estonia	Estonie	Estland
F	France	France	Frankreich
FIN	Finland	Finlande	Finnland
FL	Liechtenstein	Liechtenstein	Liechtenstein
FO	Faroe Islands	Iles Féroé	Färöer-Inseln
GB	United Kingdom GB & NI	Grande-Bretagne	Grossbritannien
GBA	Alderney	Alderney	Alderney
GBG	Guernsey	Guernsey	Guernsey
GBJ	Jersey	Jersey	Jersey
GBM	Isle of Man	île de Man	Insel Man
GBZ	Gibraltar	Gibraltar	Gibraltar
GR	Greece	Grèce	Griechenland
H	Hungary	Hongrie	Ungarn
HR	Croatia	Croatie	Kroatien
I	Italy	Italie	Italien
IRL	Ireland	Irlande	Irland
IS	Iceland	Islande	Island
L	Luxembourg	Luxembourg	Luxemburg
LT	Lithuania	Lituanie	Litauen
LV	Latvia	Lettonie	Lettland
M	Malta	Malte	Malta
MA	Morocco	Maroc	Marokko
MC	Monaco	Monaco	Monaco
MD	Moldova	Moldavie	Moldawien
MK	Macedonia (F.Y.R.O.M.)	Ancienne République yougoslave de Macédoine	Ehemalige jugoslawische Republik Mazedonien
MNE	Montenegro	Monténégro	Montenegro
N	Norway	Norvège	Norwegen
NL	Netherlands	Pays-Bas	Niederlande
P	Portugal	Portugal	Portugal
PL	Poland	Pologne	Polen
RKS	Kosovo	Kosovo	Kosovo
RO	Romania	Roumanie	Rumänien
RSM	San Marino	Saint-Marin	San Marino
RUS	Russia	Russie	Russland
S	Sweden	Suède	Schweden
SK	Slovakia	République slovaque	Slowakei
SLO	Slovenia	Slovénie	Slowenien
SRB	Serbia	Sérbie	Serbien
TN	Tunisia	Tunisie	Tunisien
TR	Turkey	Turquie	Türkei
UA	Ukraine	Ukraine	Ukraine

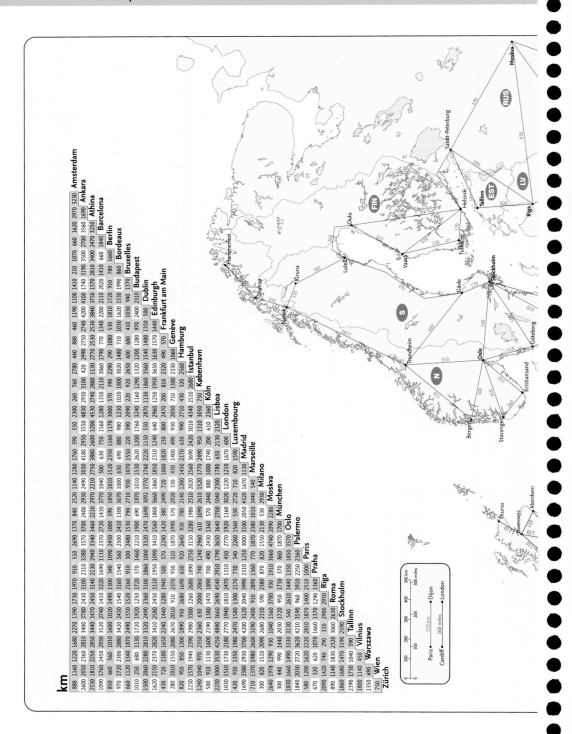

km

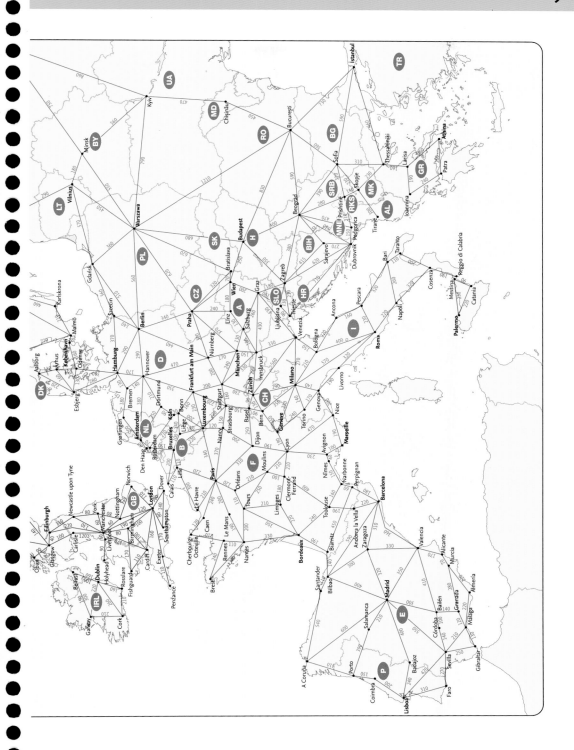

Motorway
Autoroute
Autobahn

 Motorway
Autoroute
Autobahn

 End of motorway
Fin d'autoroute
Ende der Autobahn

 End of motorway
Fin d'autoroute
Ende der Autobahn

 Lane for slow vehicles
Voie pour véhicules lents
Fahrsspur für langsam
  fahrende Fahrzeuge

 'Semi motorway'
Route pour automobiles
Kraftfahrstraße

 End of 'Semi motorway'
Fin de route pour automobiles
Ende der Kraftfahrstraße

 European route number
Numéro européen de route
Nummernschild für
  Europastraßen

 Priority road
Route prioritaire
Vorfahrtstraße

 End of priority road
Fin de route prioritaire
Ende der Vorfahrtstraße

 Priority over oncoming vehicles
Priorité par rapport aux véhicules
  venant en sens inverse
Gegenverkehr muss warten

 One way street
Rue à sens unique
Einbahnstraße

 One way street
Rue à sens unique
Einbahnstraße

 No through road
Route sans issue
Sackgasse

 Hospital
Hôpital
Krankenhaus

 Parking
Parking
Parkplatz

 Pedestrian crossing
Passage pour piétons
Fußgängerüberweg

 First aid post
Premiers secours
Erste Hilfe

 Information
Informations
Fremdenverkehrsbüro
  oder Auskunftsstelle

 Hotel/Motel
Hôtel
Autobahnhotel

 Restaurant
Restaurant
Autobahngasthaus

 Mechanical help
Assistance mécanique
Pannenhilfe

 Filling station
Station essence
Tankstelle

 Telephone
Téléphone
Fernsprecher

 Camping site
Zone de camping pour tentes
Zeltplatz

 Caravan site
Zone de camping pour caravanes
Wohnwagenplatz

 Youth hostel
Auberge de jeunesse
Jugendherberge

 Right bend
Virage à droite
Kurve (rechts)

 Left bend
Virage à gauche
Kurve (links)

 Double bend
Succession de virages
Doppelkurve

 Roundabout
Circulation en sens giratoire
Kreisverkehr

 Intersection with
  non-priority road
Intersection avec
  une route non-prioritaire
Vorfahrt

 Traffic merges from left
Rétrécissement sur la gauche
Verkehr ordnet sich von links ein

 Traffic merges from right
Rétrécissement sur la droite
Verkehr ordnet sich von
  rechts ein

 Road narrows
Chaussée rétrécie
Verengte Fahrbahn

 Road narrows at left
Chaussée rétrécie à gauche
Einseitig (links) verengte
  Fahrbahn

 Road narrows at right
Chaussée rétrécie à droite
Einseitig (rechts) verengte
  Fahrbahn

 Give way
Cédez le passage
Vorfahrt gewähren

 Slippery road
Chaussée glissante
Schleudergefahr

 Uneven road
Cassis
Unebene Fahrbahn

 Steep hill – descent
Descente ou montée à
  forte inclinaison
Gefälle

 Tunnel
Tunnel
Tunnel

 Opening bridge
Pont mobile
Bewegliche Brücke

 Road works
Travaux
Baustelle

Loose chippings
Projection de gravillons
Splitt, Schotter

 Level crossing with barrier
Passage à niveau avec barrière
Bahnübergang mit Schranken
oder Halbschranken

 Level crossing without barrier
Passage à niveau sans barrière
Unbeschrankter Bahnübergang

 Tram
Tramway
Straßenbahn

 'Count down' posts
Balises pour passage à niveau
Bake vor Autobahnausfahrt

 'Danger' level crossing
Attention au train !
Achtung Bahnübergang

 Low flying aircraft
Avions volant à basse altitude
Flugbetrieb

 Falling rocks
Chutes de pierre
Steinschlag

 Cross wind
Vents contraires
Seitenwind

 Quayside or river bank
Débouché sur un quai
ou une berge
Ufer

 Two-way traffic
Circulation dans les deux sens
Gegenverkehr

 Traffic signals ahead
Annonce de feux tricolores
Lichtzeichenanlage

 Pedestrians
Piétons
Fußgänger

 Children
Endroit fréquenté par
les enfants
Kinder

 Animals
Passages d'animaux
Viehtrieb, Tiere

 Wild animals
Passage d'animaux sauvages
Wildwechsel

 Other dangers
Autres dangers
Gefahrstelle

 Beginning of regulation
Début de prescription
Anfang

 Repetition sign
Panneau de rappel
Wiederholung

 End of regulation
Fin de prescription
Ende

 End of all restrictions
Fin de toutes les limitations
Ende sämtlicher Streckenverbote

 Halt sign
Stop
Halt! Vorfahrt gewähren!

 Customs
Douanes
Zollstelle

 No stopping ("clearway")
Arrêt interdit
Halteverbot

 No parking/waiting
Arrêt et stationnement interdits
Eingeschränktes Halteverbot

 Priority to oncoming vehicles
Priorité aux vehicules venant
en sens inverse
Dem Gegenverkehr Vorrang
gewähren!

 Use of horns prohibited
Avertisseur sonore interdit
Hupverbot

 Roundabout
Circulation en sens giratoire
Kreisverkehr

 Direction to be followed
Obligation de suivre la direction
indiquée par la flèche
Vorgeschriebene Fahrtrichtung

 Pass this side
Obligation de suivre la direction
indiquée par la flèche
Rechts/Links vorbei

 Minimum speed limit
Vitesse minimum autorisée
Vorgeschriebene
Mindestgeschwindigkeit

 End of minimum speed limit
Fin de vitesse minimum
Ende der vorgeschriebenen
Mindestgeschwindigkeit

 All vehicles prohibited
Interdit à tous les véhicules
Verbot für Fahrzeuge aller Art

 No entry for all vehicles
Interdiction d'entrer pour
tous les véhicules
Verbot der Einfahrt

 No right turn
Interdiction de tourner à droite
Rechtsabbiegen verboten

 No u-turns
Interdiction de faire demi-tour
Wendeverbot

 No entry for motor cars
Accès interdit aux
automobiles motorisées
Verbot für Kraftwagen

 No entry for all motor vehicles
Accès interdit à tous
les véhicules motorisés
Verbot für Kraftfahrzeuge
und Kraftwagen

 Motorcycles prohibited
Interdit aux motocycles
Verbot für Krafträder

 Mopeds prohibited
Interdit aux motocyclettes
Verbot für Mofas

 No overtaking
Interdiction de dépasser
Überholverbot für
Kraftfahrzeuge aller Art

 End of no overtaking
Fin d'interdiction de dépasser
Ende des Überholverbots für
Kraftfahrzeuge aller Art

 Maximum speed limit
Vitesse maximum
Zulässige
Höchstgeschwindigkeit

 End of speed limit
Fin de limitation de vitesse
Ende der zulässigen
Höchstgeschwindigkeit

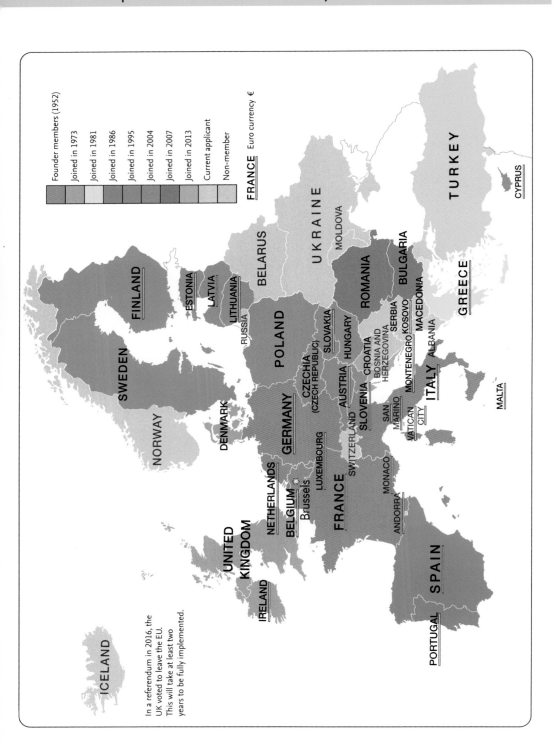

Founder members (1952)
Joined in 1973
Joined in 1981
Joined in 1986
Joined in 1995
Joined in 2004
Joined in 2007
Joined in 2013
Current applicant
Non-member

FRANCE Euro currency €

In a referendum in 2016, the UK voted to leave the EU. This will take at least two years to be fully implemented.

ICELAND

NORWAY

SWEDEN

FINLAND

ESTONIA

LATVIA

LITHUANIA

RUSSIA

BELARUS

UKRAINE

MOLDOVA

DENMARK

UNITED KINGDOM

IRELAND

NETHERLANDS

BELGIUM

Brussels

LUXEMBOURG

GERMANY

POLAND

CZECHIA (CZECH REPUBLIC)

SLOVAKIA

HUNGARY

AUSTRIA

SWITZERLAND

FRANCE

MONACO

ANDORRA

SPAIN

PORTUGAL

SLOVENIA

CROATIA

BOSNIA AND HERZEGOVINA

SAN MARINO

VATICAN CITY

ITALY

MONTENEGRO

SERBIA

KOSOVO

MACEDONIA

ALBANIA

ROMANIA

BULGARIA

GREECE

TURKEY

MALTA

CYPRUS

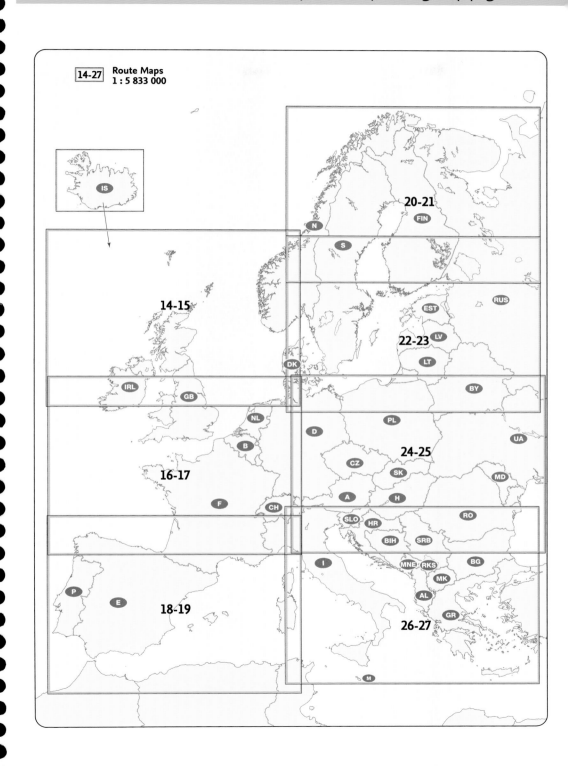

14-27 Route Maps
1 : 5 833 000

66° Straumnes Horn 22° 20° 18° 16° 62° Eysturoy
24°
Ísafjörður
Bjargtangar Reiphólsfjöll Grímsey FO
 e 81 FAROE Vágar
Reykhólssveit Rifstangi ISLANDS Sandoy
Breiðafjörður Húnaflói Sauðárkrókur Öxarfjörður (FØROYAR) Gluggarnir 610
Eyjafjörður Arctic Circle DK Suðuroy
Hafursfjörður Borgarnes Akureyri Fontur
Faxaflói
REYKJAVÍK 66° 60°
64° Keflavík 41k 1763 Ódáðahraun
Reykjanestá IS
Borgarfjörður
Bárðarbunga Seyðisfjörður
2009 Egilsstaðir
491 Grímsvötn 1719 Snæfell Breiðdalsvík
Vestmannaeyjar Sviahnúkar 1833
Vestmannaeyjar Surtsey Vík 2119 Breiðdalsvík
Kötlutangi Hvannadalshnúkur Vesturhorn
Skaftárós
20° 18° 16° 14°

56° 16° 14° 12° 10° Lewis Cape
Wrath
St Kilda 58° Western South Stornoway
Isles Harris Clisham The Minch
North Uist Ullapool
Benbecula Little Minch A835
South Uist Portree
Barra Skye 993 Carn Eighe
A L A N T I C Rum 1183 A87
Coll Beg Nevis
Tiree Fort William 1345
Mull A82 Grampian
Colonsay Oban A85 Lawers

O C E A N Jura Loch Stirling
Colonsay Lomond Greenock Glasgow
54° Islay Kintyre 873 Paisley Ham
Tory Island Malin Head Arran Kilmarnock
Errigal 753 Coleraine Campbeltown Ayr South
Letterkenny Londonderry Ballymoney Merrick Dumfries
Donegal (Derry) Ballymena 843 Stranraer
Donegal Magherafelt Larne Solway Firth
Bay Sligo Enniskillen Omagh Belfast Newtownards Workington
Nephin 806 Lough Lisburn Pe
Castlebar Erne Armagh Peel Snaefell Barrow-
765 Carrick-on- Monaghan 852 621 in-Furness
Lough Shannon Cavan Slieve Donard Isle Lancaster
Mask Longford Dundalk of Man DOUGLAS
Roscommon Dundalk B. Blackpool
Galway Athlone Mullingar Navan Drogheda IRISH Preston
52° Galway Drogheda SEA Southport
Bay IRL Tullamore DUBLIN Anglesey Colwyn St Helens
Ennis Naas Dun Holyhead Bay Liverpool
Loop Head Laoghaire Bangor Chester
Limerick Carlow Wicklow 926 Snowdon A55
16 Kilkenny (Yr Wyddfa) 1085 A5 Crew
Slea Tralee 920 Wrexh
Dingle Bay 1041 Clonmel Penycadair
Head Killarney N25 Shrew
14° 12° 10° 8° Waterford Wexford Cardi

0 100 200 km
0 50 100 miles

6° 4° 2° 0° 2° 4° 6° 8°

64°
Frohavet
Helløvik
Frøya
Smøla · Hitra
Slåttarøtindur · Kliksvík · Bordoy Tron
882
Torshavn · Kristiansund
65
Molde
Ålesund · Andalsnes
70
Stranda
Volda Storskrymten
1985
Måløy E39
Sandane 15
N
Floro
Gaidhøpiggen
2470 Dtt
Førde
Sula Hoyanger 55 Lilleha
Valdres
50
E16
E16 13 7
Bergen 1690 Hardangervidda
Hartoigan Numedal
40
Bømlo E39 E134 Møsvatnet Vestfjorddalen 60° San
Haugesund 11 Dramme Kor
Karmøy Setesdal 36 Tønsb
1443 Skien Ho
Sandnes · Stavanger 22 -grunn
E39 42
Egersund 42
Arendal
E18 36
E39 Kristiansand 58°
Lindesnes
SKAGERRAK Ska

Unst
Yell
Shetland
Islands
Foula · Lerwick

Fair Isle

Hoy Kirkwall
Orkney
Islands
Thurso

Moray Firth Elgin
Inverness
Peterhead
Ben Macdui
1309
Mountains Aberdeen

Dundee · Arbroath

Kirkcaldy
Firth of Forth
Edinburgh Berwick-upon-Tweed
Uplands
840 Galashiels
Hawick 816

Morpeth
Newcastle South Shields
upon Tyne Sunderland
Durham
Hartlepool
Darlington · Middlesbrough
Northallerton
GB
York Scarborough
Bradford · Leeds Bridlington
Huddersfield Kingston
Manchester upon Hull
Stockport · Sheffield Grimsby
on-Trent · Mansfield Lincoln

NORTH

SEA

Hirtshals
Hjørring
Brønderslev
Hanstholm
Thisted Aalborg
Skive · Hob
Struer
Viborg 16
Holstebro
Herning Silkeb
Ringkøbing Ikast Ska
62
DK 173
Varde Vejle
Frederici
Esbjerg Kolding Middelf
Ribe Odense
Rømø Haderslev Ny
Aabenraa
Syt · Sønderborg
Flensburg
Husum Schleswig
Eckernförde
Helgoländer Rendsburg
Bucht Heide · Kiel
Helgoland Nord Neumünster 54° Ba
Ostfriesische Inseln Cuxhaven Itzehoe
Nordfriesische Inseln

14° 12° 10° 8° 6°

Loop Head Ennis Tullamore Naas DUBLIN
L. Derg Dun Laoghaire
Slea Head 953 Tralee Limerick Carlow Wicklow Mts △926 Wicklow
Dingle Bay 1041△ 920△ Kilkenny M11 Anglesey Colwyn St Hel
Killarney N21 N20 Clonmel Holyhead Bay Southpo
N22 Cork Waterford Wexford A55 Snowdon △ 1085 Liver
N25 Carnsore (Yr Wyddfa) A5 Bangor Chest
Bantry Bay Pt A470 Shrews
St George's Channel Cardigan Penygadair 893△ Camb Wolverha
Fishguard Aberystwyth Bay Bir
Haverfordwest A487 Wor
Carmarthen A40 A70
Merthyr A449 Glouces
Swansea Neath Tydfil Chel
Port M4 Newport Cardi Bath
Talbot Bristol Channel
Barnstaple Exmoor M5 Sal
Taunton
Tiverton Yeov
Bodmin Exeter Dorchester Pod
A30 Dartmoor A30 Lyme Bo
Penzance Truro A38 Exmouth Weym
Land's End A30 Torquay
Isles of Scilly Plymouth Start Point
Lizard Point

ATLANTIC

OCEAN

Engli

Guernsey Cherbourg
Channel Octevil
Islands St Peter Po
CB Jersey
St Helier

Golfe de
St-Malo
Morlaix
Brest N12 St-Brieuc Dinan St-Mal
Guipavas
Quimper N164 Loudéac N12 D17
Quimperlé N24 Rennes
Lorient A11
Vannes E60 Châteaub
La Baule- N165
Escoublac E03
St-Nazaire Loire Nant
Vertou
A83
La Roche-
sur-Yon
Les Sables- E03
d'Olonne

100 200 km
0 50 100 miles
0

La Rochelle
A837
Rochefort SAIN

BAY OF BISCAY

Royan
MÉDOC
Mérignac Pessac Bo
Arcachon La Teste

Ferrol
A Coruña AP9 N
A8 E01 Gulf
Cabo Fisterra A6 Avilés Gijón/ of
A8 Xixón Costa Verde Gascony Dax Mon
A Estrada Santiago Cangas del Oviedo A63
Vilagarcía Lalín Lugo Narcea Mieres E70 Santander A824 Arcangues Bayonne
de Arousa AP53 A8 Pola de Torrelavega Dax
Pontevedra Monforte Siero Picos de Europa Algorta Irún A63 Orthez
de Lemos 2450 Bilbao Donostia Biarritz Pa
CORDILLERA CANTÁBRICA San Sal A1
Vigo Ponferrada El Telen 18 A7
Ourense León Laudio/Llodio E70 Adour
8° 6° 4° A8

IRL
E
14
18

ATLANTIC OCEAN

BAY OF BISCAY

Gulf of Gascony

CORDILLERA CANTÁBRICA

A Coruña · Ferrol · Cabo Fisterra · Avilés · Gijón/Xixón · Costa Verde · Oviedo · Santander · Torrelavega · Bilbao · Algorta · Laudio/Llodio · Donostia/San Sebastián · Biarritz · Irun · Pamplona/Iruña · Vitoria/Gasteiz · Logroño

Cangas del Narcea · Mieres · Pola de Siero · Picos de Europa · Mirando de Ebro · Tudela

Vigo · A Estrada · Santiago · Lugo · León · Palencia · Burgos · Aranda de Duero · Soria · Zar...

Vilagarcía de Arousa · Pontevedra · Ourense · Monforte de Lemos · Ponferrada · Calatayud

Viana do Castelo · Póvoa de Varzim · Matosinhos · Braga · Guimarães · Vila Real · Chaves · Bragança · Zamora · Valladolid · Segovia · Ávila · MADRID

Porto · São João da Madeira · Viseu · Salamanca · Guadalajara · Alcalá de Henares · Teruel

Ovar · Aveiro · Coimbra · Figueira da Foz · Leiria · Guarda · Covilhã · Plasencia · Cuenca

Marinha Grande · Torres Novas · Tomar · Castelo Branco · Cáceres · Talavera de la Reina · Toledo

Peniche · Torres Vedras · Caldas da Rainha · Santarém · Portalegre · Elvas · Badajoz · Mérida · Villanueva de la Serena · Almendralejo · LA MANCHA · Albacete · Requena · Val...

Amadora · Cascais · Almada · LISBOA · Vila Franca de Xira · Évora · Beja · Tomelloso · Ciudad Real · Valdepeñas · Hellín · Villena · Elda · Alicante/A...

Setúbal · Baía de Setúbal · SIERRA MORENA · Peñarroya-Pueblonuevo · Puertollano · Linares · Caravaca de la Cruz · Cieza · Orihuela · Elche/Elx · Murcia

ALGARVE · Lagos · Cabo de São Vicente · Faro · Olhão · Portimão · Huelva · Sevilla · Carmona · Córdoba · Andújar · Jaén · Úbeda · Lorca · Cartagena · Cabo de Palos

GULF OF CADIZ · Lebrija · Utrera · Écija · Martos · Granada · Guadix · Almería · Costa Blanca

Jerez de la Frontera · Sanlúcar de Barrameda · Morón de la Frontera · Antequera · Loja · Guadix · Aguilas

Cádiz · Chiclana de la Frontera · San Fernando · Ronda · Coín · Vélez-Málaga · El Ejido · Motril

Barbate de Franco · Cabo Trafalgar · Algeciras · Marbella · Estepona · Costa del Sol · Málaga · Golfo de Almería

Tanger · Strait of Gibraltar · Gibraltar · Ceuta · La Línea de la Concepción

MEDITERRANEAN

Larache · Ksar el Kebir · Tétouan · Chaouèn · Al Hoceima · Isla de Alborán · Baie d'Al Hoceima · Nador · Melilla · Oran · Mostaganem · Beni-Saf

Kénitra · RABAT · Souk el Arbaâ du Rharb · Taounate · Ghazaouet · Aïn Tembuchent · Sidi Bel Abbès

CASABLANCA · Khemisset · Sidi Kacem · Fès · Meknès · Taza · Taourirt · Oujda · Tlemcen

Map labels (France, Spain, Italy, Mediterranean Sea region):

Angoulême, Limoges, Clermont-Ferrand, Roanne, sur-Saône, Villeurbanne, Lyon, Riom, Thiers, Issoire, Ambérieu-en-Bugey, Sion, Martigny, Domodossola, Lugano, Com, Cluses, Mt Blanc, Annecy, Aosta, Novara, Mon, Mi

Périgueux, Brive-la-Gaillarde, Tulle, St-É..., Aurillac, Le Puy-en-Velay, Plomb du Cantal, Annonay, Aix-les-Bains, Albertville, Gran Paradiso, Ivrea, Vercelli, Pavia, Stradella

Bordeaux, Bergerac, Figeac, MASSIF CENTRAL, Mont Mézenc, Tournon-sur-Rhône, Vienne, Grenoble, Massif de la Vanoise, Torino, Alessandria, Asti, Voghera, Tortona, Novi Ligure

Mérignac, Pessac, Isle-Jourdain, Marmande, Agen, Cahors, Aubenas, Mende, Valence, Romans-sur-Isère, Dauphiné, Mt Pelvoux, Moncalieri, Acqui Terme, Genova

Dax, Mont-de-Marsan, Montauban, Moissac, Rodez, Millau, Pierrelatte, Alès, Montélimar, Digne-les-Bains, Gap, Briançon, Borgo San Dalmazzo, Cuneo, Cima, Rapallo, La Spe

Orthez, Pau, Auch, Colomiers, Gaillac, Albi, Carmaux, Cévennes, Bollène, Orange, Avignon, Cavaillon, Alpes-Maritimes, Argentera, Imperia, San Remo, Albenga, Savona, Golfo di

Tarbes, Lourdes, Muret, Toulouse, Montpellier, Nîmes, Arles, Salon-de-Provence, Aix-en-Provence, Grasse, Nice, MONTE CARLO, Antibes, Cannes, Côte d'Azur

PYRÉNÉES, Pic Long, St-Gaudens, Foix, Pamiers, Mazamet, Carcassonne, Béziers, Sète, CAMARGUE, Marignane, Marseille, Aubagne, St-Raphaël, Brignoles, LIGURIAN SEA

Huesca, ANDORRA LA VELLA, Cotiella, Pic d'Estats, Narbonne, Durban-Corbières, Golfe du Lion, La Ciotat, Toulon, Îles d'Hyères, Rosigna, Cap Corse, Monte Stello

zaragoza, Monzón, Lleida, Étang de Leucate, Leucate, Perpignan, Port-Vendres, Figueres, CORSE (CORSICA), Monte Padro, Monte Rotondo

Vic, Olot, Girona, Costa Brava, Ajaccio, Golfe de Sagone

Manresa, Igualada, Sabadell, Blanes, El Prat de Llobregat, Reus, Mataró, Barcelona, Capo Pertusato, Strait of Bonifacio

Ebro, Tortosa, Tarragona, Golf de Sant Jordi, Vilanova i la Geltrú, Golfo dell'Asinara, Porto Torres, Sassari, Alghero, Ozieri, Tempio Pausania

Castellón de la Plana/Castelló de la Plana, Burriana, MALLORCA (MAJORCA), Cap de Formentor, Menorca (Minorca), SARDEGNA (SARDINIA), Macomer, Nuor

sagunto, golfo de Valencia, Puig Major, Inca, Ciutadella, Maó (Mahón), ILLES BALEARS (BALEARIC ISLANDS), Palma de Mallorca, Manacor, Oristano, Terralba

encia, Eivissa (Ibiza), Illa de Cabrera, Guspini, Villacidro, San Gavino Monreale, Iglesias

Denia, Cabo de la Nao, Eivissa (Ibiza), Formentera, Carbonia, Cagliari, Quartu Sa, Sant'Antioco, Golfo di Cagliari

dorm, osa/La Vila Joiosa, Alacant

MEDITERRANEAN SEA

Scale:
0 — 100 — 200 km
0 — 50 — 100 miles

ALGER, Aïn Taya, Dellys, Collo, Skikda, Annaba, Mateur, Téboursouk

Ténès, Gouraya, Tipasa, Koléa, Boumerdes, Bejaïa, Jijel, El Milia, El Hadjar, El Tarf, El Kala, Béja, L'Ar

led Farès, Kerba, Cherchell, Blida, Larbaa, Tizi Ouzou, Akbou, El Arrouch, Azzaba, Dréan, Jendouba, Bi

Aïn Defla, Miliana, Médéa, Boufarik, Tazmalt, Bougaa, Mila, Guelma, Oued Zénati, Souk Ahras, Le Kef, Siliana

Ech Chélif, Berrouaghia, Sour el Ghozlane, Sétif, Chelghoum el Aïd, Constantine, Sédrata, M'Daourouch, Aïn Beïda, TN

elizane, Theniet El Had, Ksar el Boukhari, Sidi Aïssa, Bordj Bou Arréridj, El Eulma, Aïn M'Lila, El Aouinet, Mofsott

nora, Tissemsilt, Chahbounia, Mahdia, Aïn el Hadjel, M'Sila, Aïn Oulmene, Aïn Azel, Oum el Bouaghi, Khenchela, Kala

Tiaret, Souagueur, Aïn Oussera, Zenzach, Batna, DZ, Atlas Tellien, Chott el Hodna, Barika, Tébessa

hemaret, Frenda, Ksar Chellala, Bou Saâda, Zabrez, Khe

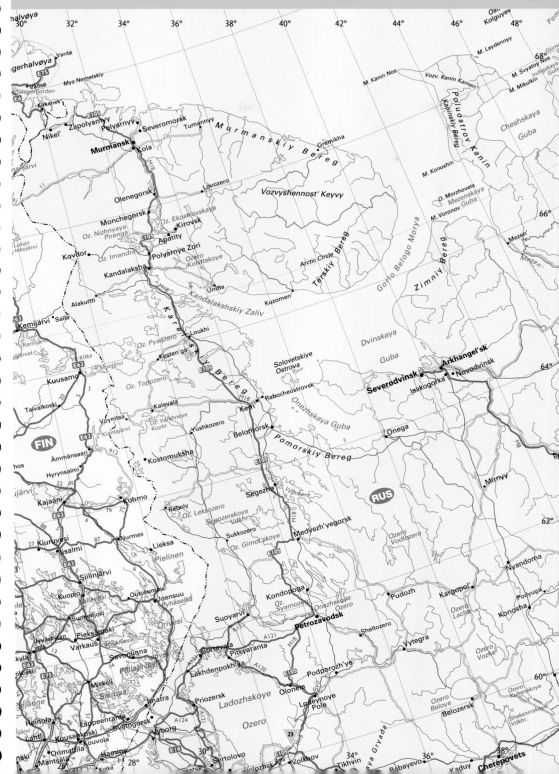

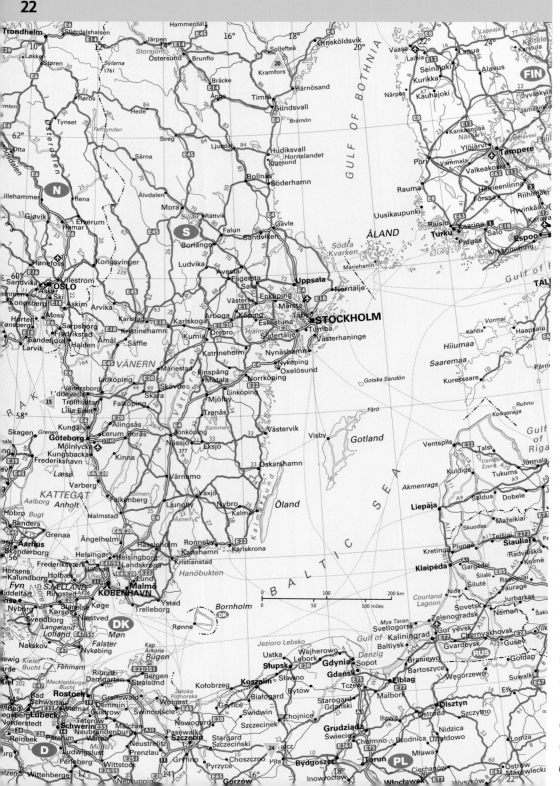

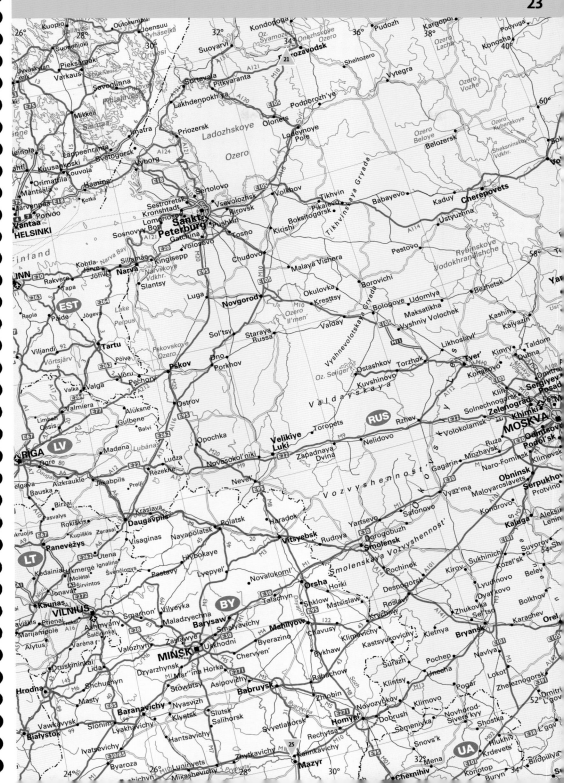

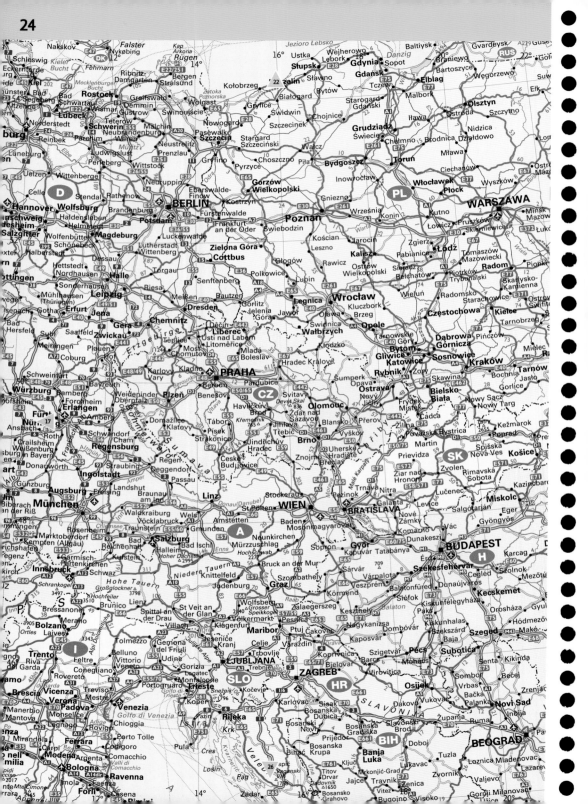

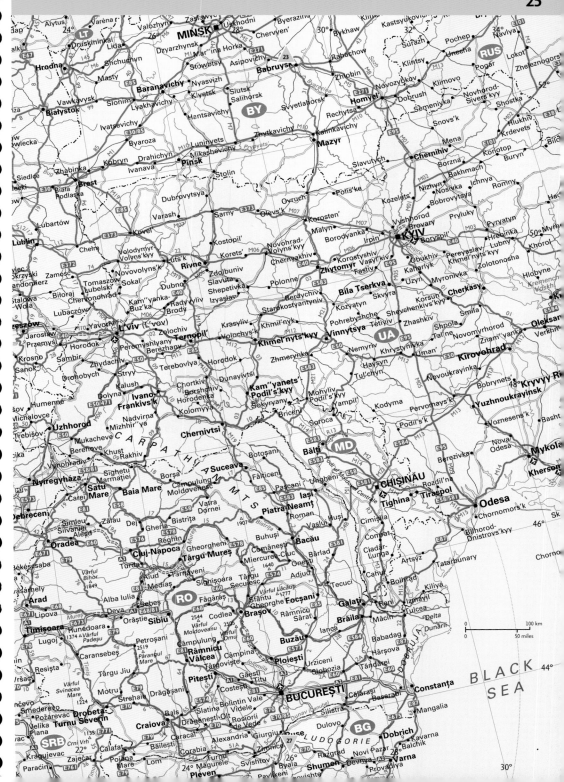

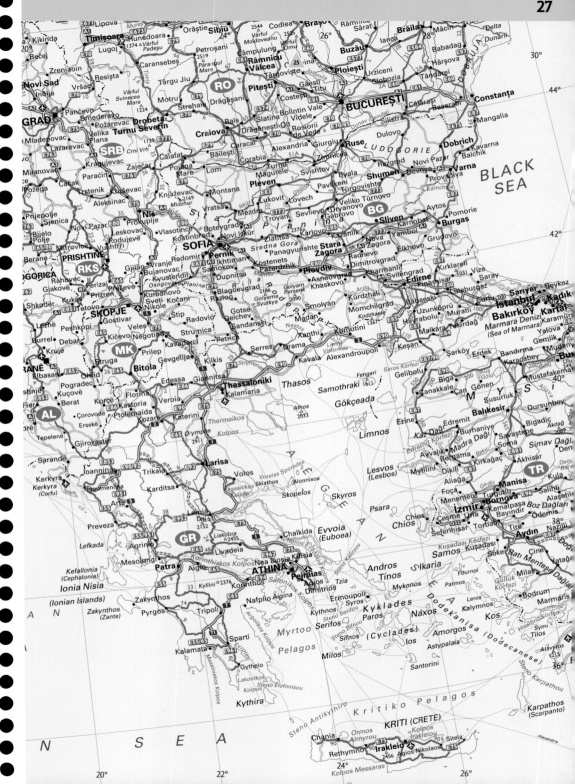

Road maps

Carte routière

Straßenkarten

	Road maps	Carte routière	Straßenkarten
E55	Euro route number	Route européenne	Europastraßennummer
A13	Motorway	Autoroute	Autobahn
	Motorway – toll	Autoroute à péage	Gebührenpflichtige Autobahn
37	Motorway junction – full access	Echangeur d'autoroute avec accès libre	Autobahnauffahrt mit vollem Zugang
12	Motorway junction – restricted access	Echangeur d'autoroute avec accès limité	Autobahnauffahrt mit beschränktem Zugang
	Motorway services	Aire de service sur autoroute	Autobahnraststätte
309	Main road – dual carriageway	Route principale à chaussées séparées	Hauptstraße - Zweispurig
	Main road – single carriageway	Route principale à une seule chaussée	Hauptstraße - Einspurig
516	Secondary road – dual carriageway	Route secondaire à chaussées séparées	Zweispurige Nebenstraße
	Secondary road – single carriageway	Route secondaire à une seule chaussée	Einspurige Nebenstraße
	Motorway tunnel	Tunnel (autoroute)	Tunnel (Autobahn)
	Main road tunnel	Tunnel (route principale)	Tunnel (Hauptstraße)
	Motorway/road under construction	Autoroute/route en construction	Autobahn/Straße im Bau
	Road toll	Route à péage	Gebührenpflichtige Straße
2587	Mountain pass (height in metres)	Col (altitude en mètres)	Pass (Höhe in Metern)
	International airport	Aéroport international	Internationaler Flughafen
	Railway	Chemin de fer	Eisenbahn
	Tunnel	Tunnel	Tunnel
Rotterdam	Car ferry	Bac pour autos	Autofähre
▲2587	Summit (height in metres)	Sommet (altitude en mètres)	Berg (Höhe in Metern)
▲	Volcano	Volcan	Vulkan
	Canal	Canal	Kanal
	International boundary	Frontière d'état	Landesgrenze
	Disputed International boundary	Frontière litigieuse	Umstrittene Staatsgrenze
D	Country abbreviation	Abréviation du pays	Nationalitätszeichen
	Urban area	Zone urbaine	Stadtgebiet
28	Adjoining page indicator	Indication de la page contiguë	Randhinweis auf Folgekarte
	National Park	Parc national	Nationalpark
	Scenic route	Parcours pittoresque	Landschaftlich schöne strecke

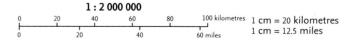

1 : 2 000 000

0	20	40	60	80	100 kilometres

0	20	40	60 miles

1 cm = 20 kilometres
1 cm = 12.5 miles

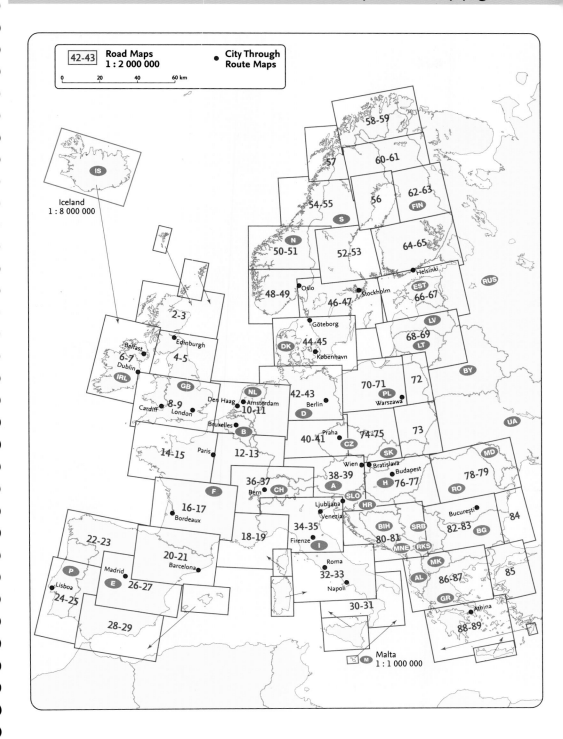

Road Maps
1 : 2 000 000

42-43

City Through Route Maps

0   20   40   60 km

Iceland
1 : 8 000 000

IS

58-59

57

60-61

54-55

56

62-63

FIN

S

N

50-51

52-53

64-65

Helsinki

48-49

Oslo

46-47

Stockholm

EST

66-67

RUS

2-3

Göteborg

LV

68-69

LT

Belfast

Edinburgh

DK

44-45

BY

6-7

Dublin

4-5

København

IRL

GB

NL

42-43

70-71

72

Cardiff

8-9

Den Haag

Amsterdam

10-11

Berlin

PL

Warszawa

London

Bruxelles

D

B

14-15

Paris

12-13

40-41

Praha

74-75

73

CZ

SK

UA

MD

38-39

Wien

Bratislava

Budapest

36-37

A

H

76-77

78-79

Bern

CH

SLO

RO

16-17

Ljubljana

HR

Bucureşti

Bordeaux

Venezia

BIH

SRB

82-83

84

22-23

18-19

34-35

Firenze

I

80-81

BG

MNE

RKS

P

20-21

Madrid

Barcelona

E

26-27

Roma

MK

85

Lisboa

32-33

AL

86-87

24-25

Napoli

GR

28-29

30-31

Athina

88-89

Malta

M

1 : 1 000 000

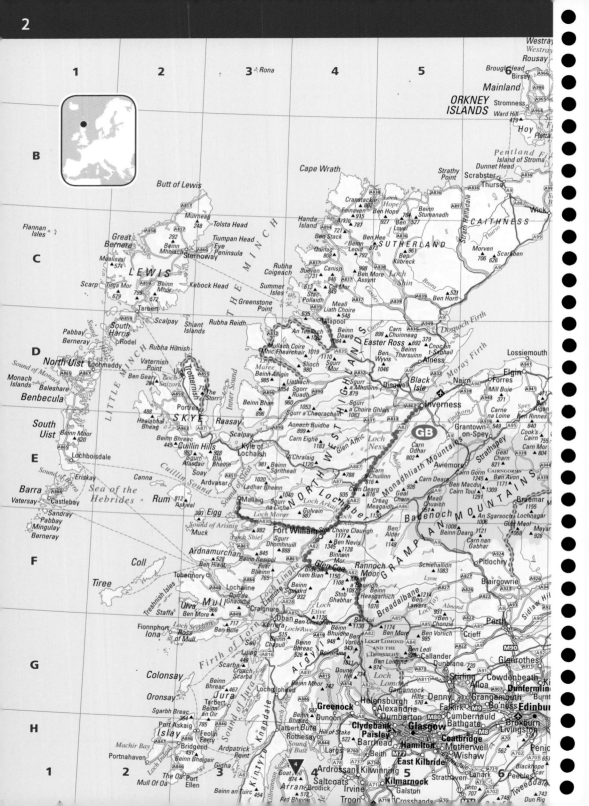

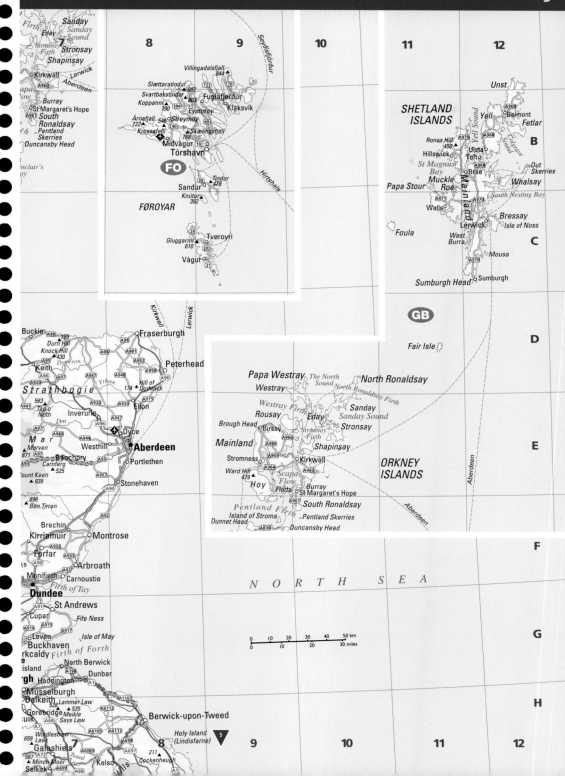

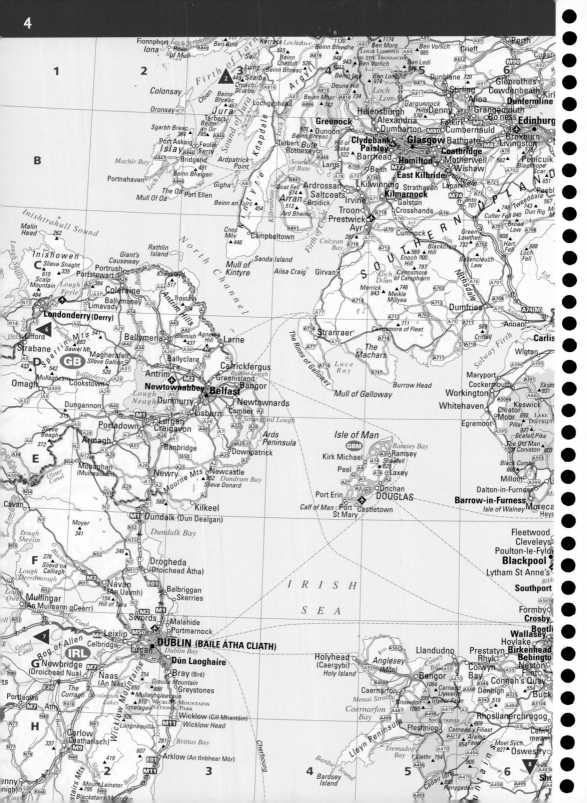

A B C D E F G

Scotland / Northern Ireland / Ireland map

Scotland (top)
Ben Cruachan, Beinn Bhuidhe 948, Ben More 966, Ben Lui, Loch Lomond, Ben Vorlich 943, Loch Awe, Oban, Kerrera, Seil, Luing, Scarba, Jura, Beinn an Oir, Craighouse, Islay, Port Askaig, Bridgend, Port Ellen, The Oa, Mull of Oa, Colonsay, Oronsay, Staffa, Iona, Ross of Mull, Finnphort, Portnahaven, Machir Bay, Gigha, Ardpatrick Point, Tarbert, Crinan, West Loch Tarbert, Knapdale, Kintyre, Campbeltown, Mull of Kintyre, Sanda Island, Ailsa Craig, Kilbrannan Sound, Arran, Goat Fell 874, Brodick, Ard Bheinn 512, Rothesay, Bute, Largs, Firth of Clyde, Dunoon, Helensburgh, Greenock, Ardrossan, Saltcoats, Irvine, Troon, Prestwick, Ayr, Girvan, Stranraer, The Rinns of Galloway, Mull of Galloway, Luce Bay, Wigtown Bay, Douglas, Isle of Man, Port Erin, Port St Mary, Liverpool (Birkenhead)

GB

North Channel / Northern Ireland
Rathlin Island, Giant's Causeway, Portrush, Portstewart, Coleraine, Ballymoney, Ballycastle, Knocklayd 517, Antrim Hills, Agnew's Hill 484, Trostan 554, Slemish Hill 437, Larne, Carrickfergus, Greenisland, Newtownabbey, Belfast, Lisburn, Bangor, Newtownards, Comber, Ards Peninsula, Strangford Lough, Downpatrick, Newcastle, Slieve Donard 852, Mourne Mts, Kilkeel, Dundrum Bay, Dundalk (Dún Dealgan), Dundalk Bay, Ballyclare, Antrim, Ballymena, Lough Neagh, Magherafelt, Maghera, Slieve Gallion 528, Cookstown, Dungannon, Portadown, Lurgan, Craigavon, Banbridge, Armagh, Newry Mts, Slieve, Monaghan (Muineachán), Moyer 341

Londonderry (Derry), Sperrin Mts, Sawel Mt 683
Limavady, Roe, Dungiven, Strabane, Omagh, Enniskillen, Upper Lough Erne, Lower Lough Erne, Lough Macnean, Doughmt, Slieve Beagh 372, Cavan, Carrick-on-Shannon, Clogher

GB
IRL

Donegal / NW Ireland
Inishowen, Malin Head, Scalp Mountain 615, Inishtrahull Sound, Lough Swilly, Lough Foyle, Letterkenny, Glenveagh National Park, Muckish Mountain 670, Errigal 752, Derryveagh Mts, Dooish 652, Horn Head, Gweedore, The Rosses, Croaghgorm 598, Blue Stack Mts, Blue Stack 674, Aghla Mountain 593, Croagh 504, Sligeanakila 494, Slieve League 601, Donegal, Donegal Bay, Lough Derg, Lough Melvin, Tory Sound, Tory Island, Aran Island, Rosses Bay, Gweebarra Bay, Loughros More Bay, Slieve Gamph or the Ox Mts, Truskmore 647, Benbulbin 526, Benwiskin, Lough Gill, Sligo (Sligeach), Lough Arrow, Lough Key, Lough Gara, Lough Allen, Knockalongy 542, Ballina (Béal an Átha), Killala Bay, Nephin Beg Range, Nephin 806, Nephin Beg 627, Maumakeogh 380, Slieve Car 721, Corraun Peninsula 714, Achill Island, Achill Head, Slieve Mór 671, Croaghaun 688, Blacksod Bay, Broad Haven, Benmore or Ballycroy National Park, Maumtrasna

ATLANTIC OCEAN

Scale bars: 100 km / 60 miles; 50 km / 30 miles

Iceland inset (IS)
Tórshavn, Fontur, Grímsey, Straumnes, Horn, Rifstangi, Kópasker, Ísafjörður, Akureyri, Sauðárkrókur, Borgarfjörður, Seyðisfjörður, Egilsstaðir, Breiðdalsvík, Vesturhorn, Langjökull, Hofsjökull 1763, Vatnajökull 2119, Öræfajökull 2109, Hvannadalshnúkur, Vestmannaeyjar, Surtsey, Vík, Kötlutangi, Svartsengi, Reykjavík, Keflavík, Reykjanestá, Borgarnes, Snæfell, Breiðafjörður, Bjargtangar, Húnaflói, Faxaflói, Kerlingarfjöll, Bárðarbunga 2009, Hekla 1491, Öskjufell

ATLANTIC OCEAN

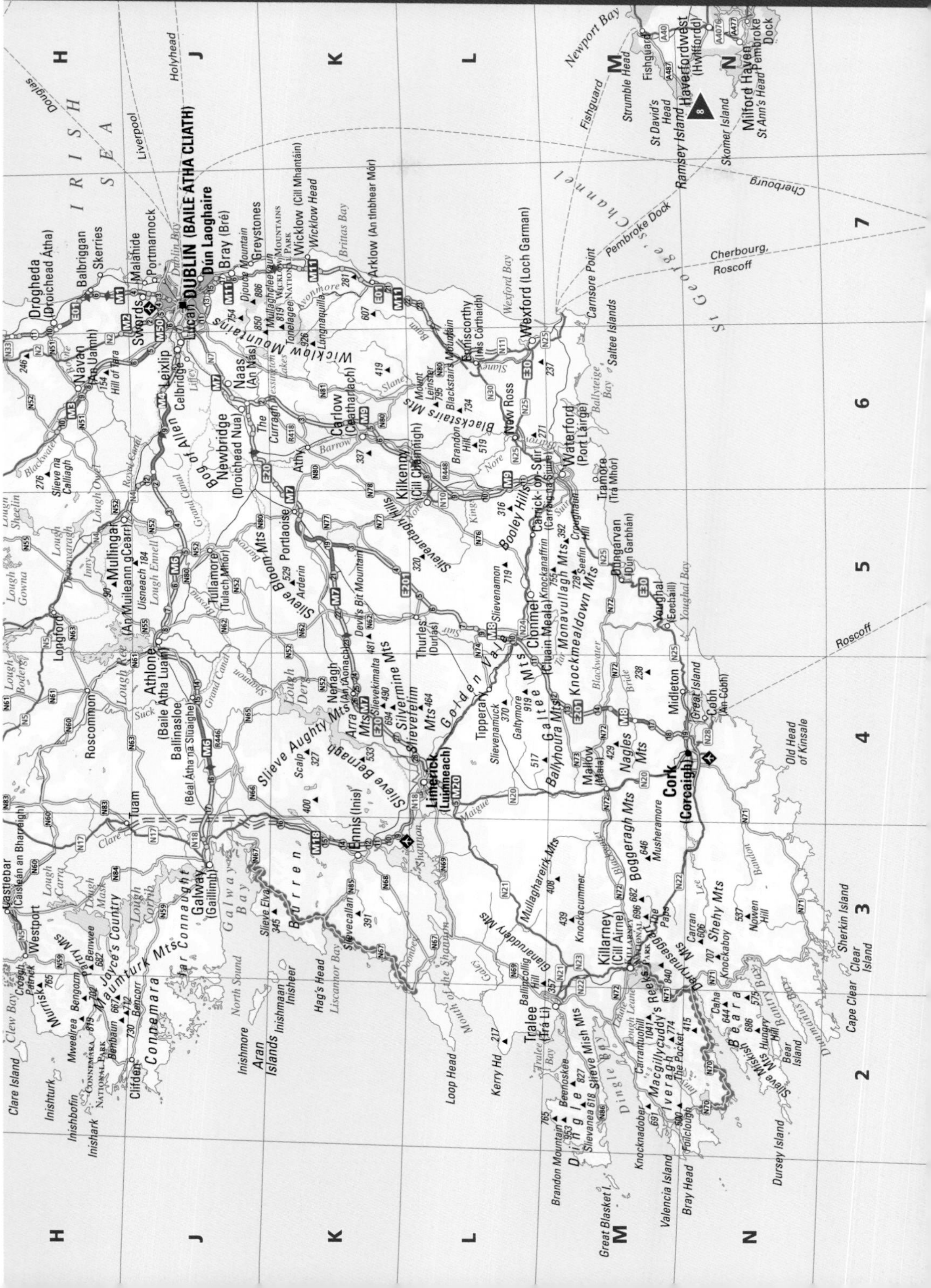
H
J
K
L
M
N
2
3
4
5
6
7
IRISH SEA
Douglas
Liverpool
Holyhead
DUBLIN (BAILE ÁTHA CLIATH)
Dún Laoghaire
Drogheda (Droichead Átha)
Balbriggan
Skerries
Malahide
Portmarnock
Swords
Lucan
Leixlip
Celbridge
Navan (An Uaimh)
Hill of Tara
Bray (Bré)
Greystones
Wicklow (Cill Mhantáin)
Wicklow Head
Wicklow Mountains
Arklow (An tInbhear Mór)
Brittas Bay
Naas (An Nás)
Newbridge (Droichead Nua)
Bog of Allen
The Curragh
Carlow (Ceatharlach)
Athy
Kilkenny (Cill Chainnigh)
Blackstairs Mts
Mount Leinster
Enniscorthy (Inis Corthaidh)
Wexford (Loch Garman)
Wexford Bay
Carnsore Point
Saltee Islands
New Ross
Waterford (Port Láirge)
Tramore (Trá Mhór)
Carrick-on-Suir
Dungarvan (Dún Garbhán)
Youghal (Eochaill)
Youghal Bay
Cobh (An Cóbh)
Great Island
Midleton
Cork (Corcaigh)
Old Head of Kinsale
Mullingar (An Muileann gCearr)
Tullamore (Tulach Mhór)
Portlaoise
Slieve Bloom Mts
Longford
Athlone (Baile Átha Luain)
Lough Ree
Roscommon
Ballinasloe (Béal Átha na Sluaighe)
Tuam
Galway (Gaillimh)
Galway Bay
Castlebar (Caisleán an Bharraigh)
Westport
Clew Bay
Croagh Patrick
Clifden
Connemara
Joyce's Country
Maumturk Mts
Iar Connaught
Aran Islands
Inishmore
Inishmaan
Inisheer
Burren
Ennis (Inis)
Limerick (Luimneach)
Shannon
Mouth of the Shannon
Loop Head
Kerry Hd
Tralee (Trá Lí)
Dingle
Slieve Mish Mts
Killarney (Cill Airne)
Macgillycuddy's Reeks
Carrantuohill
Iveragh
Valencia Island
Bray Head
Great Blasket I.
Brandon Mountain
Beara
Bantry Bay
Dursey Island
Cape Clear
Clear Island
Sherkin Island
Mallow (Mala)
Nagles Mts
Boggeragh Mts
Galtee Mts
Ballyhoura Mts
Knockmealdown Mts
Monavullagh Mts
Comeragh Mts
Clonmel (Cluain Meala)
Tipperary
Golden Vale
Thurles (Durlas)
Nenagh (An tAonach)
Slieve Aughty Mts
Slieve Bernagh
Silvermine Mts
Devil's Bit Mountain
Slievenamon
St George's Channel
Pembroke Dock
Cherbourg, Roscoff
Rosslare
Fishguard
Newport Bay
Strumble Head
St David's Head
Ramsey Island
Haverfordwest (Hwlffordd)
Skomer Island
Milford Haven
St Ann's Head
Pembroke
8

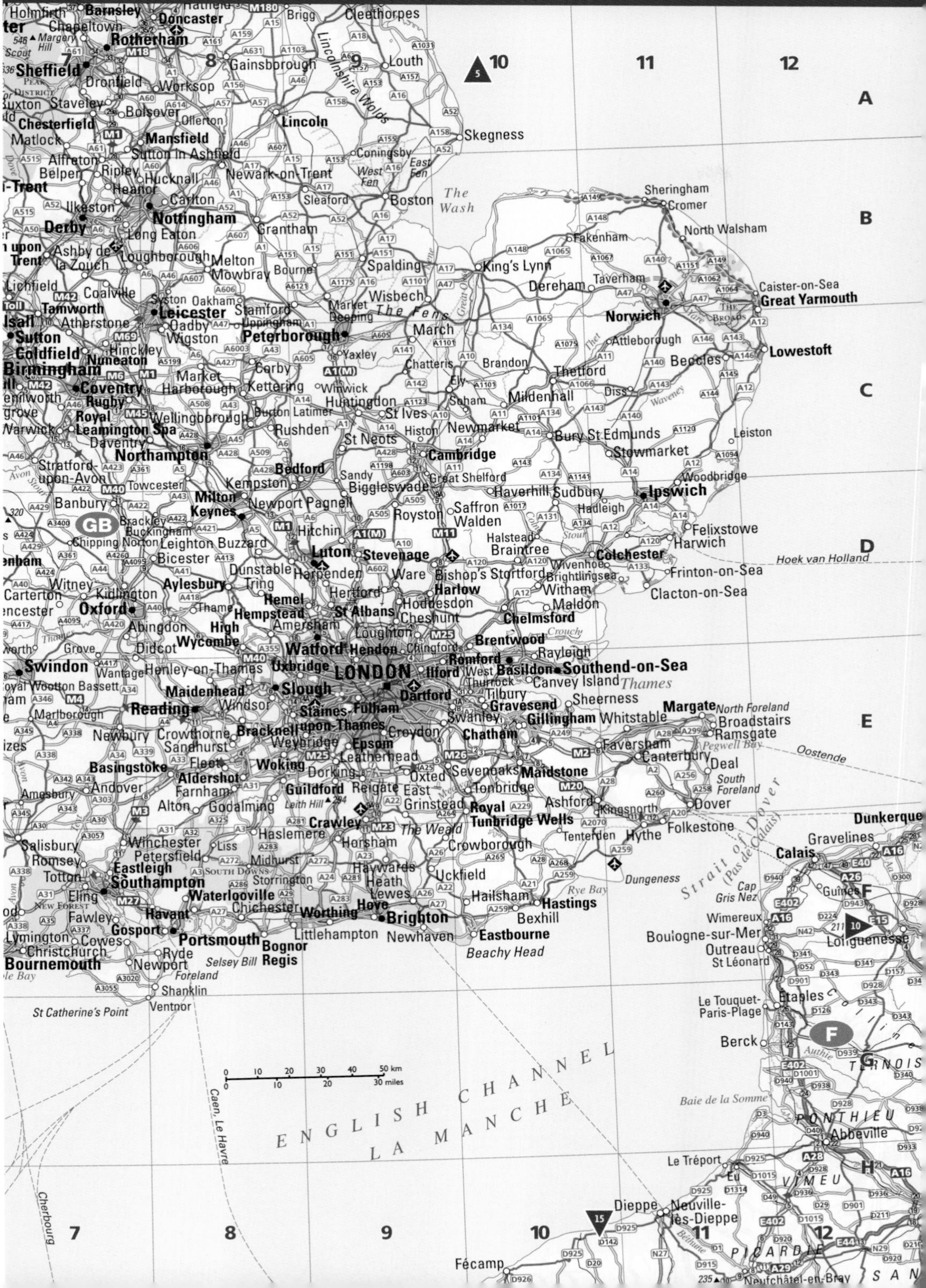
Barnsley
Doncaster
Rotherham
Sheffield
Cleethorpes
Brigg
Gainsborough
Louth
Lincolnshire Wolds
Worksop
Chesterfield
Bolsover
Lincoln
Skegness
Mansfield
Sutton in Ashfield
Coningsby
Newark-on-Trent
Matlock
Alfreton
Belper
Ripley
Hucknall
Heanor
West Fen
East Fen
Sleaford
Boston
The Wash
Ilkeston
Carlton
Nottingham
Derby
Long Eaton
Grantham
Sheringham
Cromer
North Walsham
Fakenham
Ashby de la Zouch
Loughborough
Melton Mowbray
Bourne
Spalding
King's Lynn
Dereham
Taverham
Caister-on-Sea
Great Yarmouth
Lichfield
Coalville
Tamworth
Syston
Oakham
Leicester
Stamford
Market Deeping
Wisbech
The Fens
Norwich
Atherstone
Oadby
Wigston
Uppingham
Peterborough
March
Attleborough
Sutton Coldfield
Nuneaton
Hinckley
Yaxley
Lowestoft
Beccles
Birmingham
Corby
Chatteris
Brandon
Thetford
Coventry
Market Harborough
Kettering
Winwick
Ely
Diss
Kenilworth
Rugby
Huntingdon
Soham
Mildenhall
Royal Leamington Spa
Wellingborough
Burton Latimer
St Ives
Warwick
Daventry
Rushden
St Neots
Histon
Newmarket
Bury St Edmunds
Leiston
Northampton
Cambridge
Stowmarket
Stratford-upon-Avon
Bedford
Sandy
Biggleswade
Great Shelford
Woodbridge
Towcester
Kempston
Haverhill
Sudbury
Ipswich
Banbury
Milton Keynes
Newport Pagnell
Royston
Saffron Walden
Hadleigh
GB
Brackley
Buckingham
Hitchin
Felixstowe
Chipping Norton
Leighton Buzzard
Halstead
Harwich
Bicester
Luton
Stevenage
Braintree
Colchester
Hoek van Holland
Dunstable
Harpenden
Ware
Bishop's Stortford
Wivenhoe
Brightlingsea
Frinton-on-Sea
Witney
Kidlington
Aylesbury
Tring
Hertford
Harlow
Witham
Clacton-on-Sea
Oxford
Thame
Hemel Hempstead
St Albans
Hoddesdon
Maldon
Abingdon
High Wycombe
Amersham
Cheshunt
Chelmsford
Loughton
Brentwood
Swindon
Grove
Didcot
Watford
Hendon
Chingford
Romford
Rayleigh
Wantage
Henley-on-Thames
Uxbridge
LONDON
Ilford
Basildon
Southend-on-Sea
Wootton Bassett
Maidenhead
Slough
West Thurrock
Canvey Island
Thames
Dartford
Tilbury
Windsor
Reading
Staines-upon-Thames
Fulham
Gravesend
Sheerness
Margate
North Foreland
Broadstairs
Marlborough
Swanley
Gillingham
Whitstable
Ramsgate
Newbury
Crowthorne
Bracknell
Croydon
Chatham
Pegwell Bay
Sandhurst
Weybridge
Epsom
Faversham
Canterbury
Oostende
Leatherhead
Basingstoke
Fleet
Woking
Dorking
Sevenoaks
Maidstone
Deal
Aldershot
Oxted
South Foreland
Andover
Farnham
Guildford
Reigate
East Grinstead
Tonbridge
Amesbury
Alton
Godalming
Leith Hill
Royal Tunbridge Wells
Ashford
Kingsnorth
Dover
Crawley
Dunkerque
Salisbury
Winchester
Haslemere
Horsham
The Weald
Tenterden
Hythe
Folkestone
Gravelines
Romsey
Petersfield
Liss
Midhurst
Crowborough
Strait of Dover
(Pas de Calais)
Calais
Eastleigh
Haywards Heath
Southampton
South Downs
Storrington
Uckfield
Dungeness
Totton
Lewes
Rye Bay
Cap Gris Nez
Guînes
Eling
New Forest
Waterlooville
Hailsham
Hastings
Fawley
Havant
Chichester
Worthing
Hove
Brighton
Bexhill
Wimereux
Gosport
Portsmouth
Littlehampton
Newhaven
Eastbourne
Lymington
Cowes
Bognor Regis
Boulogne-sur-Mer
Longuenesse
Christchurch
Ryde
Beachy Head
Outreau
Bournemouth
Newport
Selsey Bill
Foreland
St Léonard
Shanklin
Ventnor
St Catherine's Point
Le Touquet-Paris-Plage
Étaples
F
Berck
Authie
0 10 20 30 40 50 km
0 10 20 30 miles
ENGLISH CHANNEL
LA MANCHE
Caen, Le Havre
Baie de la Somme
PONTHIEU
Abbeville
Le Tréport
Eu
VIMEU
Cherbourg
Dieppe
Neuville-lès-Dieppe
PICARDIE
Fécamp
Neufchâtel-en-Bray
7
8
9
10
11
12
A
B
C
D
E
F
G
H

1 2 3 4 5 6

NORTH SEA

NORDSEE

Newcastle upon Tyne

Kingston upon Hull

0 10 20 30 40 50 km
0 10 20 30 miles

Wadden

Terschelling

Vlieland

Engelschmangat

Texel

Den Burg

Den Helder

Anna Paulowna

Schagen Medemblik

Langedijk

Bergen Alkmaar Hoorn

Heiloo

Castricum Marker

Heemskerk Wormerveer

Beverwijk

ZUID-KENNEMERLAND Zaandam

Haarlem AMSTERDAM

Heemstede

Hoofddorp

Noordwijk-Binnen

Katwijk aan Zee Leiden Hilversum

Wassenaar Zoetermeer Utrecht

'S-GRAVENHAGE
(DEN HAAG)

Monster Delft Gouda Veen

's-Gravenzande

Europoort Rotterdam

Vlaardingen

Spijkenisse

Dordrecht

Middelharnis

Made

Zierikzee Zevenbergen Breda Oosterhout

Tilburg

Middelburg Goes Roosendaal

Vlissingen Essen Eindho

Terneuzen Zandvliet Brecht Turnhout

Knokke-Heist Zelzate Antwerpen Kasterlee

Blankenberge Damme (Anvers) Geel

De Haan Zwijndrecht Borsbeek

Oostende (Ostend) Brugge Beernem Lier Beringen

(Bruges) Wichelen Mechelen

Westende Gistel Gent Dendermonde (Malines)

Koksijde (Gand) Zemst Hasselt

Staden St-Martens-Latem Aalst (Alost) Schaerbeek

Dunkerque Roeselare Tielt BRUXELLES St-Truiden

Gravelines (Roulers) Deinze (BRUSSEL)

Calais Zulte Kortrijk Anzegem Dilbeek

Guînes Wormhout Ieper Halle Grez-Doiceau

Cap Gullegem Wevelgem Brakel Braine- Hannut

Gris Nez Comines Mouscron Alleud

Wimereux Longuenesse Bailleul Tourcoing Soignies Eghezée

Boulogne-sur-Mer Roubaix Hernex Tubize

Outreau Lille Mons Namur

St Léonard Seclin Tournai Leuze-en- CONDRO

Étaples Béthune Hainaut

Le Touquet- Divion Anzin Charleroi Ciney

Paris-Plage Avion

Berck Arras Mons Namur

Baie de la Rochefort

Somme Abbeville Maubeuge

PONTHIEU Cambrai Aulnoye-Aymeries

Le Doullens L'Eau d'Heure Fagne

Tréport Caudry Avesnes- Couvin

Eu Albert sur-Helpe

VIMEU Fourmies Revin

Amiens PÉronne VERMANDOIS Oise Plateau de

Margate North Foreland

Broadstairs

Ramsgate

Canterbury Pegwell Bay

Deal

South

Foreland

Dover

Folkestone

Strait of Dover
(Pas de Calais)

Sheringham

Cromer

North Walsham

Caister-on-Sea

Norwich Great Yarmouth

Attleborough Beccles Lowestoft

Diss GB

Stowmarket Leiston

Ipswich Woodbridge

Felixstowe

Harwich

Frinton-on-Sea

Clacton-
on-Sea

Zuid-Kennemerland

B C D E G H

F B

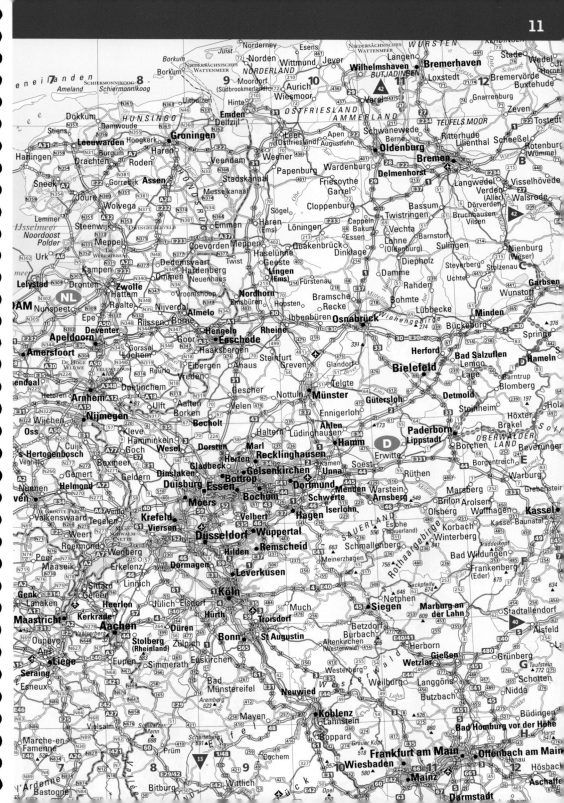

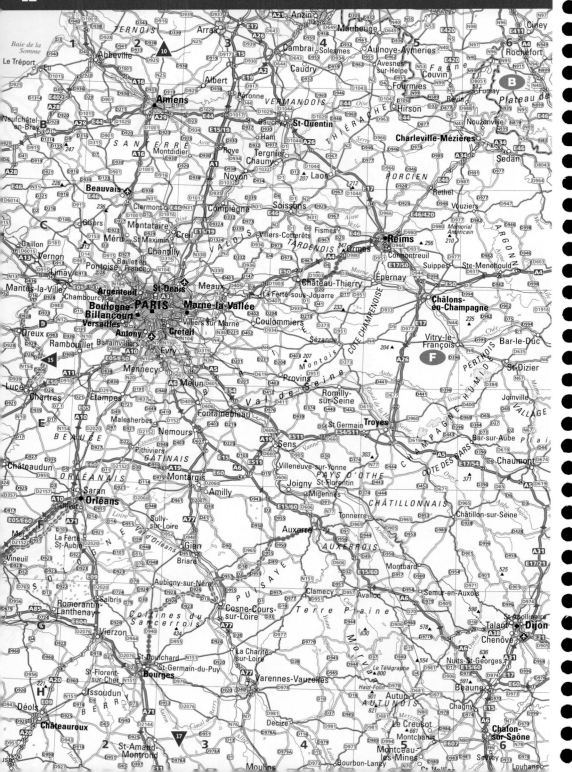

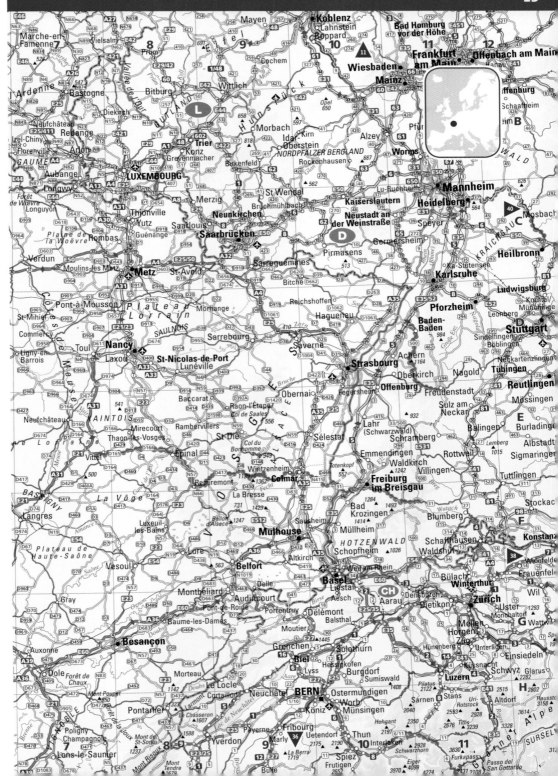

Redruth · Truro **GB** · St Austell · Saltash · Ivybridge · **Plymouth** · Paignton · Brixham · Dartmouth
Camborne · Helston · Falmouth · Start Bay
Mount's Bay · Lizard

A 1 2 3 4 ▲ 8 5 6 · Poole · Portsmouth

Dublin, Rosslare

B E N G L I S H   C H A N N E L   Alderney **GBA** · Cap de la Hague · Cherbourg-Octeville · Tour
L A   M A N C H E

Rosslare · Cork

Guernsey · Vale · St Sampson · St Peter Port **GBG** · Sark · Valognes · COTEN
C CHANNEL ISLANDS · Jersey · St Saviour · 113 · Carteret
St Brelade · St Helier **GBJ** · Coutances

D Perros-Guirec · Paimpol · Golfe de St-Malo · Granville
Roscoff · Lannion · TRÉGORROIS · Baie de St-Brieuc · Dinard · St-Malo · Baie du Mont-St-Michel
Plouguerneau · St-Pol-de-Léon · Ploubazlanec · Menez Bré 301 · Guingamp · Plérin · St-Brieuc · Dinan · Dol-de-Bretagne
Île d'Ouessant · Ploudalmézeau · PAYS DE LÉON · Landivisiau · Morlaix · Ploufragan · Lamballe · PENTHIÈVRE
St-Renan · Gouesnou · Landerneau · Monts d'Arrée · Carhaix-Plouguer · Bel Air 339 · La Mézière · Betton
E Plouzané · **Brest** · Guipavas · Montagne St-Michel 380 · Mer d'Iroise · Le Conquet · Pte de St-Mathieu · Crozon · Châteaulin · Roc de Toullaéron 326 · Montagnes Noires · 320 · Loudéac · Vezin le Coquet · **Rennes** · Cesson-Sévigné
Douarnenez · Le Cap · Menez Hom 330 · 289 · Ergué-Gabéric · Scaër 182 · Pontivy · B R E T A G N E · Ploërmel · Broz · Guichen
Pte du Raz · CORNOUAILLE · **Quimper** · Rosporden · Guer · Bain-de-Bretagne
Pont-l'Abbé · Penmarch · Concarneau · **Quimperlé** · Hennebont · Landes de Lanvaux · 180 · St-Avé · Redon
F Pte de Penmarch · **Lorient** · Lanester · Auray · Vannes · Sarzeau
Ploemeur · Larmor-Plage · Île de Groix · Ploeren · Presqu'île de Quiberon · Baie de Quiberon · Blain · Nort-sur-Erdre
Quiberon · Passage de la Teignouse · Pontchâteau · GRANDE BRIÈRE · Savenay · Carquefou · Orvault
G Belle-Île · Guérande · Trignac · La Baule-Escoublac · **St-Nazaire** · St-Herblain · **Nantes** · Rezé · Bouguenais · PAYS DE
Pornic · St-Philbert-de-Grand-Lieu · Vertou
Noirmoutier-en-l'Île · Île de Noirmoutier · Machecoul
H 2 3 4 5 St-Jean-de-Monts · 16 · Challans · Aizenay
Île d'Yeu · St-Hilaire-de-Riez · St-Gilles-Croix-de-Vie · La Roche

0 10 20 30 40 50 km
0 10 20 30 miles

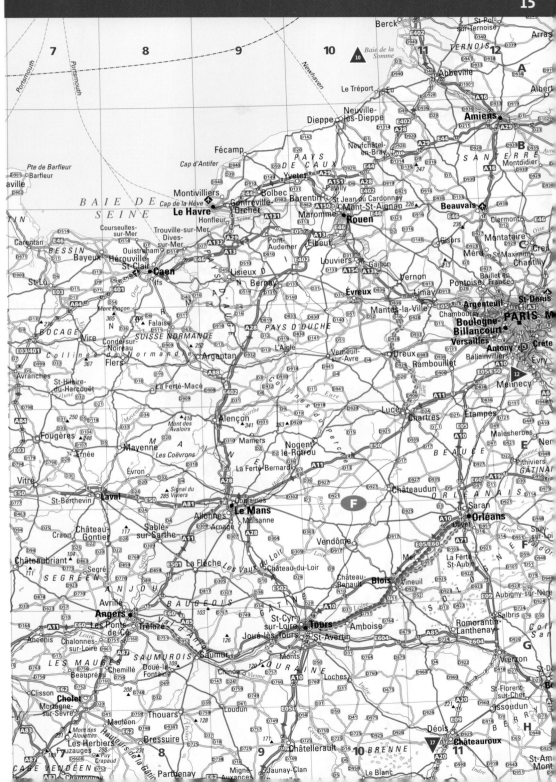

Noirmoutier-en-l'Île
Machecoul
St-Philbert-de-Grand-Lieu
Clisson
Cholet
Mortagne-sur-Sèvre
Mauléon
Thouars
Loudun
Loches
Île de Noirmoutier
Marais breton
Mont des Alouettes
Les Herbiers
Bressuire
Hauteurs de la Gâtine
St-Jean-de-Monts
Challans
Île d'Yeu
St-Hilaire-de-Riez
Aizenay
La Roche-sur-Yon
Pouzauges
Puy Crapaud
Châtellerault
St-Gilles-Croix-de-Vie
Chantonnay
Parthenay
Jaunay-Clan
Buxerolles
Olonne-sur-Mer
Château-d'Olonne
Les Sables-d'Olonne
Terrier de St-Martin
Migné-Auxances
Poitiers
St-Benoît
Chauvigny
Le Blanc
POITOU
Fontenay-le-Comte
Luçon
St-Maixent-l'École
Fontaine le Comte
Montmorillon
BRANDES
Niort
Plaines et Seuil du Poitou
AUNIS
Île de Ré
Lagord
La Rochelle
Aytré
Surgères
Bellac
Pte de Chassiron
CONFOLENTAIS
St-Pierre-d'Oléron
Rochefort
Tonnay-Charente
St-Jean-d'Angély
Île d'Oléron
St-Junien
ANGOUMOIS
Saintes
Le Gond Pontouvre
SAINTONGE
Royan
Cognac
Angoulême
Ruelle-sur-Touvre
Soyaux
La Couronne
Le-Verdon-sur-Mer
Barbezieux-St-Hilaire
0 10 20 30 40 50 km
0 10 20 30 miles
MÉDOC
Pauillac
DOUBLE
Coulounieix-Chamiers
Périgueux
St-Astier
Boulazac
PÉRIGORD BLANC
Lacanau-Océan
St-André-de-Cubzac
Coutras
Montpon-Ménestérol
PÉRIGORD
Blanquefort
St-Médard-en-Jalles
Bordeaux
Libourne
Causse de
Lège-Cap-Ferret
Pessac
Bègles
Talence
Cestas
ENTRE-DEUX-MERS
Bergerac
Andernos-les-Bains
Arcachon
Biganos
Cap Ferret
La Teste-de-Buch
Gujan-Mestras
GRAVES
PÉRIGORD NOIR
LANDES
Langon
Marmande
Fumel
Villeneuve-sur-Lot
Biscarrosse
Tonneins
Ste-Livrade-sur-Lot
Casteljaloux
Agenais
Mimizan
Agen
Le Passage
Nérac
Moissac
PAYS DE BORN
GRANDE LANDE
Valence
Castelsarrasin
Condom
GASCOGNE
LOMAGNE
Mont-de-Marsan
Soustons
Fleurance
St-Paul-lès-Dax
Dax
Aire-sur-l'Adour
Capbreton
ARMAGNAC
Tarnos
Auch
L'Isle-Jourdain
Côte d'Argent
Bayonne
Boucau
Biarritz
Anglet
Orthez
Salies-de-Béarn
BÉARN
St-Jean-de-Luz
Donostia-San Sebastián
Hendaye
Irún
Hasparren
Mourenx
Vic-en-Bigorre

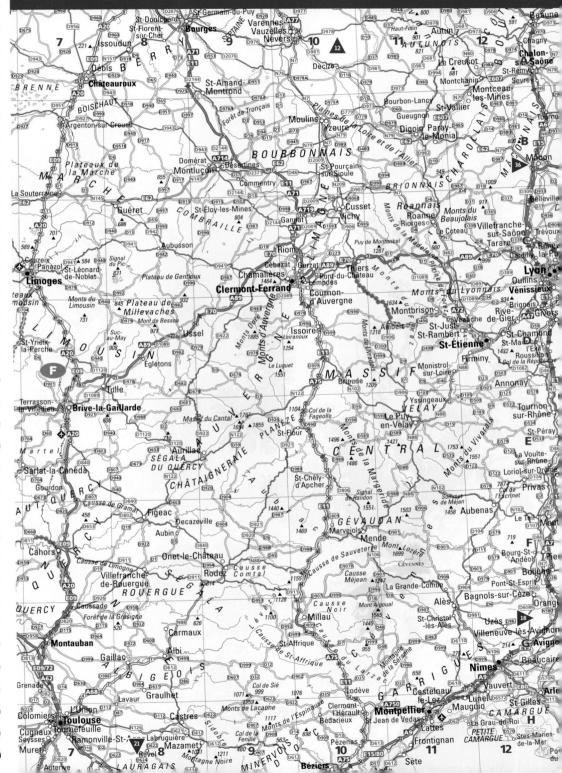

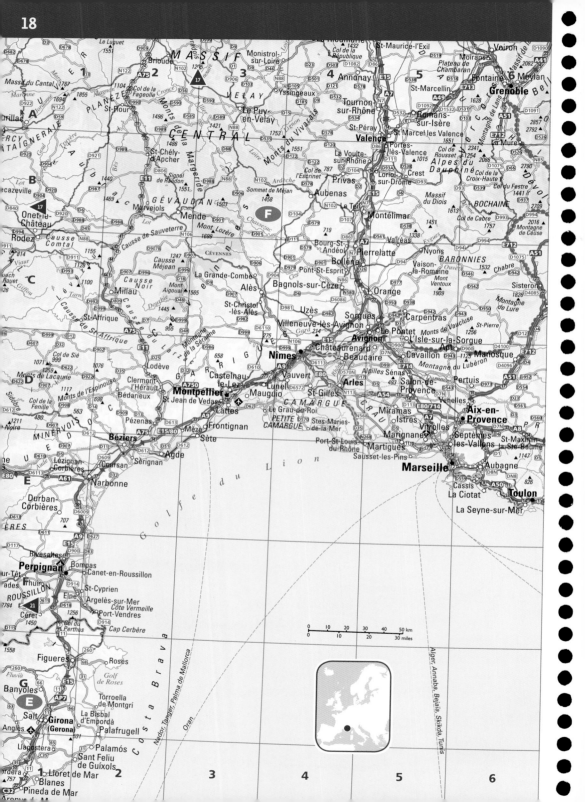

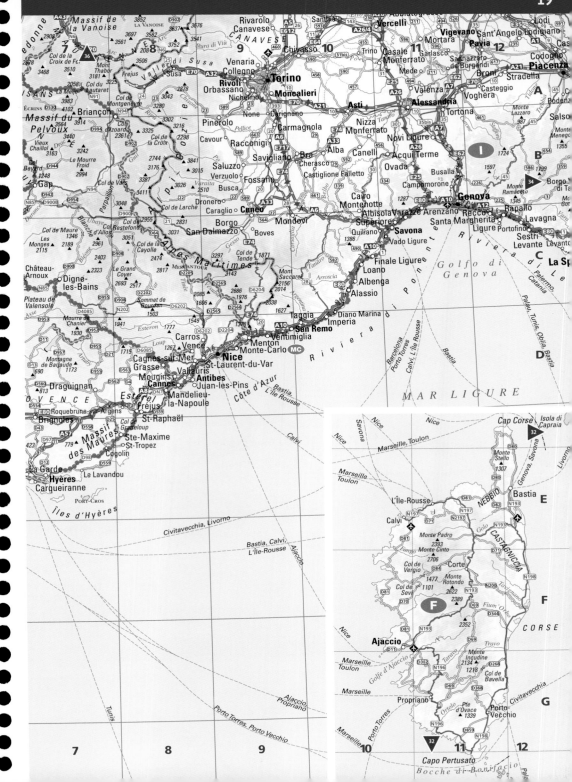

1 2 3 4 5 6

Golfe de Gascogne
Golfo de Gascuña

Portsmouth

Mont-de-Marsan

Soustons
Capbreton
St-Paul-lès-Dax
Dax
Aire-sur-l'Adour

Côte d'Argent
Tarnos
Bayonne Boucau
Biarritz Anglet
St-Jean-de-Luz
Hendaye
Salies-de-Béarn
Orthez
Vic-en-Bigorre

Santoña
Laredo Castro-Urdiales
Bermeo
Algorta
Portugalete
Barakaldo
Bilbao (Bilbo)
Santurtzi
Arizgoiti
Basauri
Amorebieta
Durango
Gernika-Lumo
Ondarroa
Zarautz
Donostia/San Sebastián
Irun
Errentaria
Hasparren
Mourenx
Oloron-Ste-Marie
Billère Pau
Jurançon
Tarbes

Balmaseda
Laudio/Llodio
Villasana de Mena
Arrasate
Eibar
Ermua
Zumarraga
Tolosa
Anoeta
Andoain
Billabona
Elizondo
Col d'Ispéguy
Lourdes

Medina de Pomar
Urduña
Legazpi
Beasain
Altsasu
Berriozar
Barañain
Pamplona/Iruña (Iruñea)
Ansó
Col du Somport
Col du Pourtalet

Miranda de Ebro
Vitoria-Gasteiz
Puerto de Azáceta
Estella
Burlada
Jaca
Sabiñánigo
Torla

Briviesca
Haro
Tafalla
Logroño
Nájera
Santo Domingo de la Calzada

Calahorra
Arnedo
Tudela
Ejea de los Caballeros
Huesca

Puerto de Piqueras
Corella
Cintruénigo
Tarazona
Tauste
Zuera

Ardal
Soria
Alto del Moncayo
Sierra del Moncayo
LLANO DE PLASENCIA
Alagón
Zaragoza

El Burgo de Osma
Almazán
Alto Cruz
Cabezo de Morés
La Almunia de Doña Godina
LLANOS DE

MARQUESADO DE BERLANGA
Calatayud
CAMPO DE CARIÑENA
Caspe

Cuatro Mojones
Santa Cruz
Herrera
Cucutas
DESIERTO DE CALANDA
Alcañiz

La Bodera
Miedla
Judes
Sigüenza
Aragoncillo
Valdellosa
Andorra

Puerto de Marañchón
Pinoso
LA ALCARRIA
Aquila
Puerto de Minguez

Guadalajara
Berninches
Bienvenida
San Ginés
San Just
Puerto de Cabrillas
Ares

Alcalá de Henares
Caimodorro
Puerto de Pozondón
Zaragozana
Peñarroya
EL MAESTRAZGO

Embalse de Buendía
San Felipe
Teruel
Puerto de Escalón
Peñagolosa

Javalón
Collado Bajo

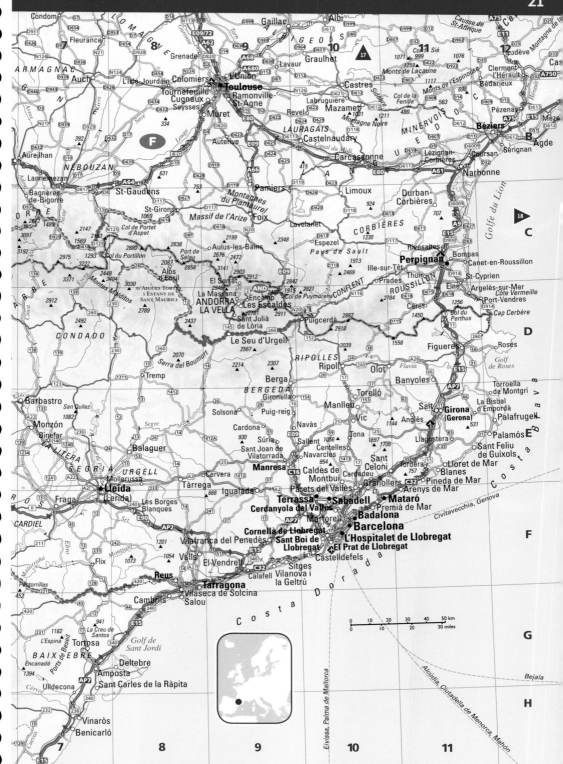

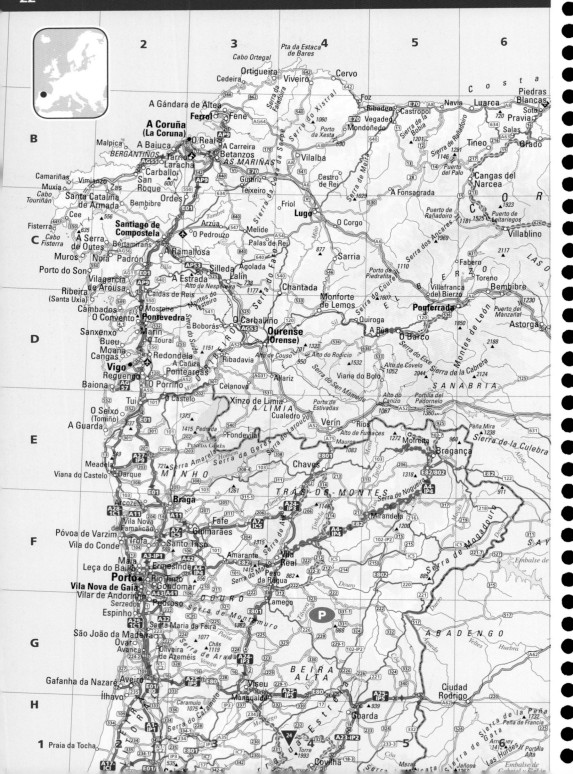

Aveiro
Gafanha da Nazaré
Ílhavo
Viseu
Mangualde
Guarda
Ciudad Rodrigo
Béjar
Plasencia
Coimbra
Covilhã
Castelo Branco
Fundão
Coria
Cáceres
Navalmoral de la Mata
Trujillo
Miajadas
Don Benito
Villanueva de la Serena
Campanario
Castuera
Mérida
Montijo
Badajoz
Elvas
Olivenza
Vila Viçosa
Estremoz
Portalegre
Abrantes
Tomar
Entroncamento
Vila Nova de Ourém
Fátima
Leiria
Torres Novas
Santarém
Almeirim
Marinha Grande
Nazaré
Alcobaça
Caldas da Rainha
Rio Maior
Cartaxo
Benavente
Vila Franca de Xira
Torres Vedras
Peniche
Ericeira
Sintra
Mafra
Oeiras
Moscavide
LISBOA
Cascais
Estoril
Amadora
Almada
Barreiro
Setúbal
Évora
Montemor-o-Novo
Vendas Novas
Reguengos de Monsaraz
Moura
Azuaga
Zafra
Villafranca de los Barros
Almendralejo
Fuente de Cantos
Peñarroya-Pueblonuevo
Hinojosa del Duque

RIBATEJO
BEIRA BAIXA
BEIRA ALTA
ESTREMADURA
LLANOS DE OLIVENZA
TIERRA DE BARROS
LA SERENA
CAMPO ARAÑUELO

Costa do Sol
Costa da Caparica
Costa da Galé
Baía de Setúbal
Cabo Espichel

0 10 20 30 40 50 km
0 30 miles

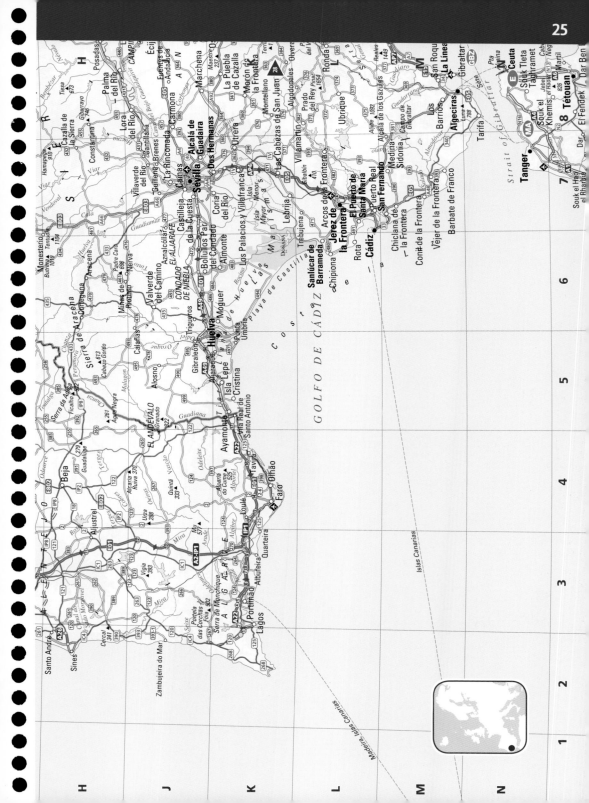

1 **2** **3** **4** **5** **6**

Valladolid
Laguna de Duero
Zamora
Salamanca
Segovia
MADRID
Ávila
Guadalajara
Alcalá de Henares
Torrejón de Ardoz
Alcobendas
San Sebastián de los Reyes
Las Rozas de Madrid
Majadahonda
Pozuelo de Alarcón
Móstoles
Alcorcón
Leganés
Getafe
Fuenlabrada
Parla
Coslada
Mejorada del Campo
Arganda del Rey
San Martín de la Vega
Pinto
Valdemoro
Ciempozuelos
Aranjuez
Ocaña
Tarancón
Colmenar de Oreja
Talavera de la Reina
Toledo
Ciudad Real
Puertollano
Valdepeñas
Manzanares
La Solana
Tomelloso
Socuéllamos
Villarrobledo
San Clemente
Mota del Cuervo
Pedro Muñoz
Campo de Criptana
Alcázar de San Juan
Madridejos
Consuegra
Daimiel
Almagro
Bolaños de Calatrava
Miguelturra
Aranda de Duero
El Burgo de Osma
Almazán
Sigüenza
Soria
Peñafiel
Cuéllar
Íscar
Arévalo
Béjar
Talayuela
Pozoblanco
Villanueva de Córdoba
Peñarroya-Pueblonuevo
Hinojosa del Duque
Cabeza del Buey
Almadén
Castuera
Campanario
La Carolina

B E R

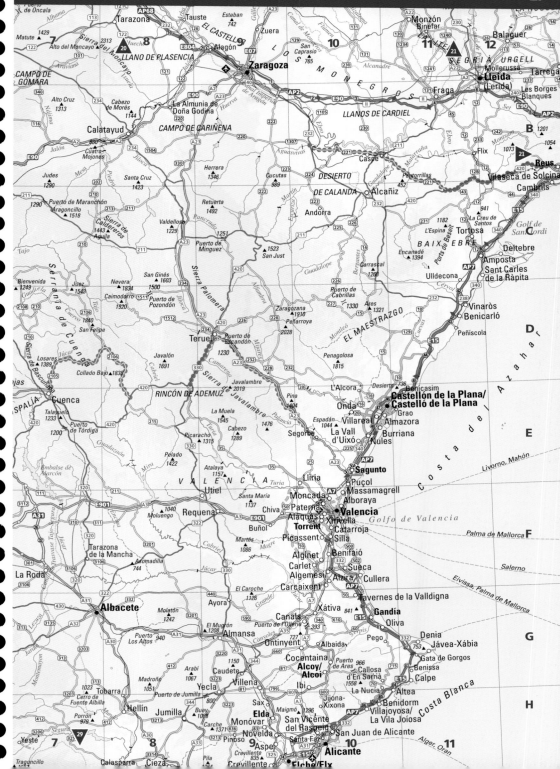

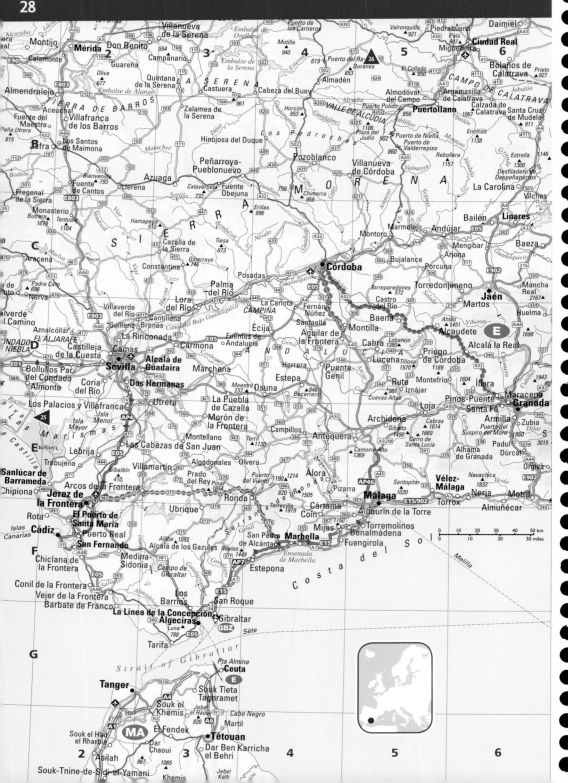

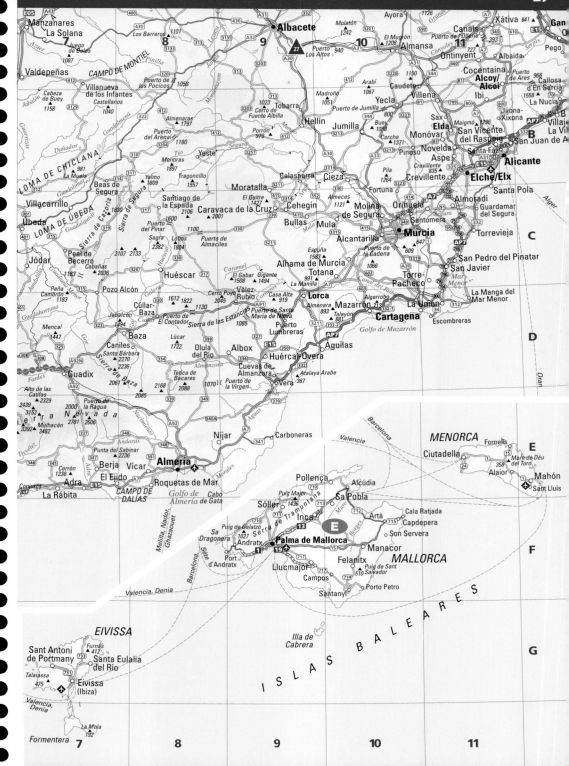

E05 A43

Manzanares
La Solana
Juego de Bolos
1087

Valdepeñas

CAMPO DE MONTIEL

Villanueva
de los Infantes
Cabeza
de Buey
1158
Castellanos
1040

LOMA DE CHICLANA

Villacarrillo

Úbeda

LOMA DE ÚBEDA

Jódar

Peal de
Becerro

Peña del
Cambrón
1183

Guadix

Alto de las
Cañfias
2439
3152
3392

Berja   Vícar

Adra
La Rábita

CAMPO DE
DALÍAS

Los Barreros

Puerto de
los Pocicos 1058

Tobarra

Cerro de
Fuente Albilla

Almenaras
1797

Puerto
del Arenal
3204

Mentiras
1897

Yeste

La Muela
312

Guadalimar

Beas de
Segura

Yelmo
1809

Santiago de
la Espada
2106

Caravaca de la Cruz
2001

Sagra
2382

Sierra de Cazorla
1890

Puerto
del Pinar
1600

Puerto de
Almaciles

Lobos
1804

Huéscar

Pozo Alcón

Cúllar-
Baza

Jabalcón
1494

1612 1822

Puerto de
El Contador

Baza

Caniles

Santa Bárbara
2270
2236

Lúcar
1722

Olula
del Río

Albox

Mencal
1447

Guadix

Tetica de
Bacares
2168
2088

Cuevas de
Almanzora

Vera

S i e r r a   N e v a d a
2000
2781 2606
Mulhacén
3482

Punta del Sabinar
2236

Níjar

Carboneras

Roquetas de Mar

Almería

Golfo de
Almería

Cabo
de Gata

Albacete

27 Puerto
Los Altos

Molatón
1242

El Mugrón
1208

Ayora

1126
Grande

Canals

Xátiva 841

Almansa

Arabí
1067

Caudete

Villena

Yecla

Madroño
1051

Puerto de Jumilla

Jumilla

Buey
1088

Carche
1371

Hellín

Porrón
979

Calasparra

Cieza

Moratalla

Cehegín

El Buitre
1427

Almeces
1121

Bullas   Mula

Alcantarilla

Alhama de Murcia

Totana

España
1583

Espuña
991

La Manilla

Lorca

Vélez-
Rubio

Casa Alta
919

Almenara

Talayón
881

Puerto
Lumbreras

Águilas

Huércal-Overa

Atalaya Árabe

Puerto de
la Virgen
367

Ontinyent

Puerto de l'Olleria

Cocentaina

Alcoy/
Alcoi

Ibi

Sax
Monóvar

Elda

Novelda

Aspe

Pinoso

Pila
1264

Fortuna

Molina
de Segura

Orihuela

Santomera

Murcia
647
609

Puerto de
la Cadena

1066

Torre-
Pacheco

La Unión

Cartagena

Golfo de Mazarrón

Mazarrón

Escombreras

Albaida

Pego

Albaida

Callosa
d'En Sarrià
966

La Nucia

Villaj
La Vi

San Juan de A

Alicante

Elche/Elx

Santa Pola

Almoradí

Guardamar
del Segura

Torrevieja

San Pedro del Pinatar

San Javier

Mar
Menor

La Manga del
Mar Menor

MENORCA

Ciutadella

Fornells

Alaior

Mare de Déu
del Toro
358

Mahón
Sant Lluís

Pollença

Sóller

Puig Major
1436

Puig de Galatzó
1027

Sa
Dragonera

Andratx

Port
d'Andratx

Alcúdia

Sa Pobla

Inca

Puig de
715
Capdepera

Cala Ratjada

Artà

Son Servera

Manacor

Palma de Mallorca

Llucmajor

Campos

Santanyí

Felanitx

Puig de Sant
Salvador
510

Porto Petro

MALLORCA

ISLAS   BALEARES

Illa de
Cabrera

EIVISSA

Sant Antoni
de Portmany

Furnás
412

Santa Eulalia
del Río

Talaiassa
475

Eivissa
(Ibiza)

La Mola
192

Formentera

Barcelona

Valencia

Valencia, Denia

1 **2** **3** **4** **5** **6**

A

B

C

Pontinia
Sabaudia
Terracina
San Felice Circeo
Golfo di Terracina
Monte Circeo 541
Fondi
Monte delle Fate 1090
Formia
Gaeta
Golfo di Gaeta
Monti Aurunci
Monte Petrella 1533
Vairano Patenora
Mondragone
Sparanise
Teano
Piedimonte Matese
Sanframondi
Guardia
Morcone
San Bartolomeo in Galdo
Monte Mutria 1823
Monte Cornacchia 1151
Ariano Irpino
Apice
Benevento
Montesarchio
Altavilla Irpina
Mirabella Eclano
Avellino
Monti d'Avella 1598
Nusco
Lioni
Monte Cervialto 1607
Monte Mai 1809
Eboli
Salerno
Baronissi
Cava de' Tirreni
Battipaglia
Faiano
Pontecagnano
Sorrento
Anacapri
Capri
Albanella
Capaccio
Agropoli
Castellabate
Vallo della Lucania
Monte della Stella 1131
Ascea
CILENTO VALLO DI
Golfo di Salerno

Napoli
Casoria
Afragola
Portici
Torre del Greco
Torre Annunziata
Gragnano
Pozzuoli
Bacoli
Forio
Ischia
Monte Epomeo 788
Isola d'Ischia
Golfo di Napoli
Vesuvio
San Giuseppe Vesuviano
Sarno
Marigliano
Baiano
San Felice
Giugliano in Campania
Lusciano
Aversa
Calvano
Marcianise
Caserta
Capua
Maddaloni
Grazzanise
Castèl Volturno
Catazzo
Monte Taburno 1394
Montesarchio
Vasto
Aurunca
Cassino

Isole Ponziane
Isola di Ponza
CIRCEO
Olbia

MARE TIRRENO

Cagliari
Tunis
Valencia
Palermo
Catania
Messina, Valletta

D

E

F

G

Isole Lipari
Isola Salina
Isola Panarea
Isola Alicudi
Isola Filicudi
Isola Lipari
Lipari
Isola Vulcano

Capri
Genova, Livorno
Napoli, Salerno
Ustica
Cagliari

Capo San Vito
Capo Gallo
Terrasini
Capaci
Palermo
Carini
Bagheria
Cefalù
Santo Stefano di Camastra
Capo d'Orlando
Gioiosa Marea
Milazzo
Villafranca Tirrena
Barcellona
Pozzo di Gotto
Patti
Torrenova
Monti Peloritani

Monte Speciale 913
Erice
Trapani
Paceco
Castellammare del Golfo
Monreale
Partinico
Misilmeri
Termini Imerese
Golfo di Termini Imerese
Castelbuono
Mistretta
Randazzo
Taormina
Messina
Reggio Calabria

Isola Favignana
Marsala
Salemi
Calatafimi
Alcamo
San Cipirello
Marineo
Corleone
Caccamo
Cerda
Monte Soro 1847
Monte Etna 3323
Fiumefreddo di Sicilia
Santa Teresa di Riva
Linguaglossa

Mazara del Vallo
Gibellina Nuova
Partanna
Castelvetrano
Sambuca di Sicilia
Bisacquino
Prizzi
Lercara Friddi
Caltavuturo
Gangi
Troina
Nicosia
Adrano
Bronte
Zafferana Etnea
Giarre
Riposto
Aci Catena

Campobello di Mazara
Capo Granitola
Menfi
Caltabellotta
Castronovo di Sicilia
Bivona
Cammarata
Casteltermini
Villarosa
Leonforte
Assoro
Regalbuto
Biancavilla
Acireale
Aci Castello
Catania

Sciacca
Ribera
Cattolica Eraclea
Serradifalco
San Cataldo
Caltanissetta
Enna
Valguarnera
Piana di Catania
Misterbianco
Golfo di Catania

SICILIA
Raffadali
Aragona
Canicattì
Barrafranca
Pietraperzia
Piazza Armerina
Caropepe
Ramacca
Palagonia
Lentini
Augusta

Agrigento
Favara
Naro
Ravanusa
Mazzarino
Sommatino
Caltagirone
Grammichele
Golfo di Augusta

Porto Empedocle
Campobello di Licata
Butera
Vizzini
Melilli
Floridia

Palma di Montechiaro
Licata
Niscemi
Acate
Palazzolo Acreide
Siracusa
Canicattini Bagni
Avola

Gela
Golfo di Gela
Comiso
Noto
Rosolini
Pachino

Vittoria
Ragusa
Modica
Scicli
Ispica
Pozzallo

Santa Croce Camerina
Golfo di Noto

Pantelleria
Linosa, Lampedusa

2 **3** **4** **5** **6**

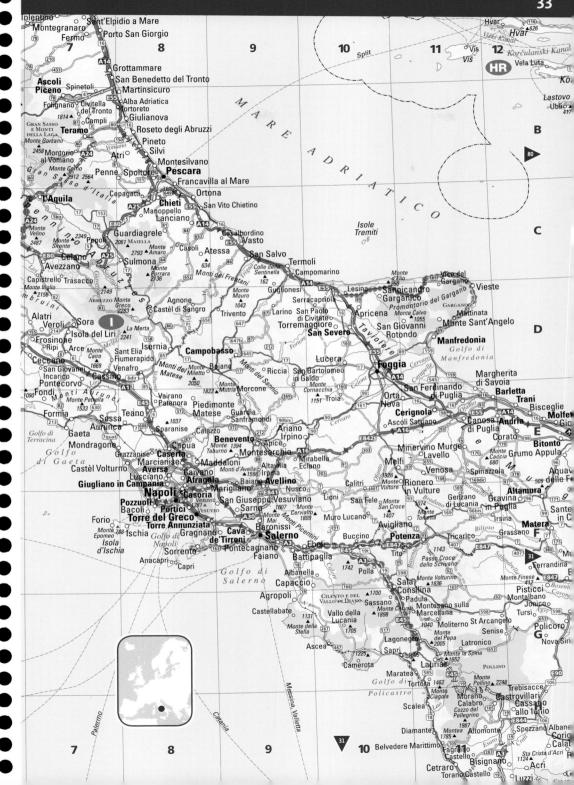

CH   CH

Montreux · Balmhorn · Bietschhorn · Campo Tencia · Passo di San Bernardino · Biasca · St Moritz · Corno di Piazzi · Cima de Piazzi

Wildhorn · Les Diablerets · Raron · Brig · Monte Leone · Basodino · Val Leventina · Piz Bernina

Aigle · Ollon · Bex · Sierre · Sion · Simplon · Locarno · Losone · Bellinzona · Giubiasco · Chiavenna · Monte Disgrazia · Monte Combolo · Sondalo

Monthey · Conthey · Weisshorn · Villadossola · Domodossola · Sondrio · Morbegno · Teglio · Tirano · Stelvio Adamello

Martigny · Dent Blanche · Cannobio · Val Grande · Luino · Lugano · Colico · Alpi Orobie

Chamonix-Mont-Blanc · Monte Rosa · Dufourspitze · Verbania · Lavena Ponte Tresa · Menaggio · Mandello del Lario · Lecco · Clusone · Darfo Boario Terme · Breno

BAGNES · Grand St Bernard · Alpi Pennine · Aosta · Corno Bianco · Gran Paradiso · Omegna · Varallo · Besozzo · Gavirate · Varese · Como · Nembro · Albino · Pisogne · Gardone Val Trompia · Lumezzane

Monte Nery · Borgosesia · Arona · Gallarate · Saronno · Seregno · Bergamo · Seriate · San Paolo D'Argon · Villa Carcina · Concesio · Gussago

Biella · Cossato · Gattinara · Oleggio · Busto Arsizio · Legnano · Lissone · Cinisello Balsamo · Rho · Sesto San Giovanni · Monza · Dalmine · Concorezzo · Treviglio · Chiari · Rovato · Brescia · Lonato

Ivrea · Galliate · Novara · Santhia · Abbiategrasso · Milano · Corsico · San Giuliano Milanese · Crema · Orzinuovi · Manerbio · Leno · Bagnolo Mella · Castiglione della Stiviere

Cuorgnè · Rivarolo Canavese · CANAVESE · Vercelli · Rozzano · Sant'Angelo Lodigiano · Pontevico · Asola · Marcaria

Venaria · Collegno · Chivasso · Trino · Mede · Vigevano · Mortara · Pavia · Casalpusterlengo · Codogno · Cremona

Rivoli · Torino · Moncalieri · Nichelino · Casale Monferrato · Garlasco · Sannazzaro de Burgondi · Broni · Stradella · Piacenza · Casalmaggiore · Colorno · Guastalla

Orbassano · Asti · Valenza · Voghera · Casteggio · Cadeo · Fiorenzuola d'Arda · Fontanellato

Pinerolo · None · Carignano · Alessandria · Tortona · Fidenza · Salsomaggiore Terme · Parma

Cavour · Carmagnola · Nizza Monferrato · Novi Ligure · Monte Lazzaro · Langhirano · Collecchio

Racconigi · Bra · Alba · Canelli · Acqui Terme · Ovada · Monte Menegosa · Borgo Val di Taro · Reggio nell'Emilia

Saluzzo · Verzuolo · Busca · Cherasco · Castiglione Falletto · Busalla · Campomorone · Monte Ramaceto · Passo della Cisa · Castelnovo ne' Monti

Dronero · Fossano · Savigliano · Cairo Montenotte · Genova · Recco · Rapallo · Monte Gottero · Pontremoli

Caraglio · Cuneo · Mondovi · Boves · Albisola · Varazze · Arenzano · Sta Margherita Ligure · Portofino · Lavagna · Sestri Levante · Levanto · Aulla · Fivizzano · Sarzana · Castelnuovo di Garfagnana

Borgo San Dalmazzo · Quiliano · Superiore · Savona · Vado Ligure · Riviera di Levante · La Spezia · Lerici · Carrara · Barga · App

Finale Ligure · Loano · Golfo di Genova · Massa · Seravezza

Alpes Maritimes · Mercantour · Albenga · Alassio · Genova · Pietrasanta · Massarosa · Lucca · Capannori

Carros · Taggia · Diano Marina · Imperia · Viareggio · San Giuliano Terme

Vence · Ventimiglia · San Remo · Menton · Nice · Monte-Carlo · MC · Riviera di Ponente · Pisa · Cascina · Pontedera · Ponsacco

St-Laurent-du-Var · Vallauris · Collesalvetti

Antibes · Juan-les-Pins · Cannes · Côte d'Azur · MAR LIGURE · Livorno · Lari

Toulon · Rosignano Marittimo · Cecina

Barcelona · Ajaccio · Arcipelago Toscano · Castagneto Carducci · San Vincenzo · Campiglia Marittima

Valencia · Porto Torres · Calvi · L'Ile Rousse · Cap Corse · Olbia, Palau · Tunis, Palermo · Isola d'Elba · Piombino · Portoferraio

Monte Stello · Bastia · Monte Capanne · Cima del Monte

0 10 20 30 40 50 km
10 20 30 miles

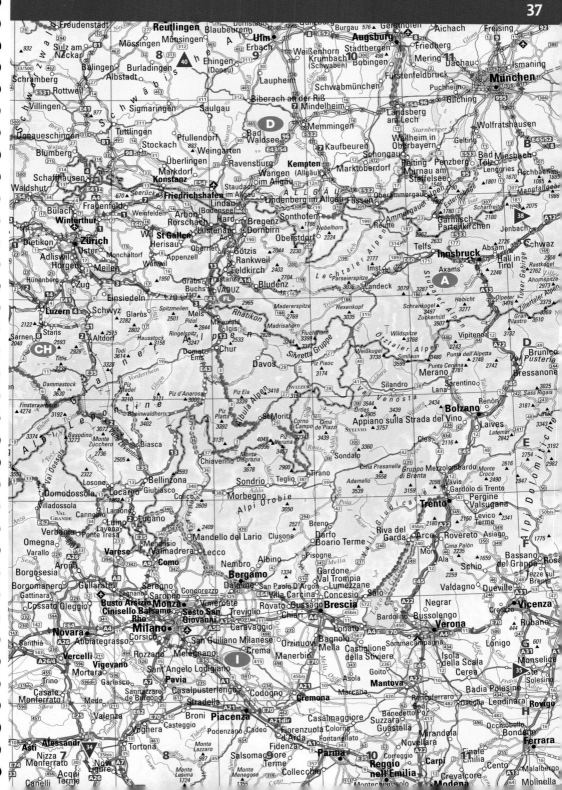

Regensburg
Pforzheim
Ludwigsburg
Gaildorf
Ellwangen
Backnang
Bissingen
Treuchtlingen
Nördlingen
Eichstätt
Kelheim
Neutraubling
Raubing
Abensberg
Schierling
Stuttgart
Esslingen am Neckar
Schwäbisch Gmünd
Aalen
Harburg (Schwaben)
Ingolstadt
Neuburg an der Donau
Mainburg
Essenbach
Dingolfing
Göppingen
Heidenheim an der Brenz
Schrobenhausen
Landshut
Niederreisbach
Böblingen
Leonberg
Hochdorf
Dillingen an der Donau
Rain
Aichach
Freising
Neumarkt-St Veit
Mühldorf am Inn
Vilsbiburg
Nagold
Tübingen
Metzingen
Langenau
Günzburg
Staufersberg
Augsburg
Stadtbergen
Friedberg
Dachau
Ismaning
Erding
Altötting
Mössingen
Reutlingen
Ulm
Erbach
Weißenhorn
Bobingen
Mering
Fürstenfeldbruck
Puchheim
München
Haar
Vaterstetten
Garching an der Alz
Trostberg
Balingen
Albstadt
Münsingen
Ehingen
Laupheim
Krumbach
Schwabmünchen
Landsberg am Lech
Grafing bei München
Traunreut
Sigmaringen
Saulgau
Biberach an der Riß
Mindelheim
Memmingen
Kaufbeuren
Weilheim in Oberbayern
Schongau
Penzberg
Bad Tölz
Miesbach
Rosenheim
Traunstein
Siegsdorf
Bruckmühl
Tuttlingen
Pfullendorf
Bad Waldsee
Schwangau
Marktoberdorf
Murnau am Staffelsee
Lenggries
Chiemgauer Alpen
Stockach
Überlingen
Weingarten
Ravensburg
Kempten
Wangen im Allgäu
Oberammergau
Mangfallgebirge
Hinteres Sonnwendjoch
Kufstein
Konstanz
Friedrichshafen
Staudach im Allgäu
Lindau
Sonthofen
Nebelhorn
Reutte
Ammergauer Alpen
Garmisch-Partenkirchen
Jenbach
Hopfgarten im Brixental
Kitzbühel
Wörgl
St Gallen
Bregenz
Dornbirn
Oberstdorf
Telfs
Innsbruck
Hall in Tirol
Schwaz
Kitzbüheler Alpen
Mittersill
Feldkirch
Bludenz
Landeck
Imst
Axams
Absam
Kreuzjoch
Rastkogel
VADUZ (FL)
Chur
Davos
St Moritz
Silvretta Gruppe
Ötztaler Alpen
Wildspitze
Zillertaler Alpen
Grosser Löffler
Hohe Tauern
Bellinzona
Chiavenna
Sondrio
Tirano
Silandro
Merano
Sarentino
Bressanone
Brunico
Cortina d'Ampezzo
Bolzano
Laives
Monte Civetta
Lugano
Como
Monza
Milano
Brescia
Sondalo
Appiano sulla Strada del Vino
Cles
Trento
Belluno
Pergine
Valsugana
Feltre
Vittorio Veneto
Sacile
Pordenone
Conegliano
Montebelluna
Oderzo
Treviso
San Donà di Piave
Venezia
Jesolo
Bassano del Grappa
Valdagno
Vicenza
Cittadella
Bussolengo
Verona
Padova
Monselice
Piove di Sacco
Saronno
Pavia
Lodi
Crema
Lonato
Castiglione della Stiviere
Lonigo
Este

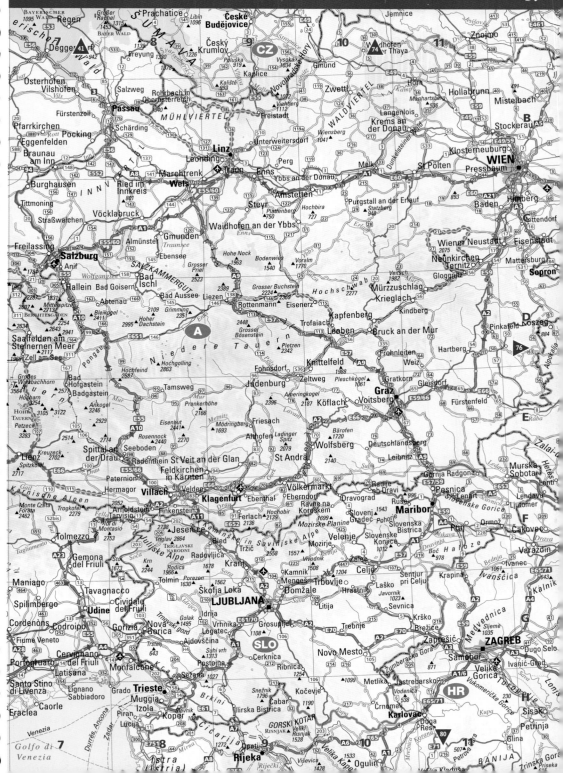

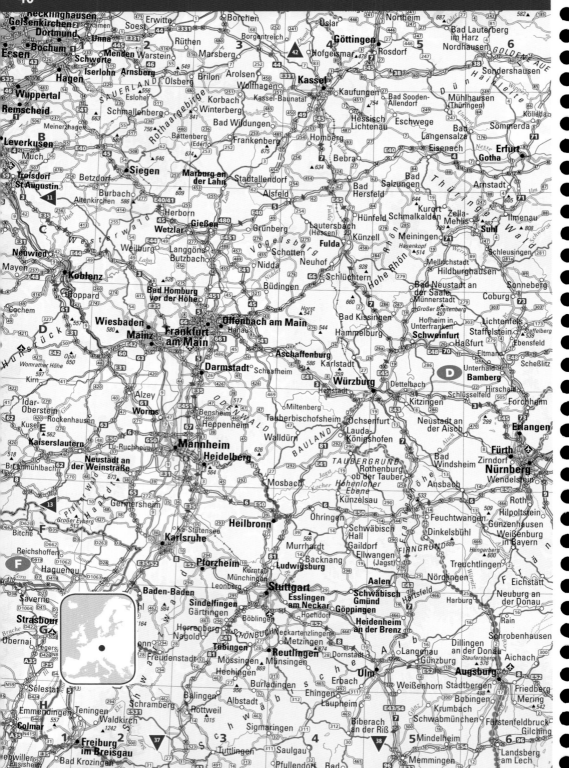

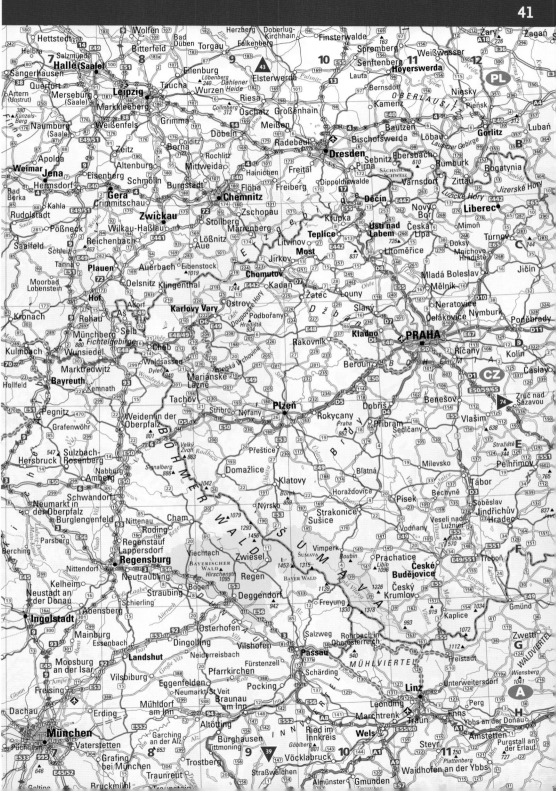

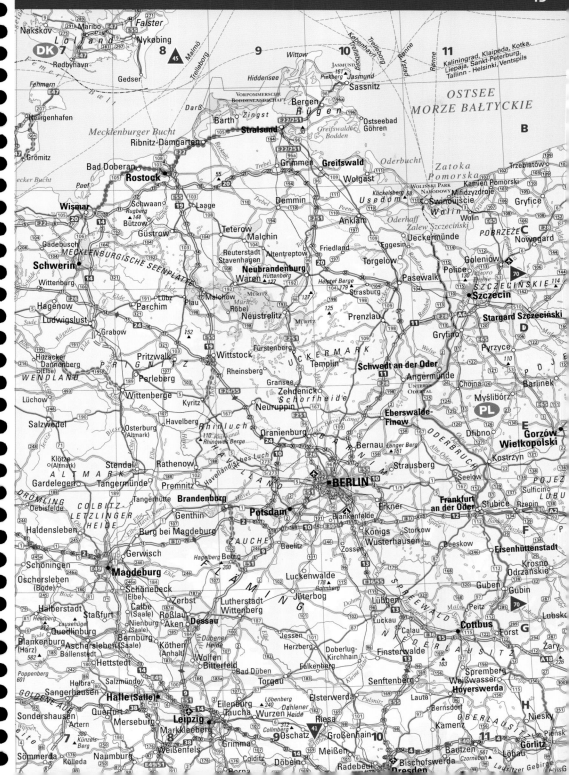

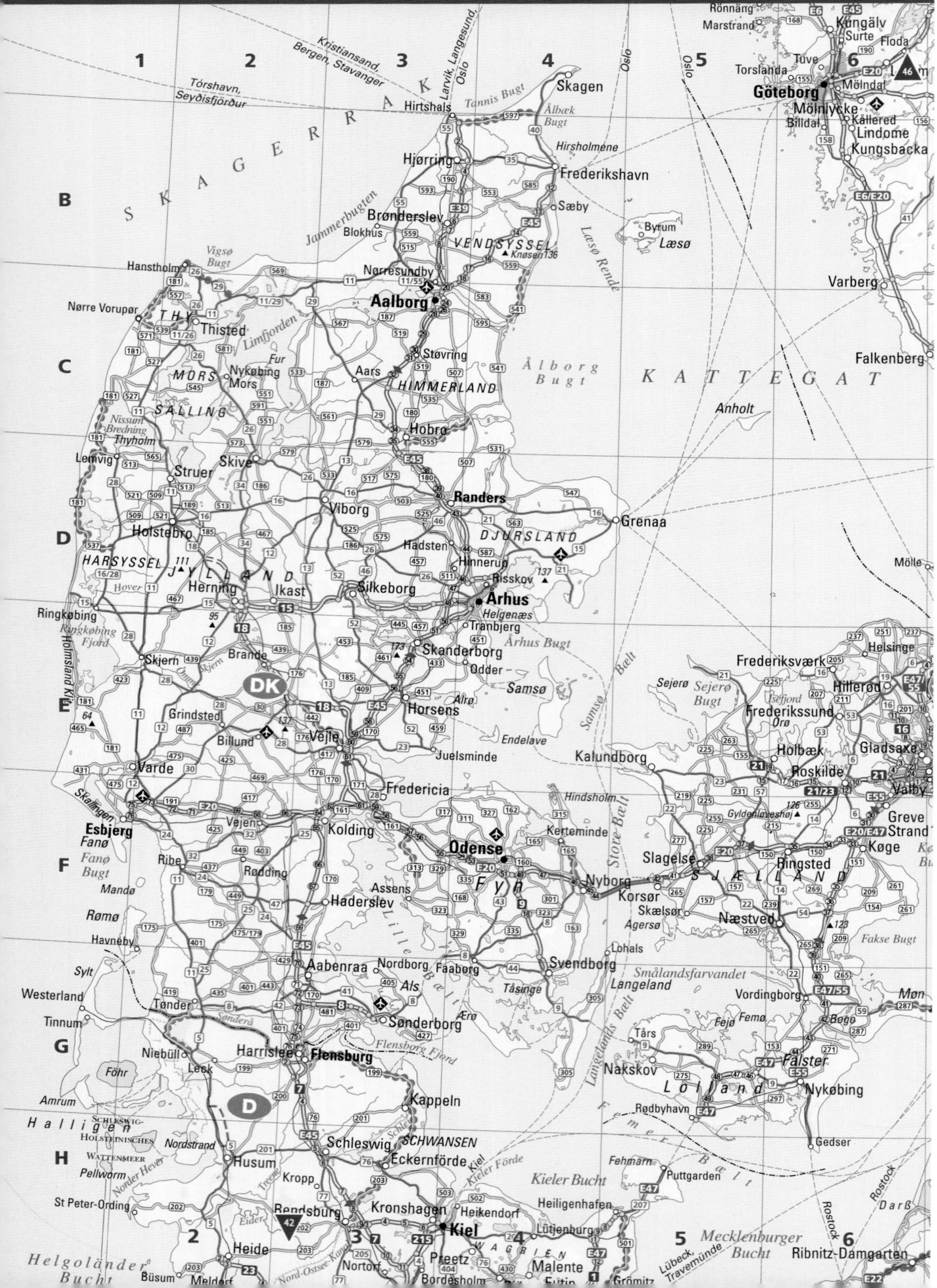

S K A G E R R A K
K A T T E G A T
Kristiansand, Bergen, Stavanger
Tórshavn, Seyðisfjörður
Larvik, Langesund, Oslo
Oslo
Rönnäng
Marstrand
Kungälv
Surte
Floda
Tuve
Torslanda
Göteborg
Mölndal
Mölnlycke
Billdal
Kållered
Lindome
Kungsbacka
Varberg
Falkenberg
Mölle
Skagen
Tannis Bugt
Ålbæk Bugt
Hirtshals
Hirsholmene
Hjørring
Frederikshavn
Sæby
Brønderslev
Blokhus
Jammerbugten
VENDSYSSEL
Knøsen 136
Byrum
Læsø
Læsø Rende
Vigsø Bugt
Hanstholm
Nørresundby
Aalborg
Nørre Vorupør
THY
Thisted
Limfjorden
Fur
Støvring
MORS
Nykøbing Mors
Aars
HIMMERLAND
Ålborg Bugt
Anholt
SALLING
Nissum Bredning
Thyholm
Hobro
Lemvig
Struer
Skive
Randers
Viborg
Grenaa
Holstebro
DJURSLAND
Hadsten
Hinnerup
HARSYSSEL
JYLLAND
Herning
Ikast
Silkeborg
Risskov
Århus
Helgenæs
Tranbjerg
Århus Bugt
Ringkøbing
Ringkøbing Fjord
Holmsland Klit
Skjern
Brande
Skanderborg
Odder
Samsø
Samsø Bælt
DK
Grindsted
Billund
Vejle
Horsens
Alrø
Endelave
Juelsminde
Kalundborg
Sejerø
Sejerø Bugt
Isefjord
Orø
Frederiksværk
Helsinge
Hillerød
Frederikssund
Holbæk
Gladsaxe
Roskilde
Valby
Greve
Strand
Køge
Varde
Skallingen
Esbjerg
Fanø
Fanø Bugt
Vejen
Kolding
Fredericia
Hindsholm
Kerteminde
Odense
Fyn
Store Bælt
Slagelse
Ringsted
SJÆLLAND
Gyldenløveshøj 126
Ribe
Rødding
Mandø
Rømø
Havneby
Haderslev
Assens
Nyborg
Korsør
Skælskør
Agersø
Næstved
Fakse Bugt
Lille Bælt
Aabenraa
Nordborg
Als
Faaborg
Svendborg
Tåsinge
Lohals
Langeland
Smålandsfarvandet
Vordingborg
Møn
Sylt
Westerland
Tinnum
Tønder
Sønderborg
Ærø
Fejø
Femø
Bogø
Niebüll
Leck
Harrislee
Flensburg
Flensborg Fjord
Langelands Bælt
Tårs
Nakskov
Lolland
Falster
Nykøbing
Rødbyhavn
Føhr
Amrum
D
Halligen
Kappeln
Femer Bælt
Schleswig-Holsteinisches Wattenmeer
Nordstrand
Husum
Pellworm
Norder Hever
Schleswig
SCHWANSEN
Eckernförde
Kieler Förde
Kieler Bucht
Fehmarn
Puttgarden
Gedser
Kropp
St Peter-Ording
Rendsburg
Kronshagen
Heikendorf
Heiligenhafen
Kiel
Lütjenburg
Rostock
Darß
Heide
Preetz
WAGRIEN
Malente
Eutin
Grömitz
Lübeck, Travemünde
Mecklenburger Bucht
Ribnitz-Damgarten
Helgoländer Bucht
Büsum
Meldorf
Nortorf
Bordesholm
Nord-Ostsee-Kanal

2 **3** **51** **4** **5** **6**

Gullenhaugen 759 · Langholsberget 521 · Björbo · Borlänge

ROMERIKE · Kongsvinger · Knästen 550

Jessheim · Oppkuven 704 · Verdehøgda 411 · Tyfors · Lejberget 546 · Sunnansjö · Ludvika 443 · Smedjebacken

Rånåsfoss · Lillestrøm · Hagfors · Bergslagen

OSLO · Strømmen · Fetsund · Elgheia 385 · Filipstad · Hällefors · Lindesberg

Sandvika · B · Asker · Sveal and · Nora

Ski · Arvika · Kil · Forshaga · S · Karlskoga · Örebro

Askim · Grums · Karlstad · Skoghall · Kristinehamn · Degerfors · Narke

Moss · 49 · Horten · Linneklepren · Skjærhalden · Kumla · Hallsberg

Sarpsborg · Säffle · VÄNERN

Fredrikstad · Halden · Åmål · Djurö · Mariestad · Tiveden · Motala · Ljungsbro · Malmslätt

Strømstad · DALBOSJÖN · Lidköping · Götene · Skövde · Tibro · Vadstena

Kungshamn · E · Vänersborg · Vargön 153 · Skara · Hjo · Mjölby

Lysekil · Uddevalla · Trollhättan · Falköping · Tidaholm · Tranås

Ellös · Lilla Edet · Stenungsund · Tjörn · Kungälv · Alingsås · Mullsjö · Habo · Bankeryd · Huskvarna · NORRA KVILL

Rönnäng · Marstrand · Surte · Floda · VÄSTERGÖTLAND · Ulricehamn · Jönköping · Eksjö

Torslanda · Tuve · Lerum · Borås · Nässjö

Göteborg · Mölndal · Mölnlycke · Kållered · Billdal · Lindome · Kinna · Vetlanda

Kungsbacka · Tomtabacken 377 · Sävsjö

Frederikshavn · Gislaved · STORE MOSS · Värnamo · Växjö

Byrum · Læsø · Varberg · Vetlanda

Falkenberg · 45 · Ljungby · Alvesta

KATTEGAT · Anholt · Bottnen · Halmstad

VÄNERN · Tiveden · Vättern

1 2 3 4 5 6

877
Sløvåg 57
Leirvåg Hope
Nordhordland
Radøy Fedjehei
Alvøy 565 570
Tjeldstø Skråmestø 567 869
Blomøy 563 566
Askøy 561 Nyborg
Store Sotra 341 556
555
Vik 552
Osøyri
Halhjem
Huftarøy 546
Sandvikvåg
Huftarøy
Tysnesøy 49

Bjørndalskamden
1402 E16
Kvitanosi Vinje 601
1433 Kaldafjellet
1411
Voss Storskavlen
13 1729 1802
Skjemmene 572
1351 Ramnabergnuten
Bruravik 1729
550 Sovrnuten
Norheimsund 13 1649
Tysse 1299 Maurset
Kinsarvik
Jondal 550
Solnut 1552 Harteigan
Fodnanuten 1690
Varaldsøy 1454 HARDANGERVIDDA
Odda Sandfløegg
Sauanuten 1719
1409 13 1639

Blaskavlen
1809
Store Raudbergskarvet
Lishovden 1819
1763
50 Folarskarnuten
1933

Vesleboltnskarvet
1778 Sælegga
1137 Fagernes

Nystølfjell
1295

Hemsedal 52 51
Hallingdal Gol
Geilo 7 40
Bjordalsnuten Dyna
1382 1212 Blåfjellet
Synhovd Fjellbunutun 1157
1438 1340
Bjørkeflåta
Borgsjåbrotet 40 Solendsfjellet
1484 1045
Reksjæggi Rollag
1478 Mæl
Filseggi 364 N
1630 Vestfjorddalen Gausta
Brattefjell 1883 Bletoppen
1541 1341

Hardangervidda

Store Skrekken
1429

B

C

Bømlo Sunde
Stord Ulvenåso
542 749 1247
Mosterhamn Halsnøy
541 48
Langevåg 514
47 541
Våg 513
Haugesund 515
Akrehamn 513
Karmøy 511
Arsvågen Vestre
Hauske Bokn
Rennesøy

Horda
Kyrkjenuten 13
1602 Vassdalsegga
Sauda 1658 Edland
Skaulen 362
Hustveit 1540 9
1188 Snønuten
1604 Snjoheii Urenosi
1438 1520
Ryfylke Bykleheiane
Lovraeid Rygnestad
Grytenuten 863 Tjomsnuten
Nedstrand 517 1269
Ombo Nomeland
Tveit Rjuvbrokkene 925
Reineknuten Rjuven
787 1443 Setesdal
Lysekammen
1304 Rienshornhei
1162

Vehuskjerringi
1356
E134 Amot 45
Brunkeberg Stor-Roan
1192
Setesdal Gvarv
355

Mælefjell Notodden
1515 Lifjell
1288 360
36
Ruglefjell
847 38

D

E Stavanger
509
Sandnes
510 13 508
Bryne Jæren 503
507 505
504 561
Lakksvela Vikeså
Dålane 906
Egersund
Eigerøya

Forsand 45
1035 Sinnes
1018 468
Tonstad 42
Risnes 465
Kvinlog
Sira 465 Storkarshei
Navrestad 465 622
542 465 460
Flekkefjord Kvinesdal 460
Kirkehamn 469 461
Hidra Kaldåskni 461
506 43
Borhaug 455
Lista Farsund 460
Våge Lindesnes Mandal

Dansevalheia
825 Tjønnefoss
Gjerstad
Vegarshei Kragerø
413 416 Risør
405 411
Evje 571
362 406 404 Arendal
403
485 402
Vennesla E18 Grimstad
453
461 452
Søgne 456 Kristiansand
401 Flekkerøy
E39

Dyna
Bjørdalsnuten

Kåldåskni
506

F

G

Tórshavn,
Seydisfjördur

0 10 20 30 40 50 km
0 10 20 30 miles

S K A G E R R
A
K

H

2 3 4 5 6

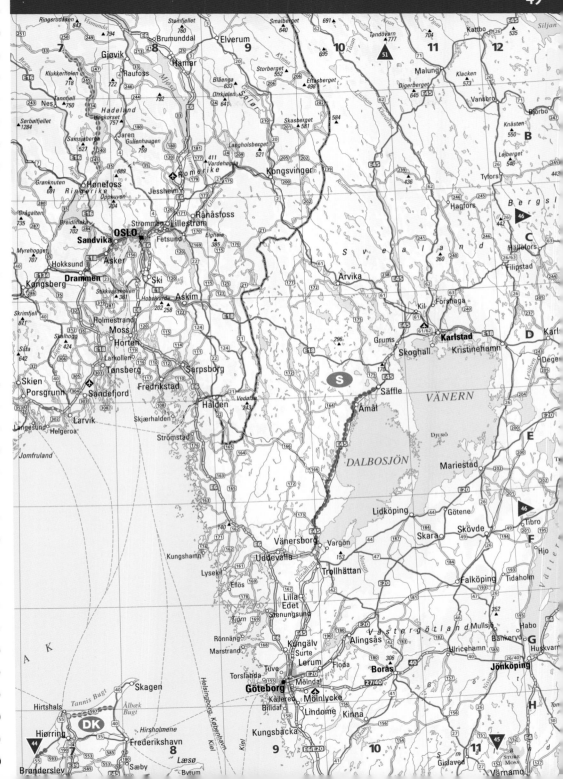

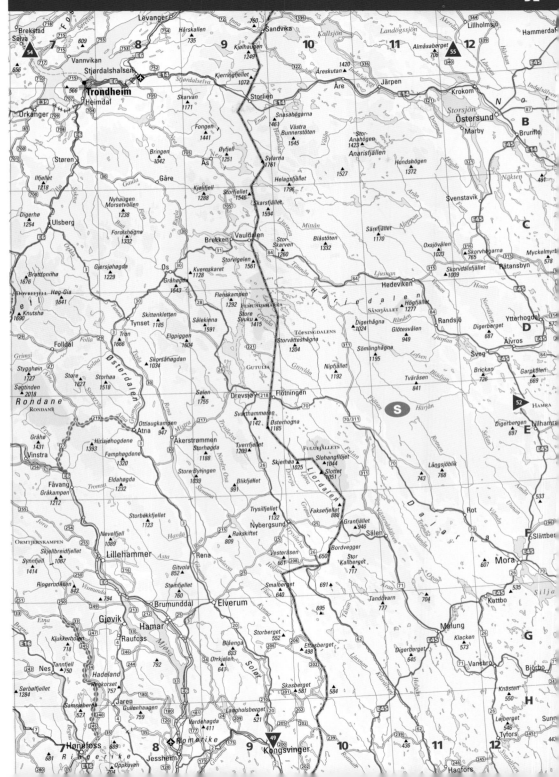

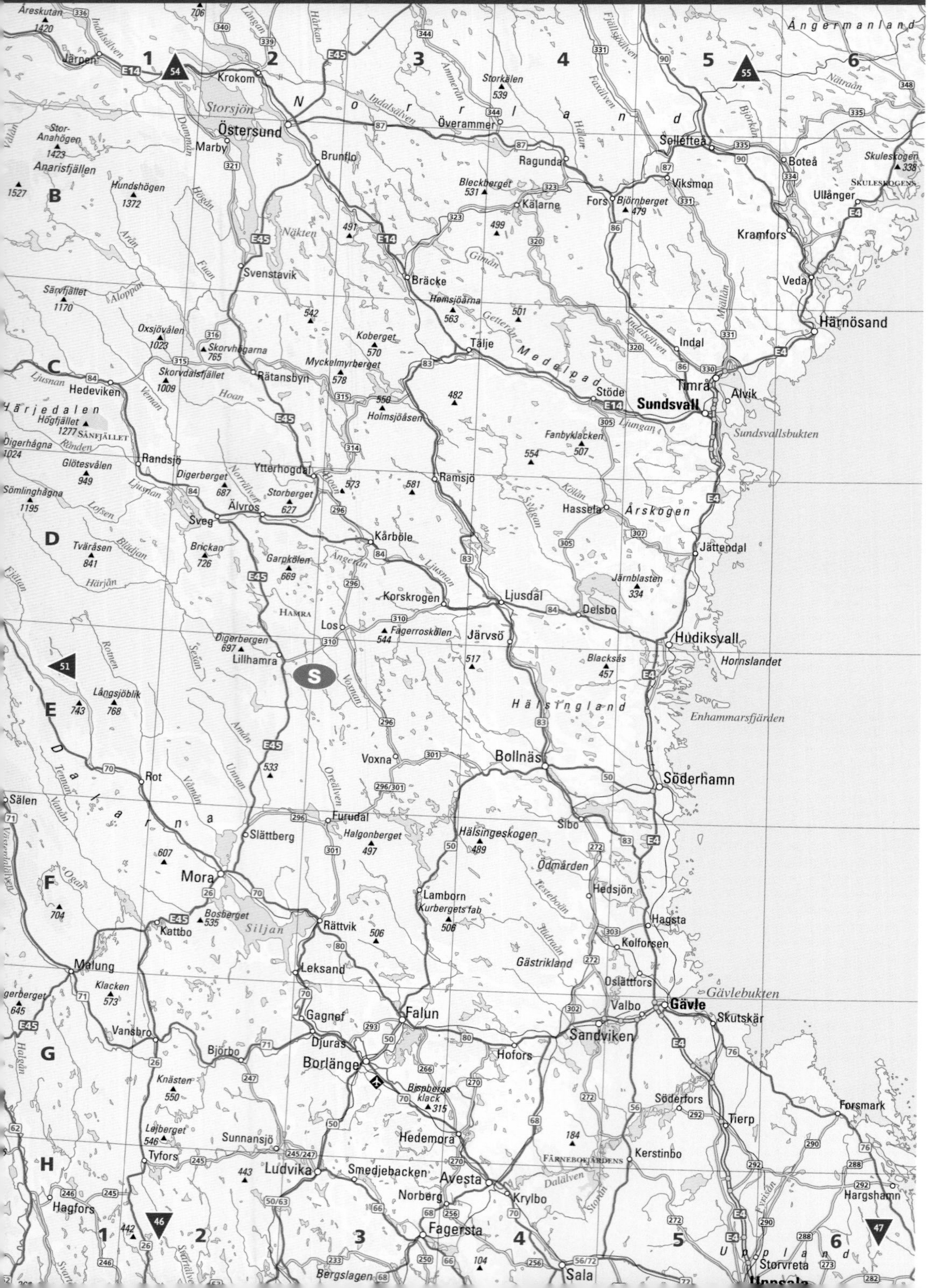
Åreskutan 1420
Järpen
Krokom
Storsjön
Östersund
Marby
Stor-Anahögen 1423
Anarisfjällen
Hundshögen 1372
Brunflo
Storkälen 539
Överammer
Ragunda
Sollefteå
Boteå
Skuleskogen 338
Viksmon
Ullånger
Bleckberget 531
Kälarne
Fors
Björnberget 479
Kramfors
Svenstavik
Bräcke
Hemsjöarna 563
Veda
Härnösand
Särvfjället 1170
Oxsjövålen 1023
Skorvhögarna 765
Koberget 570
Tälje
Indal
Skorvdalsfjället 1009
Rätansbyn
Myckelmyrberget 578
Hedeviken
Härjedalen
Högfjället 1277
Holmsjöåsen
Stöde
Sundsvall
Timrå
Alvik
Sundsvallsbukten
Digerhågna 1024
Randsjö
Glötesvålen 949
Fanbyklacken 507
Digerberget 687
Ytterhogdal
Ramsjö
Sömlinghågna 1195
Storberget 627
Älvros
Sveg
Hassela
Årskogen
Tväråsen 841
Brickan 726
Kårböle
Jättendal
Garpkölen 669
Järnblasten 334
Korskrogen
Ljusdal
Delsbo
Los
Fagerroskölen 544
Järvsö
Hudiksvall
Hornslandet
Digerbergen 697
Lillhamra
Blacksås 457
Långsjöblik 768
Hälsingland
Enhammarsfjärden
Voxna
Bollnäs
Söderhamn
Rot
Sälen
Dalarna
Furudal
Sibo
Slättberg
Halgonberget 497
Hälsingeskogen 489
Mora
Ödmården
Hedsjön
Lamborn
Kurbergets fäb 506
Bosberget 535
Kattbo
Siljan
Rättvik
Hagsta
Kolforsen
Malung
Klacken 573
Leksand
Gästrikland
Oslättfors
Gävlebukten
Gagnef
Falun
Valbo
Gävle
Skutskär
Vansbro
Djurås
Sandviken
Björbo
Borlänge
Hofors
Knästen 550
Bispbergs klack 315
Söderfors
Forsmark
Tierp
Lejberget 546
Sunnansjö
Hedemora
Kerstinbo
Tyfors
Ludvika
Smedjebacken
Avesta
Krylbo
Dalälven
Hargshamn
Hagfors
Norberg
Fagersta
Uppland
Storvreta
Bergslagen
Sala

1 2 3 4 5 6

B

C

D

E

F

G

H

Meløya
Glomsteet 1288
Ågskaret
17
1454
Blokktinden 1032
Snøtinden 1594
Jektvik
SALTFJELLET SVARTISEN
Nesøya
Hestmona
Hestmona 566
Kilboghamn
Trænfjorden
Lurøya
Høgtuva 1268
Langvatnet
619
Løvunden
Strandtinden 1173
Snøhellet 1196
Sjøn
Sjønbotn
12
Nesna
Hemnesberget
Hemnesøy
808
808
Glein
Levang
Lihødet 842
Toven 991
E6
Korgen
Dønna
Dønmannen 838
809
17
78
Sandnessjøen
806
Engan
17
Vefsnfjorda
Røssvassbukta
Tjøtta
Mosjøen
Røssvatnet
1559
Geittind
Vågsodden
Vefsna
Vega
Trolltinden 797
839
17
E6
Horn
Anddalsvågen
Trofors
73
804
17
76
Ivarrud
Bjørgefjellet
76
BØRGEFJELL
Vennesund
Holm
Gutuvikfjellet 594
Leka
Terråk
Skatollet
801
E6
Nurstfjellet
771
17
Drottendalsfjellet 927
Søre Steinfjellet
Mealhkoe 1182
593
Vikna
770
606 Kjøringvassfjellet
981
1008
Mealhkoe 1160
Røyrvik
Vikna
806
N
773
Jåavma
Geisnes
769
776
Mariafjellet 1170
Abelvær
768
Saltfjella 759
757
1056
793
Hurtigruten
769
Skorva 665
776
Skorovatn
Tømmervikfjellet 448
775
Heimdalshaugen 1150
Portfjellet 838
648
Skogmo
764
E6
Nesåpiggen 988
Sanddøla
Laueysnes
17
760
Vestre Brandsfjellet 1072
Eidet
74
Namsos
Geitfjellet 872
Formofoss
74
540
685
766
Reinsjøfjellet 726
Lura
GRESSÅMOEN
Osen
Langnesfjellet 775
Finnhůva 995
715
Snåsavatnet
Imsa
Blåfjellshatten 1332
17
E6
763
Finnvollheia 675
Sprova
Brannheiklumpen 818
Imsdalsfjellet 941
Harsvik
Kjerringheia 540
715
INNHERRAD
Stjørdøla
Måhkene 1266
723
762
Steinkjer
Løysmundhatten 1090
Storfjellet 664
720
Sandfjället 1248
Ansätten 1091
Åfjord
711
761
759
Mjölksvattsfjället 1230
Tarva
710
715
755
Verdalsøra
757
Skäckerfjällen
Åkersjön
714
Brekstad
Levanger
72
Hárskallen 735
760
336
Froya
716
Grandefjæra
609
E6
754
Sandvika
Kallsjön
Landögssjön
714
Knarrlagsund
Selva
755
753
1035
Hitra
656
717
Vannvikan
Kjølhaugen 1249
Almåsaberget 706
Sandstad
710
Stjørdalshalsen
752
Kristiansund, Ålesund, Bergen
322
Kjerringfjellet 1072
Åreskutan 1420
Åre
336
Fonna 722
566
Trondheim
E14
E14
680
Heimdal
Skarvän 1171
51
Störlien
Järpen
Omnsfjellet 847
Orkanger
704
705
E14
E14
Gråfjellet 1040
65
708
Fongen
Snasahögarna
Enan
Vinjeøra
Søva
E39

0 10 20 30 40 50 km
0 10 20 30 miles

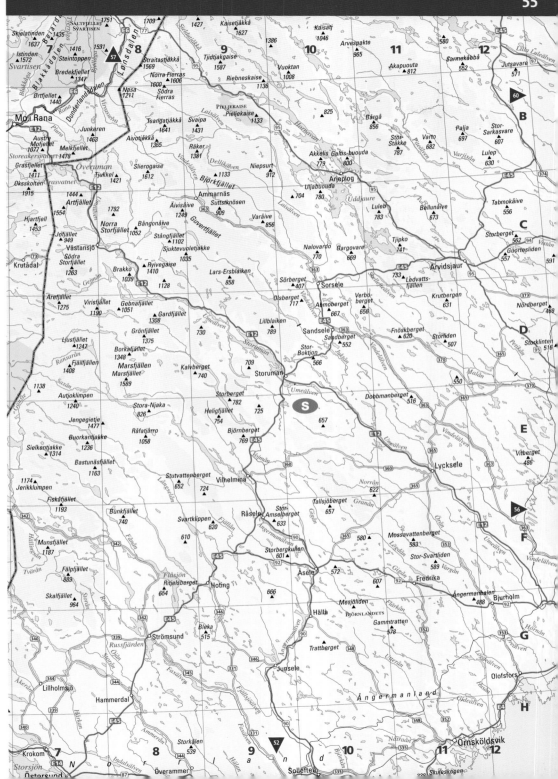

56

1 | **2** | **3** | **4** | **5** | **6**

Särmekåbbá 552
812
Jutsavare 571
Lilla Luleälven
Stora Luleälven
Vuottarauto 474
468
E10
417
Ainseväle
Tornio
932
21
Naustapuouta 636
Luottäive 603
97
97
Rödaälven
Luleälven
60
Stor Läppberget 263
392
98
930
930
B
Varto 682
Palja 697
Stor-Sarkasvare 607
E45
Vitberget 594
391
356
231
398
99
21
FIN
62
929
E8
E75
927
Lulep 630
Junkerkölen 348
97
E10
4
Kalix
398
E8
926
Pudasälven
Varjisån
673
Harrejaureliden 647
Tabmokäive 556
374
 Enstakaberget 440
Boden
383
Kalix
Haparanda
Tornio
4
Bellunäive
556
97
356
E4
Kemi
E8 E75
95
E45
Störberget 562
Nattberget 458
94
Råneälven
PERÄMEREN
Guortesliden 557
Västån 591
Älvsbyn 247
Gammelstaden
Luleå
HAPARANDA SKÄRGÅRD
C
Arvidsjaur
95
330
374
94
E4
Krutbergen 631
S
Nördberget 469
Stor-Flötuberget 426
373
Piteå
Kallfjärden
Storliden 507
55
365
Byskeälven
Peitån
95
Storklinten 516
Åbyälven
Skellefteälven
370
Mälån
550
D
365
E4
370
BOTTENVIKEN
PERÄMERI
Kågeälven
Vindelälven
95
Vitberget 486
Stor-Blåbergsliden 374
Byurälven
Skellefteå
Raahe
cksele
363
364
Risån
Sikån
8
E
E12
365
7840
787
Kalajoki
786
353
364
Rickleån
E4
7730
787
786
Kalajoki
Angermanbalen 488
363
Vindelälven
774
7720
27
F
Bjurholm
92
E12
775
Ylivieska
63
353
Hörnän
Öreälven
Umeå
28
62
155
63
Pirttiharju
Kökkola
(Karleby)
13
Lögdeälven
Olofsfors
G
Holmsund
Västra Kvarken
757
749
Jakobstad
(Pietarsaari)
748
747
63
öldsvik
Hundn
Norra Kvarken
Merenkurkku
E4
709
7450
7270
741
63
750
751
Norra Gloppet
Östra Gloppet
19
7320
738
751
7530
Björköby
240
7300
63
741
7370
2 | **3** | **4** | **5** | **6**
E8
718
725
64
711
16
Södra Gloppet
Vaasa
(Vasa)
717
Kyrönjoki
618
7210
Kauhava
723

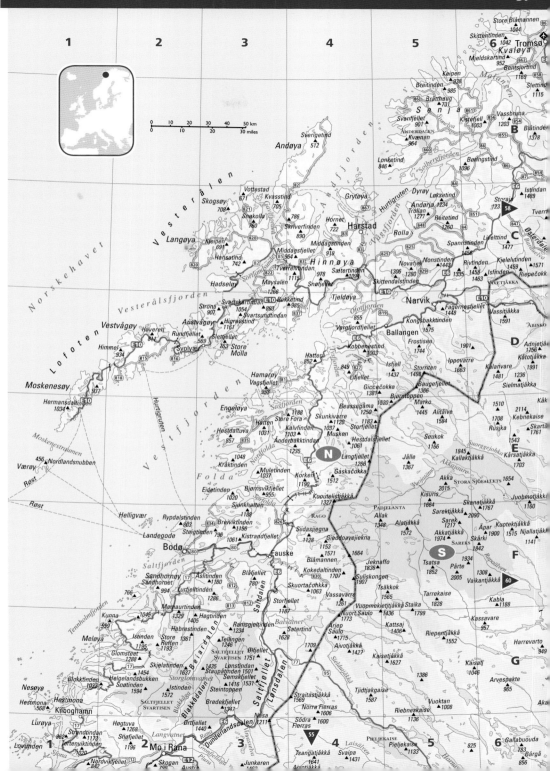

1 2 3 4 5 6

0 10 20 30 40 50 km
0   10   20   30 miles

Norskehavet

Vesterålen

Andøya 512

Sverigetind

Vottestad
Skogsøy 671 Kvasstind
708▲ 705

Snøkolla 786
760 Skriverfinden Hornet
890 722 Harstad

Langøya Kjeipen
691 Middagstinden
820 Middagsfjellet 964 83 Hinnøya
Hansatind 742▲ 82 Tverrfjellheia Sætertinden
1115 978 1094

Hadseløy Møysalen
1266 Snøfjevål

Vesterålsfjorden Strona Svartskarmutian 985
907 1054 Bukketind
Svartsundtindan Tjeldøya
Austvågøy Higravstind
Vestvågøy Haveren 1161
811 Rundfjellet 569 Vågfjordfjellet
Himmel Sletfjellet Kobbenestind
934 E10 263 Store 1003
Svolvær Molla
815 816 Hatten 849 827 Isfjell
852▲ 1437
Moskenesøy Hamarøy Lifjellet Giccecôkka
937 Vågsfjellet 1381
953

Hermansdalti Engeløya Beassegåma Bjørntoppen
1034 Store Fora ▲1188 1250 Marko
Hestdaltuva 1120 Skunkivære 1445
857 835 1031 1103 ▲ Musken Hestdalsfjellet
Anderbakktindan 1061
1235

1048 N Langtjellet
Kråktinden 1266
Muletinden Korken
Bjørnsvikfjellet 955 Gåskacôkka
Eidetinden 1512
1020 Sjunkhatten
1188 Kuoutelistjåkkå
Rypdalstinden 1327 Padjelanta
Helligvær 803 834 Breiviktinden Allak
1156 RAGO 1348
Landegode Steigtinden 796 Siidasjiegna
1061 Kistrandfjellet 1128 Gieddoavejiekna
Bodø 80 80 Fauske 1153
Saltfjorden Blåmannen 1571 1664
Sandhornøy Aslitinden 1707 Suliskongen
Sandhornet ▲180 Kokedaltinden 1907
766 994 Lurfjelltinden 830
1286 Skuortacôhkka Tsäkkok
1063 Vassavarre 1565
Mørnaurtinden Storfjellet 1261
Kunna 1329 Høgtinden 1197
599 1045 1405 Ramsgjeltinden Vuopmekietjätjåkkå
Habrestinden 1628 Satertind Nuort Saulo
Meløya 1234 1773
Istinden Store 1361 Tellingen Årjep
1454 Ruffen Øffjellet Saulo
Glomsteet 1195 1193 1709 1715
1288 Skjelatinden Lønstinden Aivotjåkkå
17 1435 Staupåtinden 1501 1427 Kaisetjäkkå
Blokktinden 1416 Semskfjellet 1627
1032 Helgelandsbukken Istinden 1531 1386
Nesøy Søøtinden 1572 Steintoppen
Hestmona 1594 Blåkkådalen
568 Kilboghamn Bredekfjellet Straitastjåkkå
1347 1569 Norra Fierras
Lůrøya Høgtuva Ørtfjellet Nåsa 1211 Sôdra 1606
1268 1440 1600 Fierras
Løvunden Strøndtinden Snøfjellet Dunderlandsdalen
862 1173 1196 55
Tertenviktinden Mo i Rana
1020 Nordvikfjellet Skogan Tsangatjåkkå Svaipa
842 1641 1431

1 2 3 4 5 6

B

NORDISHAVET

580

Hurtigruten
Rolvsøysundet

Hammerfest
Kvaløya
Svartfjellet
630

Sørøya 882
656

Lopphavet Hasvik
Sørøysundet

94

Eliassen
939 949
Stjernøya
Seiland
1079 Skinnfjellet
985 710
698

C

Nord-Kvaløy
Fugløya
Fugløykallen
753

Alangen
737
Vanna
Vanntindan
1033
Arnøya
1168
Middagsfjellet
1071
828
Økfsjord
1066
1304
Liv'luvarri
958
Fjelltindnasen
1041

Øksfjord

Navgastat
713

Rebbenesøy
Skjervøy
Kvænangen
882

E6

Lassefjellet
1166
Stuora
Hal'di
1149
Alta
740

Svartevasstind
Hansnes
Hurtigruten
Kågen
1098
Gierdoidvarri
810

Ringvassøy 876
Reinøy
Reinskartind
884
Uløya
866
Blåtind
1142
Rieppesgai'sa
1337
Nubivarri
841
Cæv'dni
672

Istind
953 863
Tverrbakktind
1390

Store Blåmannen
1044
Ulfstind
1094
Vaggastinden
1398
Bæssetindan
1312
1301
Iešjávri
Vir'dnečak'ka
590

Skittentinden
1042
Stortind
1512
Nordmannviktind
1336
N

Tromsø
Tromsdalen
Tromsdalstind
Fornesfjellet
1478
Bæccahal'di
1326
Čuonjaoai'vi
1089

Kvaløya
Mjeldskartind
952
862
91
865

Bentsjertind
1169 858
Sennedalsfjellet
1385
868
E6
Isfjellet
1375
Mållejus
975
Čáravárri
887

Breittinden
785
Slåtting
1115
Jiehkkevarri
1833
Čiččenvárri
1312

861 856
Lakselvtinden
1617
Rášśahibba
1252
1365

Senja
Klstefjell
1003
855 854
Henriktind
1219
Halti
1328

ANDERDALEN
860
Blåtinden
1378
Piggtind
1505
Mannfjellet
1533
Goahterášša
1371
Kahperusvaarat
1144
REISA

Børingstind
1096 84
Lille
Russetind
1527
Báras
1419
Saana
1029
Jollanoaivi
1029
Vuoskuvarri
527

Stormauken
1249
942
1523

Storaia
1237
Istinden
1489
Moskkugáisi
1523
Bås'tevarri
658

Divdjalen
Langfjelltind
1504
Rostadalen
Peeravaara
933

E6
851
Rostaelva
Rommaeno

Spannstinden
1456
Kjerkestinden
1677
1271
Ropi
945
Tarju
735
Urtivaara
633
491

Livelttind
1477
Njumis
1713
Jerta
1428
Paltalve
915
Ruutusoive
842

Jonstingen
1443
Rivtinden
1458
Kjelelvttind
1571
Tsáktso
1119
Tarvantovaara
591
Jierstivaara
647

Kistefjell
1633
Máissavarri
1022
Roopi
799

57
Vavetjåkka
Råkkunbárri
1659

E6
E10
Vassitjåkka
1591
Tuoptejåkkah
1604
ÖVRE DIVIDAL
Åhtevatnet
Ránddno

G
ABISKO
Pyhäkero
711
Outtakka
723

1901
Ippovaare
1663
Kåtotjåkka
1991
Rakisvare
985
Puollanáive
796
PALLAS JA OUNASTUNTURIN
KANSALLISPUISTO

Kalahvare
1481
Torneträsk
S
Taivaskero
807

H
Rassepautastjåkka
1750
Råppe
1014
Luleg-
Patsajåkel
782
Vittangivaara
836
60
612
Nunasvaara
580
Halju
551
Keimiötunturi
810

1510
Rusjka
1708
Kebnekaise
2114
1017
Leavvajohka
Rautasakara
E45
99
79

1543
Skartåive
1761
2
Piedjastjåkka
3
Kiruna
4
5
6

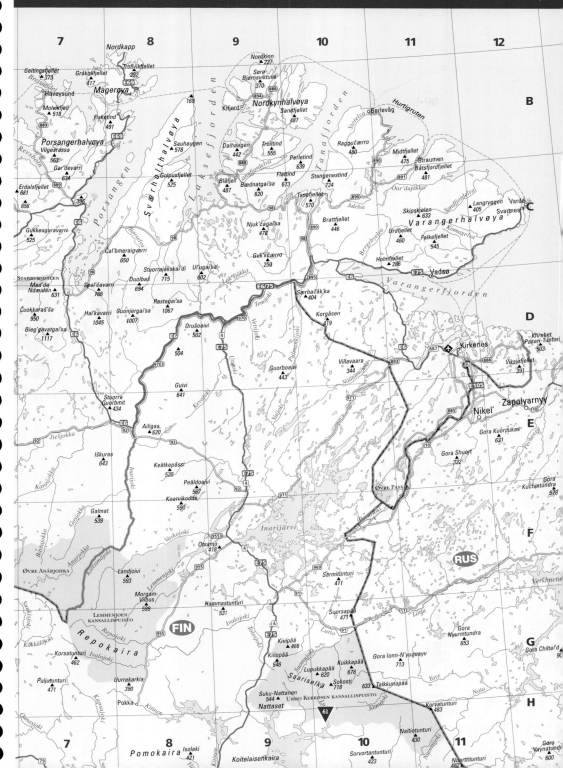

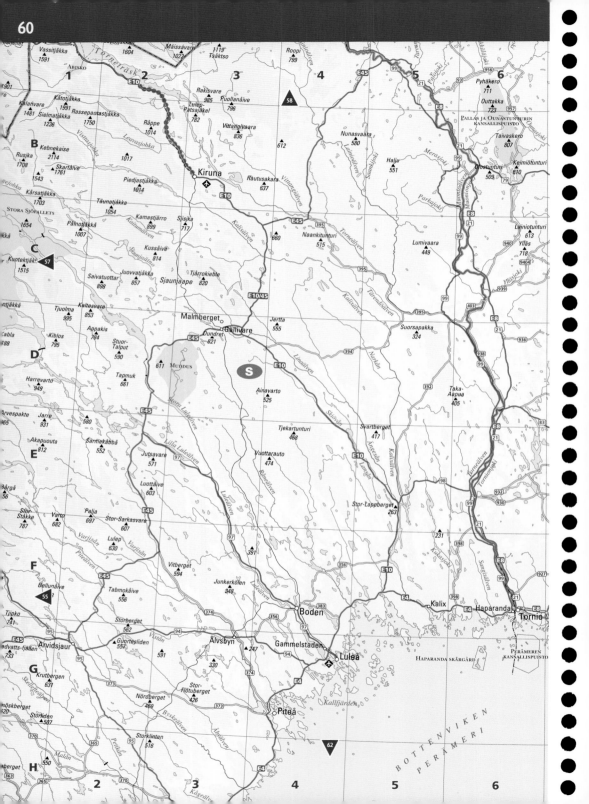

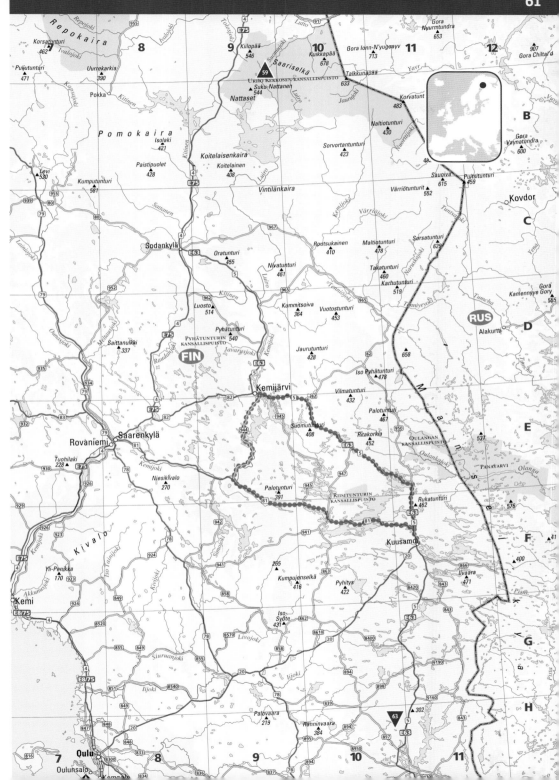

1   2   3   4   5   6

Luottåive
603

Stor-
arkasvara
807

E45

Vitberget
594
374

374

Varjisån

Piteålven
656

B

Junkerkölen
348

374

E45

Enstakaberget
440

Boden
383

Storberget
62
94

Nåttberget
458

Vistån

Älvsbyn

S

Gammelstaden

247

Luleå

391

356
97

E4

Lulealven

Luleälven

97

E10

E4

356

Stor-
Lappberget 263

60

231

398

Kalajärvi

Sangisälven

Kalix
398

21

98

392

932

930

99

Tornio

Torneå

21

929

927

E8

99

930

Saarenkylä
Rovaniemi

Tuohilaki
228

E75

926

930

926

4

Yli-
Perukka
170

Akkunusjoki

Kemijoki

923

Kivalo

Iso Tainijoki

Haparanda

E4

Tornio

E8

Kemi

924

849

Simojoki

E8/75

E4

8520

Jördberget
469

C

Storklinten
516

56

330

373

Byskeälven

Åbyälven

373

Piteå

Kallfjärden

Kågeälven

370

D

Bureälven
374

Stor-Blåbergsliden

95

Skellefteå

E4

364

Sikån

Risån

364

Rickleån

E

365

364

Sävarån

E4

364

F

Umeå

4

ölmsund

Västra
Kvarken

Degerfjärden

Norra Kvarken

Merenkurkku

G

Norra
Gloppet

Östra
Gloppet

Björköby
7240

Södra
Gloppet

Vaasa
(Vasa)

6732

679

Laihia

E12

687

6781

6785

5781

7200

E8

717

7210

7060

725

7041

E8

738

718

720

730

7300

7320

741

2   3

16

Lapua

132

66

6991

7114

7120

714

Kauhava

711

64

733

Alajärvi

16

4   5   6

BOTTENVIKEN

PERÄMERI

HAPARANDA SKÄRGÅRD

PERÄMEREN

0   10   20   30   40   50 km
0   10   20   30 miles

855

851

849

848

E8/75

848

816

Oulu

8300

Oulunsalo

Kempele

22

4

813

827

Siikajoki

8090

86

8110

8060

E75

Raahe

813

E8

807

807

822

88

88

86

807

Liminkaoja

Piipsanjoki

8060

88

E75

Kalajoki

786

7890

787

Oulainen

7970

186

793

800

786

8

774

786

798

786

7840

787

786

7730

7220

775

Ylivieska

785

786

E75

793

798

86

63

28

Nivala

58

775

Pyhäjoki

Kokkola
(Karleby)

13

E8

749

748

757

63

760

7630

775

Pirttiharju
155

28

Kalajoki

E75

Jakobstad
(Pietarsaari)

747

749

7450

63

751

775

658

E75

7270

751

7530

7370

58/775

6540

760

Kolima

58

Salamajärven
Kansallispuisto

648

Pyhä-Häkin

697

77

6501

Vaasa (Vasa)
Laihia
Kauhava
Karvala
Lapua
Alajärvi
Seinäjoki
Nurmo
Ruona
Saarijärvi
Äänekoski
Suolahti
Kurikka
Alavus
Närpes
Kauhajoki
Keuruu
Jyväskylä
Pirttimäki
Mänttä
Parkano
Jämsänkoski
Jämsä
Kankaanpää
Hämeenkangas
Orivesi
Pori
Pihlava
Reposaari
Mäntyluoto
Ylöjärvi
Friitala
Tampere
Nokia
Pirkkala
Kangasala
Harjavalta
Vammala
Lempäälä
Rauma
Kokemäki
Huittinen
Valkeakoski
Eura
Toijala
Hämeenlinna
Lahti
Hollola
Laitila
Uusikaupunki
Loimaa
Turenki
Orimattila
Forssa
Riihimäki
Mäntsälä
Somera
Hyvinkää
Kustavi
Karkkila
Järvenpää
Porvoo (Borgå)
Hakkenpää
Raisio
Naantali
Littoinen
Paimio
Tuusula
Keraya
Turku (Åbo)
Kaarina
Salo
Nummela
Klaukkala
Vantaa (Vanda)
Tikkurila
Pargas (Parainen)
Lohja
Kirkkonummi (Kyrkslätt)
Virkkala
Karis
Espoo (Esbo)
Kauniainen
HELSINKI (HELSINGFORS)
Kökar
Dalsbruk Bromary (Taalintehdas)
Ekenäs (Tammisaari)
Hanko (Hangö)
Mariehamn Stockholm

-money-lp/vip-voucher_clip_image...   01/08/2007

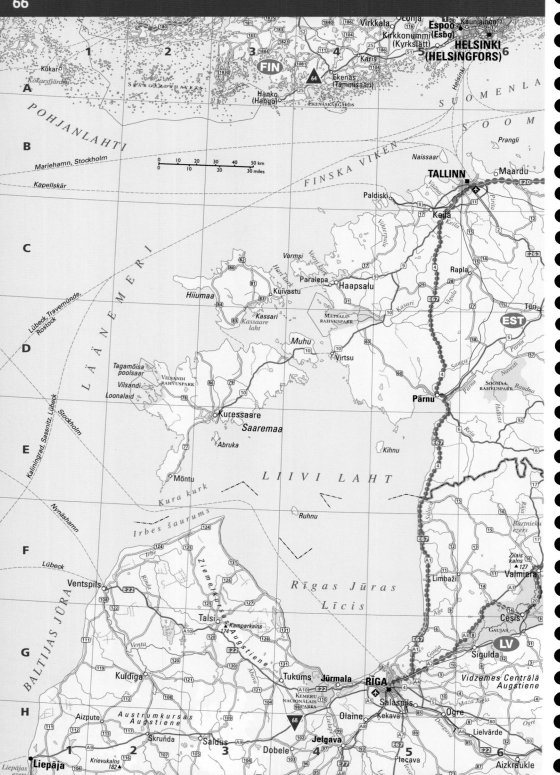

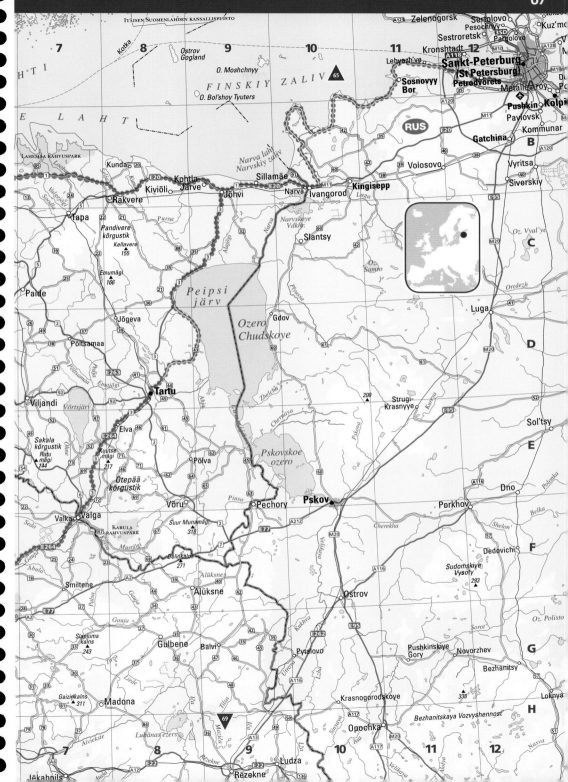

ITÄISEN SUOMENLAHDEN KANSALLISPUISTO

7   8   9   10   11   12

Zelenogorsk   A123   Sertolovo
Pesochnyy   Kuz'mo
Sestroretsk   Pargolovo
A128
Lebyazh'ye   Kronshtadt   Sankt-Peterburg
(St Petersburg)   M18
Sosnovyy   Petrodvorets   M10
Bor   Metallo   roy   Po
RUS   Pushkin   Kolpi
Pavlovsk
Gatchina   Kommunar   B
A120
Volosovo   Vyritsa
Siverskiy   C
Oz. Vyal'ye

Ostrov
Gogland
O. Moshchnyy
FINSKIY ZALIV 65
O. Bol'shoy Tyuters

HTI
E L A H T
LAHEMAA RAHVUSPARK
Narva laht
Narvskiy zaliv
Kunda   Kohtla-   Sillamäe   Narva   Ivangorod   Kingisepp
Kiviõli   Järve   Jõhvi   Luga
Rakvere   Slantsy
Tapa
Pandivere   Narvskoye
kõrgustik   Vdkhr.
Kellavere   155   Oz.
Samro
Emumägi   166
Paide   Peipsi   Gdov   Luga   D
järv   Ozero
Jõgeva   Chudskoye
Põltsamaa   Oredezh
Viljandi   Strugi-   Sol'tsy   E
Tartu   Krasnyye   200
Võrtsjärv   Pskovskoe   Zhelcha   Chernaya
Elva   ozero
Sakala   Kuutse   Põlva   Dno
kõrgustik   mägi   217   Pskov
Rutu   Otepää   Võru   Pechory   Porkhov   F
mägi   144   kõrgustik   Piusa   Suur Munamägi   318
Valka   Valga   Delinkalns   271   Dedovichi
KARULA   Sudomskiye
RAHVUSPARK   Vysoty   293
Smiltene   Alūksne   Ostrov   G
Gauja
Slanjuma   Pushkinskiye   Novorzhev
kalns   243   Gory   Bezhanitsy
Gulbene   Balvi   Pytalovo   Loknya
Gaizinkalns   311   Madona   Krasnogorodskoye   338
Bezhanitskaya Vozvyshennost'   H
Lubānas ezers   69   Opochka
7   8   9   10   11   12
Jēkabpils   Ludza   Rēzekne

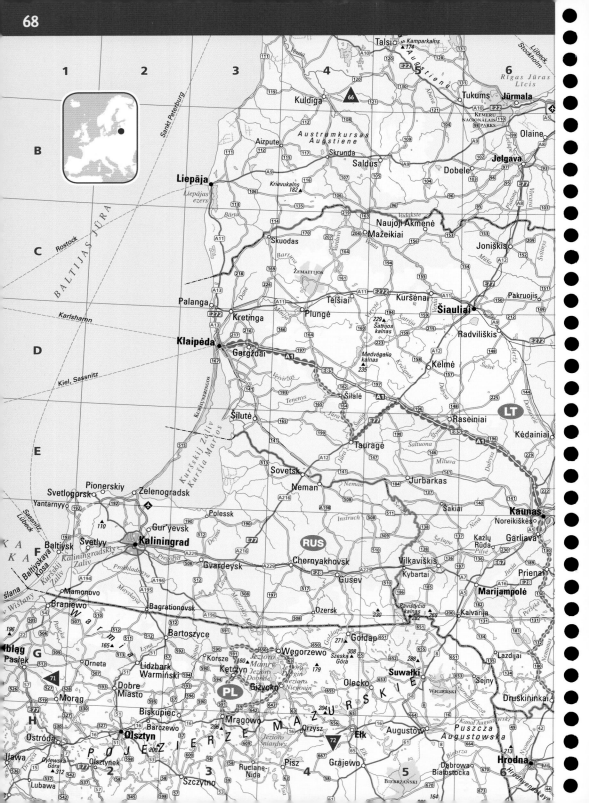

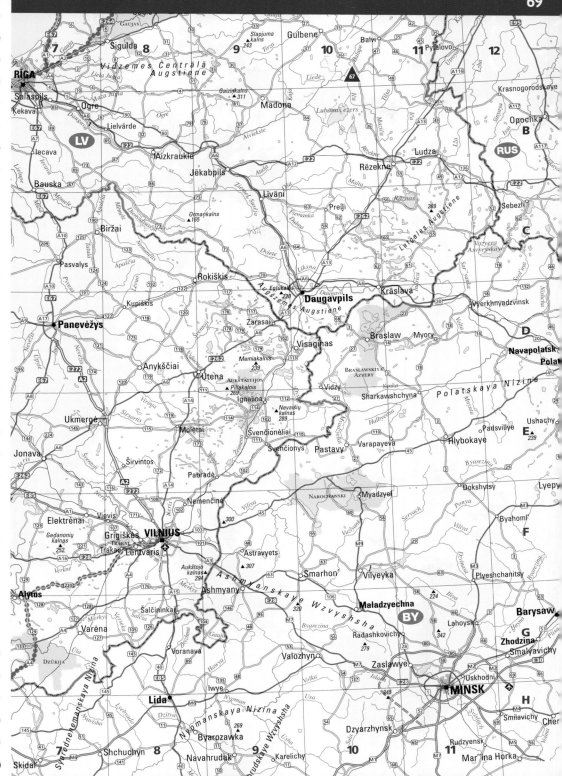

1 2 3 4 5 6

Lübeck · København · Trelleborg · Ystad · Rønne · Klaipėda, Kaliningrad, Sankt-Peterburg · Ustka

OSTSEE
MORZE BAŁTYCKIE

Wittow · Hiddensee · Piekberg · Jasmund · Sassnitz · Bergen · Rügen · Darłowo · Sławno · **Słupsk**

Zingst · Stralsund · Ostseebad Göhren · Greifswalder Bodden · Kołobrzeg · **Koszalin** · KOSZALIŃSKIE

Grimmen · Greifswald · Oderbucht · Zatoka Pomorska · Trzebiatów · Karlino · Miastko

Demmin · Anklam · Usedom · Kamień Pomorski · WOLIŃSKI · Świnoujście · Wolin · Międzyzdroje · Gryfice · Białogard · Czarne

Reuterstadt Stavenhagen · Altentreptow · Friedland · Eggesin · Ueckermünde · Zalew Szczeciński · POBRZEŻE · Nowogard · Świdwin · Połczyn Zdrój · Szczecinek

Neubrandenburg · Helpter Strasburg · Pasewalk · Police · SZCZECIŃSKIE · Drawsko Pomorskie · Złocieniec · Czaplinek · Debrzno · Złotów

Neustrelitz · Prenzlau · **Szczecin** · Stargard Szczeciński · Wałcz · Jastrowie · POJ KRA

Fürstenberg · Templin · Gryfino · Pyrzyce · Choszczno · DRAWIEŃSKI · **Piła** · Wyrzysk

Rheinsberg · Gransee · Zehdenick · Schorfheide · Schwedt an der Oder · Angermünde · Chojna · Barlinek · Trzcianka · Chodzież · Noteć

Eberswalde-Finow · Myślibórz · Strzelce Krajeńskie · Drezdenko · Wieleń · Czarnków · Wągrowiec

Oranienburg · Bernau · Wriezen · Langer Berg · Dębno · Gorzów Wielkopolski · Puszcza Natecka · Wronki · Rogoźno · Oborniki

BERLIN · Strausberg · Seelow · Kostrzyn · Skwierzyna · Sieraków · Międzychód · Szamotuły · Murowana Goślina

Potsdam · Erkner · Frankfurt an der Oder · Słubice · Rzepin · POJEZIERZE LUBUSKIE · Międzyrzecz · Pniewy · Buk · **Poznań** · Swarzędz

Blankenfelde · Königs Wusterhausen · Storkow · Beeskow · Świebodzin · Nowy Tomyśl · Opalenica · Puszczykowo · Luboń

Beelitz · Zossen · Luckenwalde · Golmberg · Eisenhüttenstadt · Krosno Odrzańskie · Grodzisk Wielkopolski · Wolsztyn · Mosina · Środa Wielkopolska · Kórnik

Jüterbog · Lübben · Guben · Gubin · Sulechów · Kościan · Śmigiel · Śrem

Herzberg · Cottbus · Peitz · Vetschau · **Zielona Góra** · Lubsko · Nowa Sól · Wschowa · Leszno · Gostyń

Falkenberg · Forst · Żary · Kożuchów · Żagań · Głogów · Góra · Rawicz

Elsterwerda · Weißwasser · Szprotawa · Przemków · Polkowice · Ścinawa · Żmigród · Milicz

Riesa · Großenhain · Hoyerswerda · Bernsdorf · Niesky · Bolesławiec · Chocianów · **Lubin** · Wołów · Brzeg Dolny · Trzebnica

Meißen · Kamenz · Pieńsk · **Legnica**

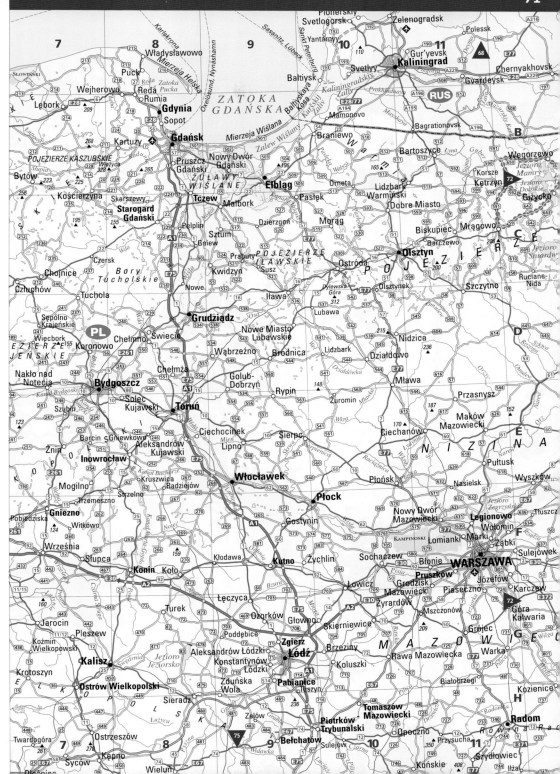

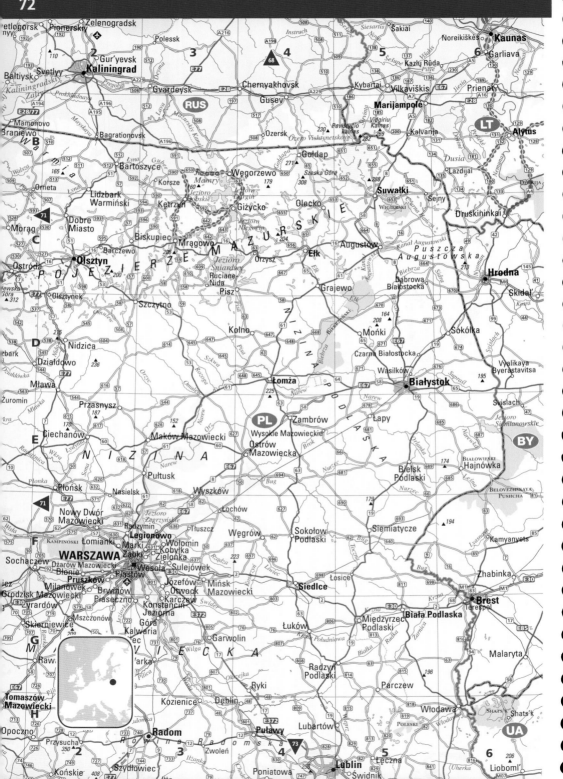

Cottbus
Forst
NIEDERLAUSITZ
Herzberg
Doberlug-Kirchhain
Bad Düben
Torgau
Falkenberg
Finsterwalde
Spremberg
Senftenberg
Hoyerswerda
Weißwasser
Żary
Żagań
Szprotawa
Przemków
Głogów
Polkowice
Ścinawa
Lubin
Wołów
Eilenburg
Elsterwerda
Wurzen
Riesa
Lauta
Bernsdorf
Kamenz
OBERLAUSITZ
Niesky
Pieńsk
Bolesławiec
Chocianów
Chojnów
Legnica
Grimma
Oschatz
Großenhain
Meißen
Döbeln
Bautzen
Bischofswerda
Löbau
Görlitz
Lubań
Lwówek Śląski
Złotoryja
Jawor
Borna
Rochlitz
Mittweida
Radebeul
Dresden
Sebnitz
Ebersbach
Lausitzer Gebirge
Gryfów Śląski
Strzegom
Burgstädt
Hainichen
Freital
Pirna
Flöha
Chemnitz
Freiberg
Dippoldiswalde
Rumburk
Bogatynia
Varnsdorf
Zittau
Jelenia Góra
Świebodzice
Kamienna Góra
Świdnica
Wałbrzych
Zwickau
Stollberg
Zschopau
Marienberg
Děčín
Krupka
Jizerské Hory
Jablonec nad Nisou
Liberec
Nový Bor
Lužické Hory
KARKONOSZE
KRKONOŠSKÝ
Lößnitz
Aue
Teplice
Ústí nad Labem
Česká Lípa
Mimoň
Vrchlabí
Trutnov
Broumov
Nowa Ruda
Eibenstock
Litvínov
Most
Litoměřice
Turnov
Doksy
Mnichovo Hradiště
Dvůr Králové
Jirkov
Chomutov
Kadaň
Klingenthal
Mladá Boleslav
Jičín
Nová Paka
Kłodzko
Karlovy Vary
Ostrov
Žatec
Louny
Mělník
Jaroměř
Hořice
Náchod
Szczytna
Orlické Hory
Doupovské Hory
Podbořany
Slaný
Neratovice
Nový Bydžov
Dobruška
Hradec Králové
Rakovník
Kladno
Čelákovice
Nymburk
Poděbrady
Rychnov nad Kněžnou
PRAHA
Pardubice
Holice
Tepelská Vrchovina
Mariánské Lázně
Beroun
BOHEMIA
Říčany
Kolín
Kutná Hora
Chrudim
Vysoké Mýto
Ústí nad Orlicí
Lanškroun
Tachov
Čáslav
CZ
Železné Hory
Litomyšl
Stříbro
Nýřany
Plzeň
Rokycany
Dobříš
Benešov
Zruč nad Sázavou
Chotěboř
Hlinsko
Svitavy
Polička
Příbram
Sedlčany
Vlašim
Světlá nad Sázavou
Nové Město na Moravě
Přeštice
Humpolec
Havlíčkův Brod
Domažlice
Klatovy
Blatná
Milevsko
Pelhřimov
Jihlava
Letovice
Bystřice nad Pernštejnem
Horažďovice
Tábor
Bechyně
Písek
Nýrsko
Strakonice
Sušice
Soběslav
Jindřichův Hradec
Velké Meziříčí
Blansko
Kuřim
Třešť
Třebíč
Cham
BÖHMER WALD
ŠUMAVA
Vodňany
Veselí nad Lužnicí
Telč
Náměšť nad Oslavou
Rosice
Brno
Viechtach
Zwiesel
Vimperk
Prachatice
Dačice
Ivančice
Moravské Budějovice
Regen
České Budějovice
Třeboň
Jemnice
Deggendorf
Český Krumlov
Znojmo
Freyung
Waidhofen an der Thaya
Osterhofen
Gmünd
Kaplice
Rohrbach in Oberösterreich
Horn
Zwettl
Hollabrunn
Mistelbach
Pfarrkirchen
MÜHLVIERTEL
WALDVIERTEL
Freistadt
Langenlois
Krems an der Donau
Braunau am Inn
Linz
Unterweitersdorf
Stockerau
Altötting
Leonding
Perg
Klosterneuburg
Marchtrenk
Traun
Enns
Ybbs an der Donau
Melk
St Pölten
Pressbaum
WIEN
Burghausen
INN
Ried im Innkreis
Wels
Tittmoning
Vöcklabruck
Steyr
Purgstall an der Erlauf
Baden
Himberg
Straßwalchen
Hochbira
Plattenberg
A
D

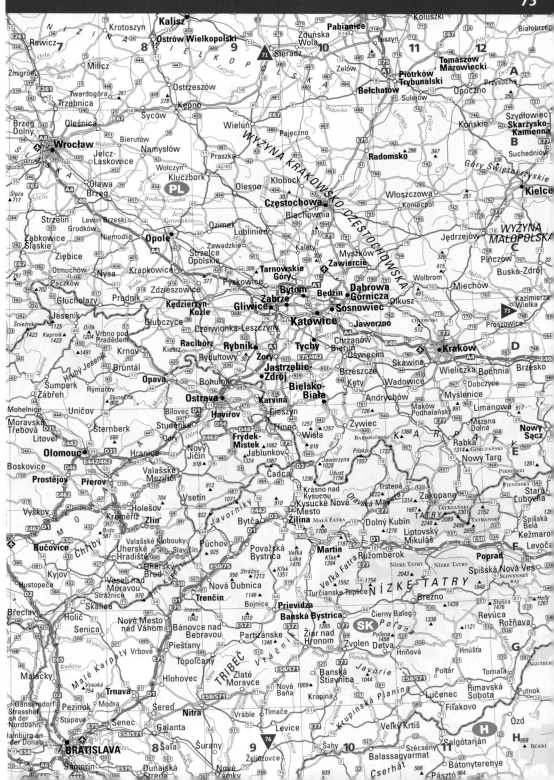

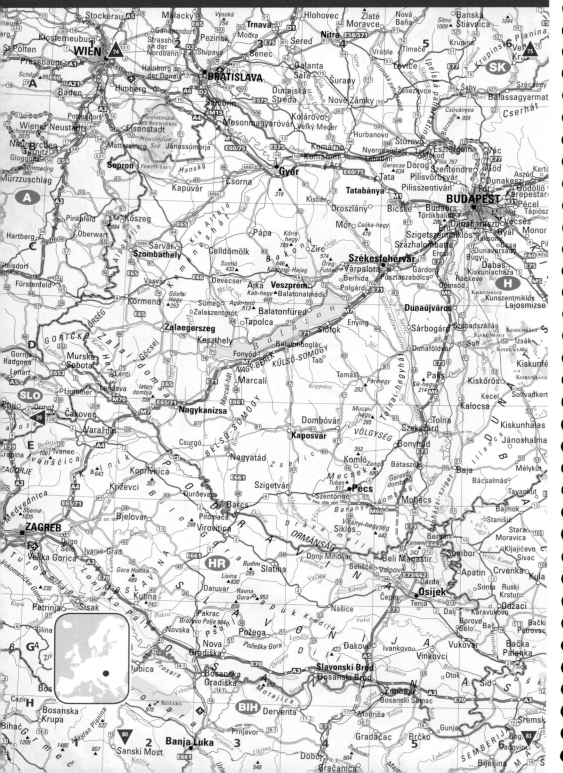

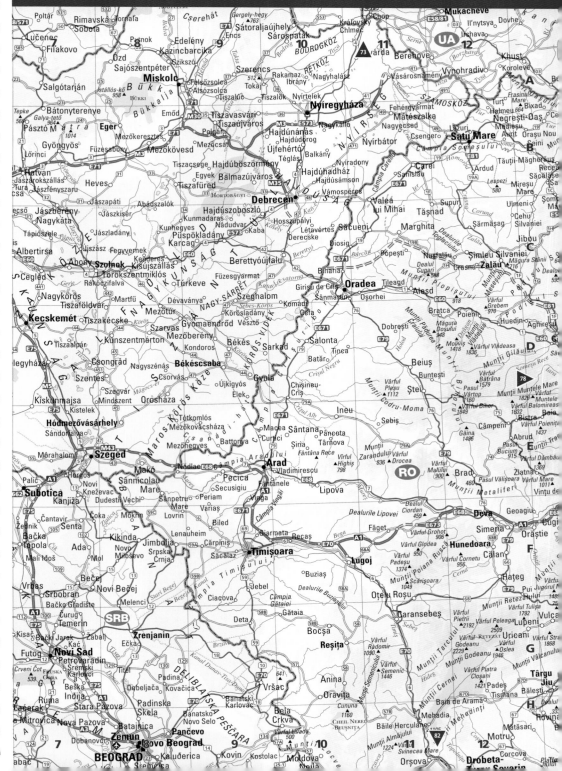

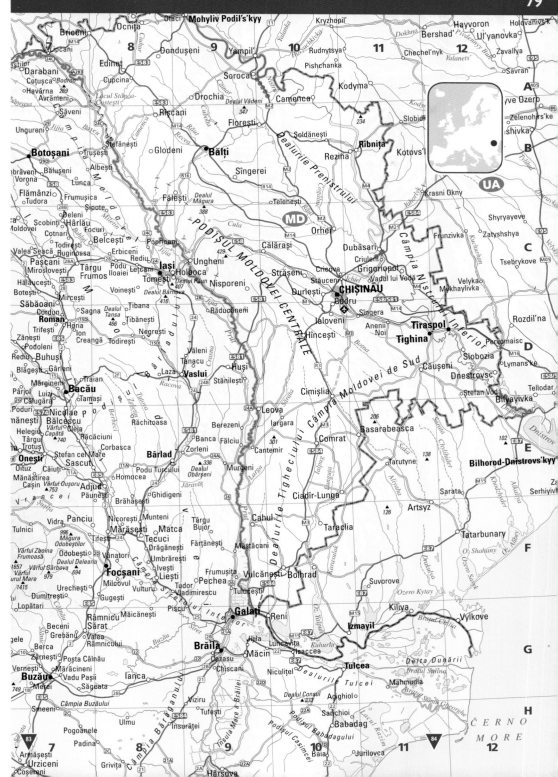

BEOGRAD · Pančevo · Zemun · Smederevo · Požarevac · Kovin · Kostolac · Moldova Noua · Orşova · Drobeta-Turnu Severin · Strehaia · Filiaşi · Craiova · Balş

Vršac · Anina · Oravita · Băile Herculane · Mehadia · Motru · Turceni · Argetoaia · Coşoveni · Leu

Târgu Jiu · Rovinari · Ticleni · Târgu Cărbuneşti · Berbeşti · Horezu · Novaci

Smederevska Palanka · Velika Plana · Lapovo · Kragujevac · Jagodina · Ćuprija · Paraćin · Bor · Negotin · Zaječar · Vidin · Calafat · Poiana Mare · Lom · Kozloduy · Oryakhovo · Miziya

Kruševac · Aleksinac · Sokobanja · Knjaževac · Belogradchik · Montana · Berkovitsa · Vratsa · Mezdra · Cherven Bryag · Byala Slatina · Knezha

Trstenik · Vrnjačka Banja · Niš · Prokuplje · Pirot · Bela Palanka · Dimitrovgrad · Godech · Svoge · Botevgrad · Etropole

Novi Pazar · Kuršumlija · Leskovac · Vlasotince · Slivnitsa · SOFIA · Kostinbrod · Novi Iskŭr · Elin Pelin · Ikhtiman

Mitrovicë · Podujevë · Vushtrri · PRISHTINË (PRIŠTINA) · Fushë Kosovë · Lipjan · Janjevë · Vranje · Surdulica · Breznik · Pernik · Radomir · Kostenets

Shtime · Gjilan · Bujanovac · Preševo · Kyustendil · Bobovdol · Dupnitsa · Samokov · Belovo · Septemvri

Prizren · Ferizaj · Kaçanik · Kumanovo · Kratovo · Probištip · Delčevo · Blagoevgrad · Yakoruda · Velingrad · Rakitovo

Gostivar · Tetovo · SKOPJE · Sveti Nikole · Štip · Veles · Kočani · Vinica · Trabotivište · Radoviš · Bansko · Razlog

Gotse Delchev · Sandanski · Kičevo

SRB · RKS · MK · Europe locator inset

Mountain and feature labels: DELIBLATSKA PEŠČARA · Munţii Godeanu · Munţii Cernei · DJERDAP · HOMOLJE · KRAJINA · Câmpia Bălţatei · Platforma Oltenţului · Câmpia Bailestilor · ŽUPA · TOPLICA · SUVA PLANINA · VRACHANSKA BALKAN · Stara Planina · Golema Planina · Sofiyska Planina · KRAJIŠTE · SLAVIŠTE · Osogovska Planina · PALAKARIYATA · RILA · PIRIN · Sar Planina · MALEŠEVO

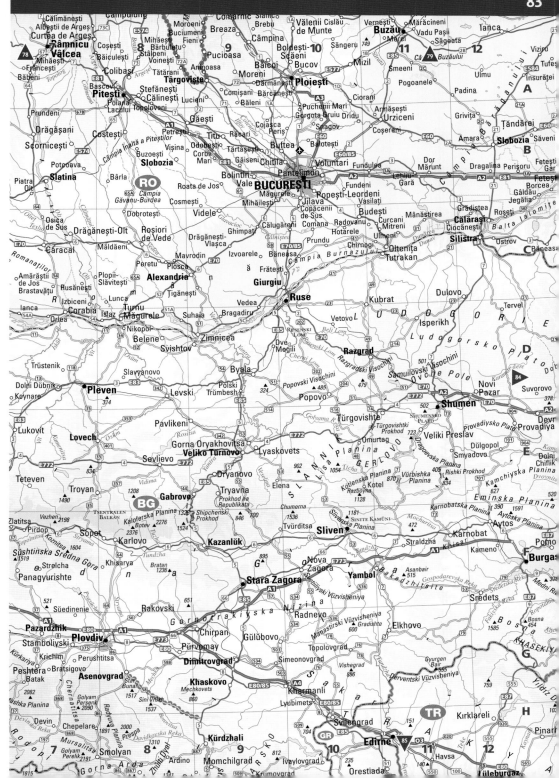

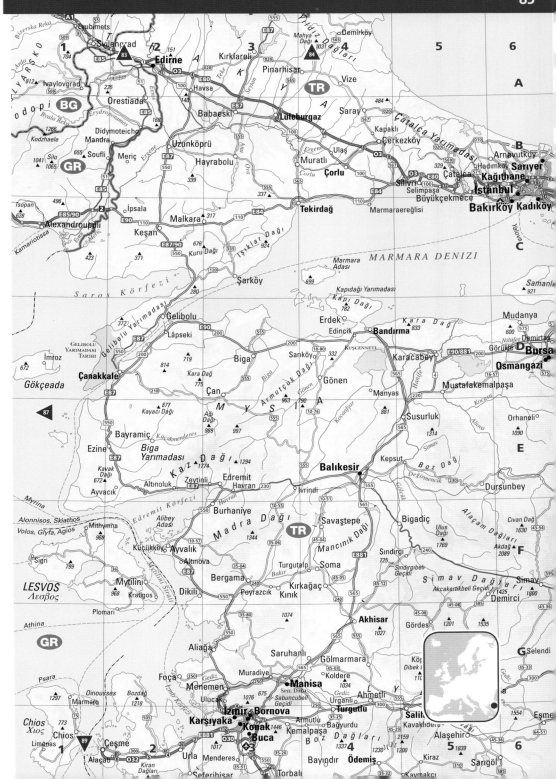

Bar
Ulcinj
Shkodër
Lezhë
Laç
Mamuras
Fushë Krujë
Krujë
Kamëz
Durrës
Shijak
TIRANË
AL
Kavajë
Kalaja e Turrës
Peqin
Cërrik
Lushnjë
Elbasan
Librazhd
Berat
Fier
Patos
Roskovec
Kuçovë
Ballsh
Selenicë
Poliçan
Vlorë
Memaliaj
Tepelenë
Përmet
Gjirokastër
Delvinë
Sarandë
Şidari
Palaiokastritsa
Kerkyra
Κέρκυρα
Igoumenitsa
Parga
Ano Lefkimmi
Paxoi
Preveza
Lefkada
LEFKADA
Λευκάς

Kukës
Tetovo
Kumanovo
Kratovo
Kočani
Probištip
SKOPJE
Vrapčište
Gostivar
Veles
Sveti Nikole
Štip
Radoviš
Negotino
Kavadarci
Peshkopi
Debar
Kičevo
Brod
Prilep
Kruševo
Demir Hisar
Bitola
Struga
Ohrid
Resen
Pogradec
Gramsh
Korçë
Bilisht
Kastoria
Florina
Edessa
Giannitsa
Naousa
Alexandreia
Veroia
Ptolemaïda
Argos Orestiko
Kozani
Siatista
Grevena
Kalampaka
Trikala
Karditsa
Sofades
Farsala
Larisa
Λάρισα
Tyrnavos
Ampelonas
Elassona
Ioannina
Ιωάννινα
GR
Arta
Agrinio
Amfissa
Lamia
Karpenisi
Thermo
Angelokastro

MK

E65   E75   E90   E92   E851   E852   E853   E55   E86   E583   E951   E952   E90/92   E55/952

BG

Grid columns: 7 8 9 10 11 12

Osogo
Rujen 2252
Beltok 1524
2729
Musala 2925
Slavov Vrŭkh 2306
Pazardzhik
Plovdiv
Pūrvomay
Gülubovo
Simeono
1187
E79
1225
7
8
Yakoruda
Alabak
84
Kŭrkariya
Peshtera
Stamboliyski
E773
1375
8
E85
534
E80
Dimitrovgrad
Delčevo
Čavka 1383
Blagoevgrad
Veliytsa 1710
Velingrad
9
Rakitovo
Bratsigovo
Krichim
Perushtitsa
10
86
588
11
83
Khaskovo
Kha
Vinica 1538
Simitli
RILA
Razlog
Golyama Syutkya 2186
Batak
Star Bryar
Mechkovets 860
1517
Sini Vrŭkh 1537
Lyubim
Trabotiviste
Pirin 2593
Bansko
Beslet 1938
2082
Batashka Planina
868
Golyam Persenk 2090
Radiuva Planina
E80/85
Kharmanliyska Reka
Lisec 1754
Kadiytsa 1924
Vikhren 2914
PIRIN
Polezhan 2850
Devinska Reka
Devin
Chepelare 1891
2000
Prespa
1310
Kürdzhali
509
Ivay
Vinica Planina
Berovo
1421
Kamenitsa 2822
Orelek 2099
197
Mursalitsa
Golyam Perelik 2191
Smolyan
Gorna Arda
Ardino
Momchilgrad
887
812
B
509
MALEŠEVO
1744
Markovi Kladéntsi 1523
Sandanski
198
Gotse Delchev
Slavyanka 2212
1815
Madan
Dzhebel
1241
Krumovgrad
960
Iztochni Rodopi
1041
Sil
106
Ograzden
Radomir 2029
A5
109
Petrich
Bistrica
Orvilos
Exochi
Nestos
1827
Vŭrbitsa
Nedelino
Zlatograd
Mugelen
Kot
126
Strumičko Pole
Belašica
1880
Kerkini
604
A25
1850
Falakro 2232
57
Papikio 1483
Mugelen
914
C
Valandovo
604
Bogdanci
702
Limni Kerkini
Sidirokastro
1963
1175
14
1406
55
1070
Komotini
E90
678
Tsopan 628
Gevgelija
1179
E79
Drama
1298
Xanthi
2
Lissa
E90
Serres
Angitis
12
Chrysoupoli
Kilkis
Polykastro
A25
Nigrita
1103
Strymonas
59
Pangaio 1956
Kavala Καβάλα
Keramoti
Paralia Avdiron
Agios Charalampos
Alexandroupoli
Koufalia
E75
569
1092
694
E90
2
Thasos
872 1203
Thasos Θάσος
69
69
800
Alexandroupoli
D
Sindos Evosmos
Lagkadas
2
E90
2
832
Thrakiko Pelagos
Kamariotissa
Fengari 1600
Ampelokipoi
1
Polichni
Thessaloniki Θεσσαλονίκη
16
16
1165
16
Samothraki
Kalamaria
Mesimeri
A25
Polygyros
Ouranoupoli
510
645
Gökçeada
672
G
Katerini
Thermaïkos Kolpos
Kolpos Agiou Orous
Athos 2033
E
1
Litochoro
E75
Kolpos Kassandras
808
Sithonia
Skopia 430
85
1588
243
Kassandra 353
Myrina
319
Limnos Λήμνος
1978
F
Agiokampos
1054
Agios Efstratios 296
Agios Efstratios
Mytilini
3
1
E75/92
Voreies Sporades Βόρειοι Σποράδες
Gioura
570
Kyra Panagia
299
Mytilini
Nea Ionia
1651
39
E79
Volos
725
Skiathos
433
Glossa
680
Alonnisos
Peristera
Chora
Sigri
30
1
E75
34
Pagasitikos Kolpos
Skiathos
Skopelos
403
Skyros
LES Λεσ
893
Platanias
Almyros
Skopelos
0 10 20 30 40 50 km
0 10 20 30 miles
1726
1
E75
77
Xiro 991
Linaria
Kochylas 792
H
1372
Voreios Evvoikos Kolpos
77
Pyxaria 1343
1743
Psara
Antipsara 631
ETHNIKOS DRYMOS PARNASSOU
7
8
89
Psachna
9
Kymi
761
Peiraias Rafina
Athina Tinos Irakleio
10
Ermoupoli
11
Atalanti
1080
E75
Nea Artaki
1189
Parnassos 2457
Orchomenos
1021
Chalkida
1171

Lefkada
LEFKADA
Λευκάδα
Elati
Karpenisi
Lamia
Xiro 991
Voreios Evvoikos
1589
893
2101
86
E75
Atalanti
Agrinio
1924
1372
Angelokastro
602
1734
2510
27
1080
E75
750
Thermo
Amfissa
ETHNIKOS DRYMOS PARNASSOU
Parnassos 2457
Kifisos
Orchomenos
930
Limni Trichonida
ETHNIKOS DRYMOS OITIS Oiti 2152
Apoxiaremi Limni Kopaidas
Voreies Echinades
Trikorfo 1545
Livadeia
Ithaki
806
Mesolongi
Nafpaktos
48
Thiva
B
KEFALLONIA
Κεφαλληνία
Patra
Πάτρα
Aigio
Korinthiakos Kolpos
Paralia Saranti
1748
1409
E962
1131
Sami
Patraikos Kolpos
1926
8A
1208
Megara
Argostoli
1628
ETHNIKOS DRYMOS AINOU
Kiato
Loutraki
Salamina
E94
Kyllini
966
2224
2341
Kyllini 2376
Korinthos
Κόρινθος
Salamina
Vrachionas 756
GR
872
Aigina
C
ZAKYNTHOS
Ζάκυνθος
Zakynthos
Porthmos Zakynthou
Amaliada
798
1446
1616
7
1199
743
Pyrgos
Peloponnisos
Πελοπόννησος
1366
1981
Argos
Nafplio
113
Kyparissiakos Kolpos
1419
Tripoli
1274
976
Argolikos Kolpos
Ermioni
Nedas
604
1254
E961
1935
Spetses
Spetses
D
Thessaloniki
Chios
Kuşadası Körfezi
Kuşadası
515
Sazlı
1224
9A
E55
Leonidio
1153
Samos
Söke
E55/65
A71
1852
Karlovasi
1433
Davutlar
Gargalianoj
Messini
1359
82
Sparti
1839
Pythagoreio
1237
Özbaşı
DILEK YARIMADASI MILLI PARKI
Sarıkemer
TR
Lykodimo 958
2404
1327
Paralia
Samos
Σάμος
Fournoi
Agathonisi
Methoni
Koroni
Messiniakos Kolpos
E961
86
Patmos
Arkoi
Yenihisar
525
Milas
916
1125
Leipsoi
1083
Dağ
Gytheio
Farmakonisi
330
E
Leros
Güllük Körfezi
879
Monemvasia
Lakki
326
Telendos
Bodrum
Yaran Dağı
716
Kalymnos
Mani
Peiraias
678
Pserimos
Kos
Gökova Körfezi
Neapoli
772
89
Kalymnos
845
748
Agia Pelagia
Kefalos
Kos
Κως
426
Datça
Reşadiye Yarımadası
400
Hisarönü Körfezi
1144
507
Astypalaia
Gyali
698
616
KYTHIRA
Κύθηρα
Kythira
F
Nisyros
Symi
Astypalaia
Dodekanisos
Δωδεκάνησος
Ancona, Bari, Brindisi
Syrna
GR
851
Rodos
378
Kissamos
Peiraias
Tilos
Trianta
G
Alimia
798
Chalki
593
Chalki
Attavyros 1215
95
RODOS
Ρόδος
Irakleio, Siteia, Agios, Nikolaos
Monolithos
Skiadi 563
458
Lindos
Steno Karpathou
Kattavia
213
Saria 630
718

2   3   4   5   6

Skyros
Linaria
Kochylas
702
403

7
8
9
10
11

Pyxaria
1343
1743
Kymi
1189
761
Psachna
Nea Artaki
Chalkida
1171
1021

Limnos, Kavala
Lesvos
Lesvos

Psara
Antipsara
531

Marmaro
1297
Oinousses
773
75
Chios
Χίος
Chios
85
505
TR
Bozdag
1218
Foça

87

85

A I G A I O N

EVVOIA
Εύβοια

Notios Evvoikos Kolpos

Avlonas
E75
PARNITHAS
1400
Agia Marina
Nea Styra
680

Limenas
Çeşme
300
O32
B
Ur
Kiran
Dağları
662

ATHINA
ΘΗΝΑΙ
Nea
Lipsia
Chalandri
Zografou
Spata
Kifisia
Nea Makri
Marmari
Petalioi
1398
Karystos

Samos, Kos, Rodos

Peiraias
ΠΕΙΡΑΙΑΣ
Kallithea
Glyfada
Voula
Keratea
89
Agios
Dimitrios
91
ETHNIKOS
DRYMOS
SOUNIOU
264
Lavrio
Aigina
532
Makronisos
Korisia
Tzia
Κέα
561
Gyaros

Gavrio
716
994
Andros
Άνδρος

Tinos
Τήνος
650

Ikaria
Ικαρία
Evdilos
1037
1433
Kar
Samo
Σάμο
C

Ydra
Ydra

PELAGOS

Kythnos
Κύθνος
Merichas
298
Syros
Σύρος
442
Ermoupoli
Rineia
Tinos
364
Mykonos
Mykonos
Μύκονος

Fournoi
Fournoi
1033

Patmos
Πάτμος
Skala
Patmos

Serifos
585

Kyklades
Κυκλάδες

Donoussa

Patmos, Rodos
88
Levitha
D

MYRTOO

PELAGOS

Antimilos

Sifnos
Σίφνος
300
Antiparos
Kamares
694

Paros
Πάρος
Paroikia
771
Naxos
Naxos
Νάξος
1001

Koufonisi
Schoinoussa
Irakleia
Keros
Katapola
607
Kinaros
821

Amorgos

E

Kimolos
325
Polyaigos
370
Adamas
751
Milos
Μήλος

Sikinos
Ios
Ιος
600
735
Ios

Astypalaia
482
Astypalaia

Folegandros
415

Oia
566
Santorini
Θήρα
484 Anafi
Anafi

Syrna

Kythira
748
762
Kissamos
Platanos
Kolpos
Chanion
E65
Chania
E75
Ormos Almyrou
Peiraias
Peiraias
Paros
Peiraias
Thira
KRITI
Κρήτη
Dia
Milos, Peiraias
Karpathos, Rodos, Lemesos
F

Elos
1182
1331
Lefka Ori
2116
2452
Palaiochora
ETHNIKOS
DRYMOS
SAMARIAS
Chora Sfakion
Rethymno
90
E75
1078
1312
984
1777
1136
Psiloreitis
2456
Irakleio
GR
Nea
Alikarnassos
811
Kolpos
Irakleiou
E75
90
Selena
1559
Agios
Nikolaos
Dikti
2148
Kolpos
Mirampellou
1237
1476
90
E75
Siteia
Palaikastro
819
Zakros
G

Matala
Kolpos
Messaras
Geropotamos
97
Kofinas
1231
97
Ierapetra

Gavdos
325

7
8
9
10
11

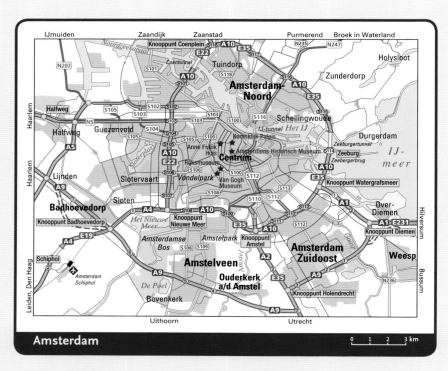

Amsterdam

0　1　2　3 km

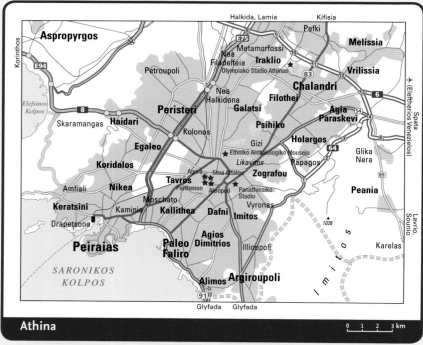

Athina

0　1　2　3 km

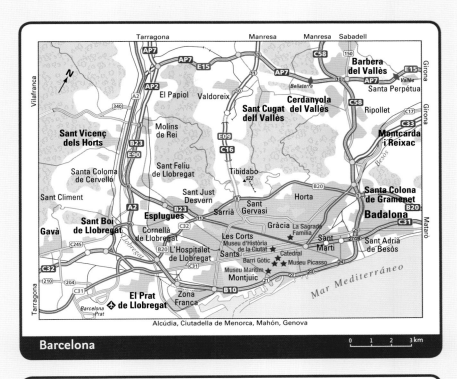

Barcelona

0 1 2 3 km

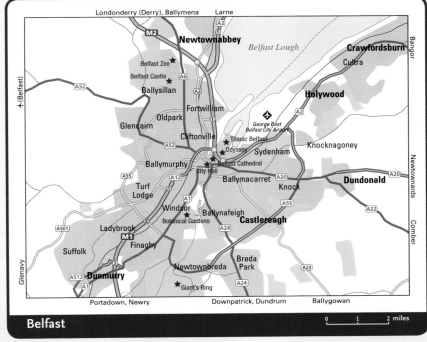

Belfast

0 1 2 miles

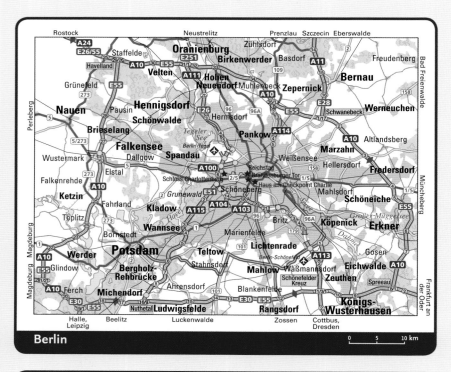

Berlin

0   5   10 km

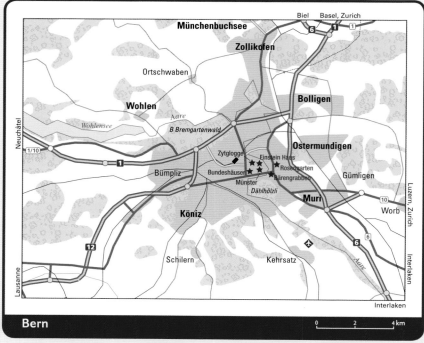

Bern

0   2   4 km

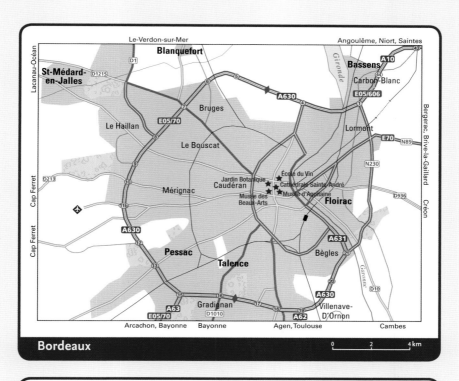

Bordeaux

0   2   4 km

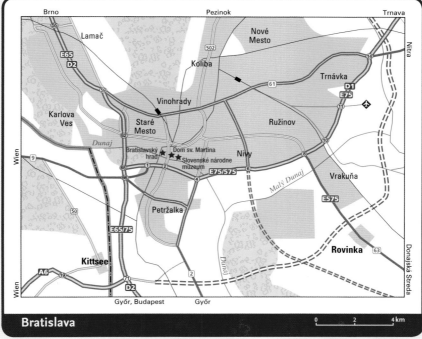

Bratislava

0   2   4 km

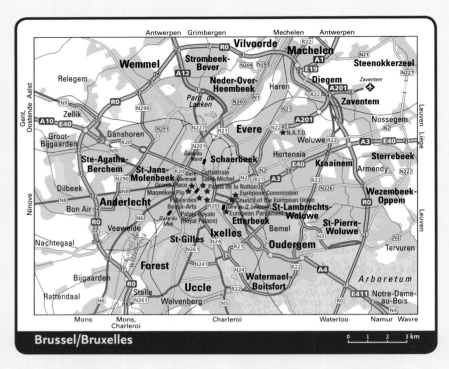

Brussel/Bruxelles

0   1   2   3 km

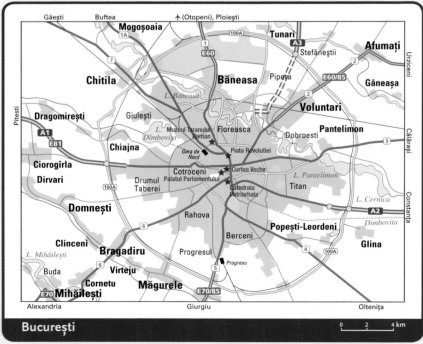

Bucureşti

0   2   4 km

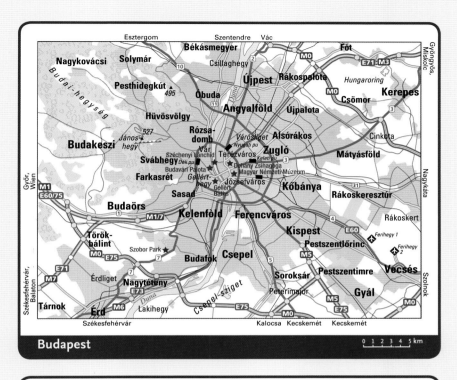

Budapest

0 1 2 3 4 5 km

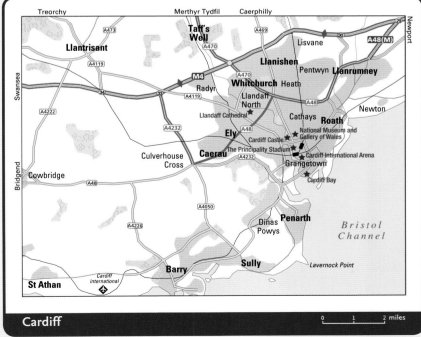

Cardiff

0 1 2 miles

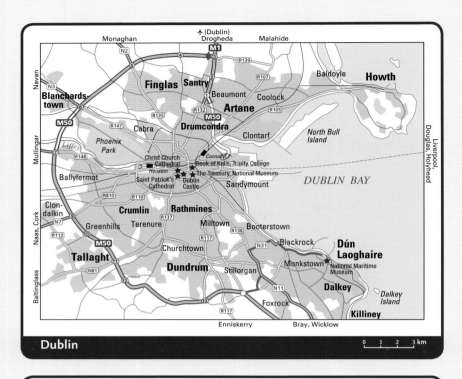

Dublin

0 1 2 3 km

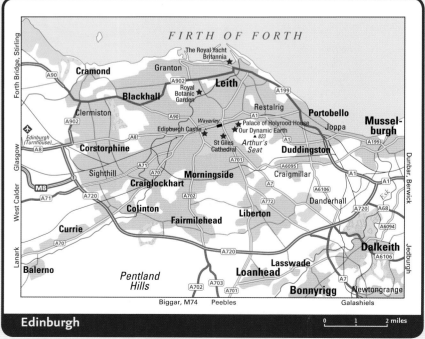

Edinburgh

0 1 2 miles

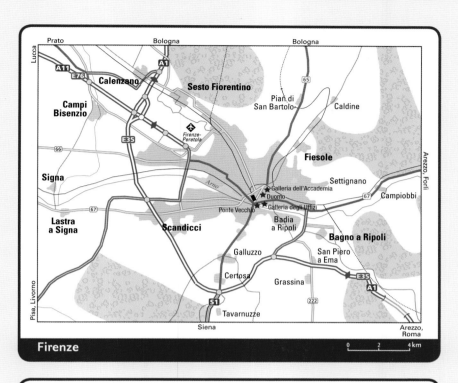

Firenze

0 2 4 km

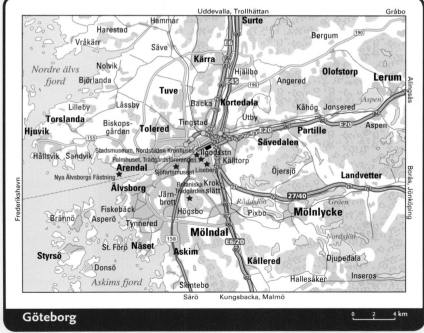

Göteborg

0 2 4 km

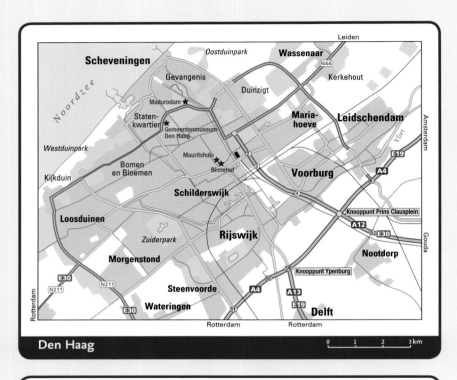

Den Haag

0 1 2 3 km

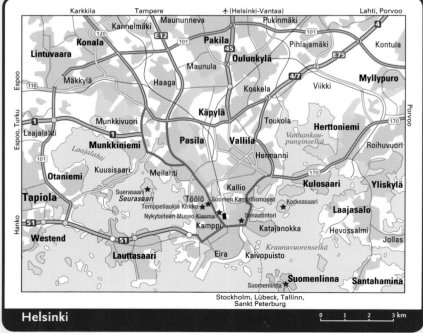

Helsinki

0 1 2 3 km

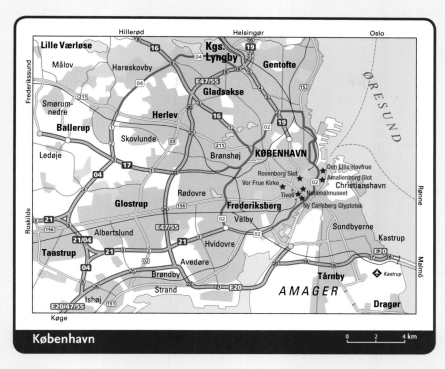

København

0   2   4 km

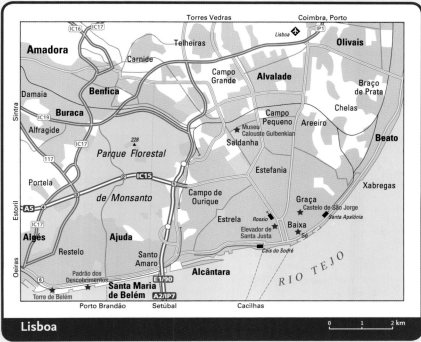

Lisboa

0   1   2 km

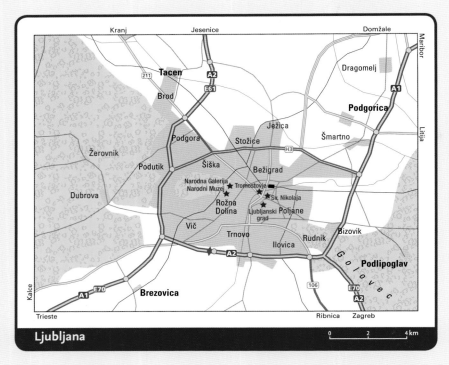

Ljubljana

0 2 4 km

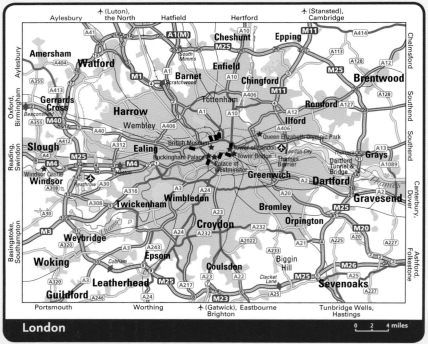

London

0 2 4 miles

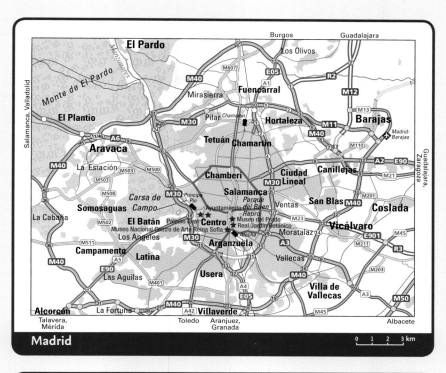

Madrid

0 1 2 3 km

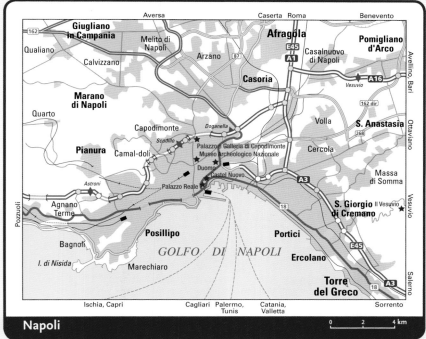

Napoli

0 2 4 km

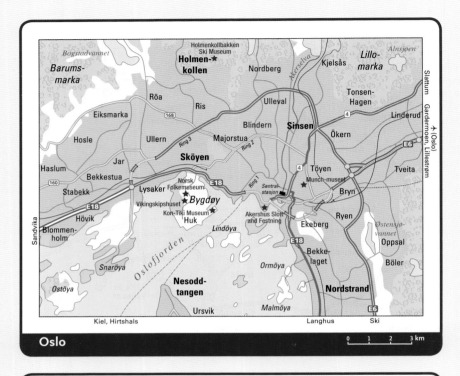

Oslo

0 1 2 3 km

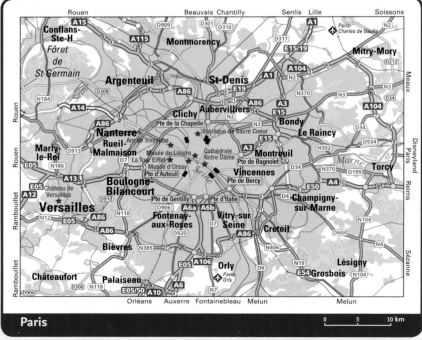

Paris

0 5 10 km

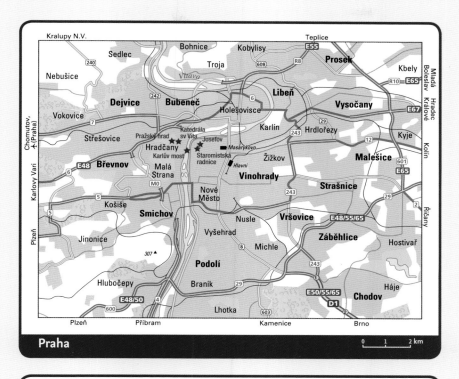

Praha

0 1 2 km

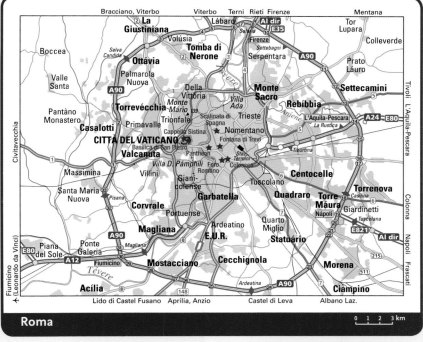

Roma

0 1 2 3 km

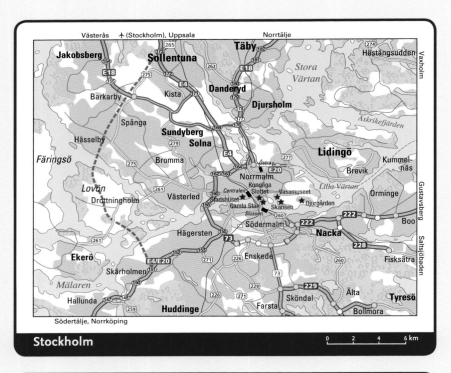

Västerås   ✈ (Stockholm), Uppsala   Norrtälje
                                              274
Jakobsberg   Sollentuna   Täby   Hästängsudden
      150   171   181   Vaxholm
   E18   275   172   262   E18
      155
            172   Stora
   Barkarby   Kista   171   Danderyd   Värtan
            E4   179
                     Djursholm
      Spånga   178
                     177
   Hässelby   Sundyberg   169 177
            279   Solna   Lidingö   Kummel-
   Färingsö   Bromma   E4   näs
      275   164   277
            162 163   Östra   Brevik   Gustavsberg
   Lovön   Norrmalm   Lilla Värtan
      261   Västerled 160 Centralen Kungliga   Vasamuseet Orminge
   Drottningholm   158 Stadshuset Slottet Skansen
               Gamla Stan   Djurgården
               Slussen   260
            Söndermalm   222   222   Boo
   Hägersten   155
            73   Nacka
   Ekerö   152 153   228
      E4/E20   271   226   260   Fisksätra
   Skärholmen 150   Enskede
   Mälaren   73
      150   48   229   Älta
   Hallunda 147   259   226 271   Sköndal 229 Tyresö
         Huddinge   Farsta   Bollmora

Södertälje, Norrköping

Stockholm   0   2   4   6 km

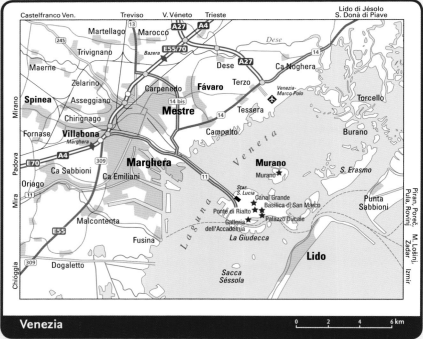

Castelfranco Ven.   Treviso   V. Véneto Trieste   Lido di Jésolo
                                      S. Donà di Piave
      Martellago Marocco 13 A27 A4
         245   A27
   Trivignano   E55/70 Bazera   Dese
   Maerne   14
   Zelarino   Carpenedo Dese Ca Noghera
      Spinea Asseggiano Fávaro Terzo Torcello
            14 bis   Venezia-
   Chirignago   Mestre   Marco Polo
   Fornase Villabona 14 Tessera Burano
      Marghera   Campalto
   E70 A4 309   Veneta Murano S. Erasmo
   Ca Sabbioni Ca Emiliani Marghera
   Oriago 11   11   Murano
            Staz.   S. Erasmo
   Malcontenta   S. Lucia Canal Grande Punta
            Basilica di San Marco Sabbioni
         Ponte di Rialto
   Fusina   Galleria Palazzo Ducale
         dell'Accademia La Giudecca
               Lido
   Dogaletto 309
         Sacca
         Séssola

Venezia   0   2   4   6 km

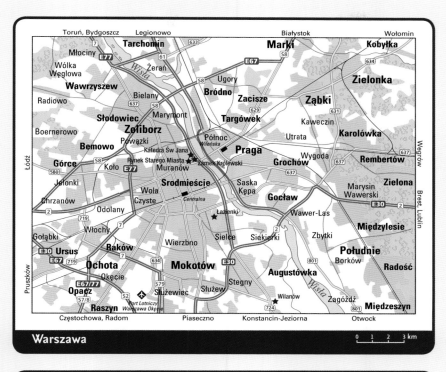

Warszawa

0 1 2 3 km

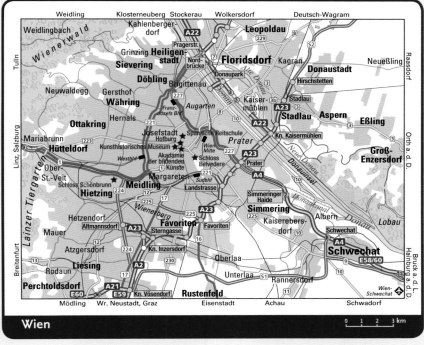

Wien

0 1 2 3 km

Index

The index contains a selection of the major towns and cities found on the reference map section of the atlas.
All indexed entries have a page and grid reference.

Entries which have a ❏ symbol instead of a grid reference are located on small insets within the appropriate page.

A	Austria		IRL	Ireland
AL	Albania		IS	Iceland
AND	Andorra		L	Luxembourg
B	Belgium		LT	Lithuania
BG	Bulgaria		LV	Latvia
BIH	Bosnia and Herzogovina		M	Malta
BY	Belarus		MA	Morocco
CH	Switzerland		MC	Monaco
CZ	Czechia (Czech Republic)		MD	Moldova
D	Germany		MK	Macedonia (F.Y.R.O.M.)
DK	Denmark		MNE	Montenegro
E	Spain		N	Norway
EST	Estonia		NL	Netherlands
F	France		P	Portugal
FIN	Finland		PL	Poland
FL	Liechtenstein		RKS	Kosovo
FO	Faroe Islands		RO	Romania
GB	United Kingdom		RSM	San Marino
GBG	Guernsey		RUS	Russia
GBJ	Jersey		S	Sweden
GBM	Isle of Man		SK	Slovakia
GBZ	Gibraltar		SLO	Slovenia
GR	Greece		SRB	Serbia
H	Hungary		TR	Turkey
HR	Croatia		UA	Ukraine
I	Italy			

A

Name	Country	No.	Grid	Name	Country	No.	Grid	Name	Country	No.	Grid
Arjona	E	28	C5	Atessa	I	33	C8	Azanja	SRB	81	C12
Arklow	IRL	4	H3	Athens	GR	89	C7	Azkoitia	E	20	B2
Arkösund	S	47	E8	Atherstone	GB	9	C7	Aznalcóllar	E	25	J7
Arles	F	17	H12	Athina	GR	89	C7	Azuaga	E	24	G8
Arlon	B	13	B7	Athlone	IRL	7	J5				
Armagh	GB	4	E2	Athy	IRL	4	H2	**B**			
Armăşeşti	RO	83	B11	Atna	N	51	E8				
Armilla	E	28	E6	Atri	I	33	B8	Babadag	RO	79	H10
Armutlu	TR	85	H4	Atripalda	I	30	B6	Babaeski	TR	85	B3
Arnage	F	15	F9	Attleborough	GB	9	C11	Băbeni	RO	78	H3
Arnavutköy	TR	85	B6	Åtvidaberg	S	47	E7	Bač	SRB	76	G6
Arnedo	E	20	D3	Au	CH	37	C9	Bacău	RO	79	D7
Arnhem	NL	11	D7	Aubagne	F	18	E6	Baccarat	F	13	E9
Arnoldstein	A	39	F8	Aubange	B	13	B7	Baciu	RO	78	D2
Arnsberg	D	11	E10	Aubenas	F	17	F12	Bačka Palanka	SRB	76	G6
Arnstadt	D	40	B6	Aubigny-sur-Nère	F	12	G2	Bačka Topola	SRB	77	F7
Arolsen	D	11	E12	Auch	F	16	H5	Bački Jarak	SRB	77	G7
Arona	I	34	B3	Audierne	F	14	E2	Bački Petrovac	SRB	77	G7
Arpino	I	33	D7	Audincourt	F	13	G9	Bačko Gradište	SRB	77	F7
Arras	F	10	H3	Aue	D	41	C9	Bacoli	I	30	B4
Arrasate	E	20	C2	Auerbach	D	41	C8	Bácsalmás	H	76	E6
Arriondas	E	23	B8	Augsburg	D	38	B4	Badajoz	E	24	F5
Arroyo de la Luz	E	24	D6	Augusta	I	30	F6	Badalona	E	21	F10
Arsta	S	47	C9	Augustfehn	D	11	B10	Bad Aussee	A	39	D8
Arsvågen	N	48	D2	Augustów	PL	68	H5	Bad Berka	D	41	B6
Arta	GR	86	G4	Aulla	I	34	E5	Bad Bramstedt	D	42	C5
Artà	E	29	F10	Aulnoye-Aymeries	F	10	H4	Bad Doberan	D	43	B8
Artena	I	32	D6	Aulus-les-Bains	F	21	C9	Bad Düben	D	43	G9
Artern (Unstrut)	D	41	A6	Auray	F	14	F4	Baden	A	39	C12
Artsyz	UA	79	F11	Aurec-sur-Loire	F	17	D11	Baden-Baden	D	13	D11
A Rúa	E	22	D5	Aureilhan	F	21	B7	Badgastein	A	39	E7
Arvidsjaur	S	55	C12	Aurich	D	11	A10	Bad Goisern	A	39	D8
Arvika	S	46	B3	Aurillac	F	17	E9	Bad Hersfeld	D	40	B4
Arzachena	I	32	D3	Auriol	F	18	E6	Bad Hofgastein	A	39	E7
Arzúa	E	22	C3	Auterive	F	21	B9	Badia Polesine	I	35	D8
Aš	CZ	41	D8	Autun	F	12	H5	Bad Ischl	A	39	C8
Ås	N	51	B9	Auxerre	F	12	F4	Bad Kissingen	D	40	D5
Ascea	I	30	C6	Auxonne	F	13	G7	Bad Krozingen	D	13	F10
Aschaffenburg	D	13	B12	Avallon	F	12	F5	Bad Lauterberg im Harz	D	42	G6
Aschersleben	D	43	G7	Avanca	P	22	G2	Bad Münstereifel	D	11	G9
Ascoli Piceno	I	33	B7	Aveiro	P	22	G2	Bad Neustadt an der Saale	D	40	C5
Ascoli Satriano	I	31	A7	Avella	I	30	B5	Badovinci	SRB	81	B9
Åsele	S	55	F10	Avellino	I	30	B6	Bad Salzuflen	D	11	D11
Asenovgrad	BG	83	G8	Aversa	I	30	B5	Bad Salzungen	D	40	B5
Åseral	N	48	E4	Avesnes-sur-Helpe	F	10	H5	Bad Sooden-Allendorf	D	40	B5
A Serra de Outes	E	22	C2	Avesta	S	47	A7	Bad Waldsee	D	37	B9
Ashby de la Zouch	GB	5	H8	Avetrano	I	31	C11	Bad Wildungen	D	11	F12
Ashford	GB	9	E10	Avezzano	I	33	C7	Bad Windsheim	D	40	E5
Ashington	GB	5	C8	Aviano	I	35	B10	Baena	E	28	D5
Ashmyany	BY	69	H9	Avigliano	I	31	B7	Baeza	E	28	C6
Asiago	I	35	B8	Avignon	F	18	C5	Bagheria	I	30	E3
Asilah	MA	28	H2	Ávila	E	23	G9	Bagnacavallo	I	35	E9
Asker	N	49	C7	Avilés	E	23	B7	Bagnara Calabra	I	31	G7
Askim	N	46	C2	Avlonas	GR	89	B7	Bagnères-de-Bigorre	F	21	C7
Askvoll	N	50	F1	Avola	I	30	G6	Bagno a Ripoli	I	35	F8
Aspe	E	27	H9	Avonmouth	GB	8	H5	Bagno di Romagna	I	35	F9
Aspropyrgos	GR	89	B7	Avrămeni	RO	79	A7	Bagnolo Mella	I	34	C6
Assemini	I	32	G2	Avranches	F	15	D7	Bagnols-sur-Cèze	F	17	G12
Assen	NL	11	B8	Avrig	RO	78	F3	Bagrationovsk	RUS	68	G2
Assens	DK	44	F4	Avrillé	F	15	F8	Bagshot	GB	9	E8
Assisi	I	32	A5	Axams	A	37	C11	Bağyurdu	TR	85	H4
Assoro	I	30	F5	Ayamonte	E	25	K5	Baia	RO	84	B5
Asti	I	19	A10	Aylesbury	GB	9	D8	Baia de Aramă	RO	77	H12
Astillero	E	23	B10	Aylsham	GB	9	B11	Baia de Arieş	RO	78	E1
Aston	GB	8	C8	Ayora	E	27	G9	Baia Mare	RO	78	B2
Astorga	E	22	D6	Ayr	GB	4	C4	Baiano	I	30	B5
Åstorp	S	45	D7	Aytos	BG	83	F12	Baia Sprie	RO	78	B2
Astravyets	BY	69	H9	Aytré	F	16	C3	Băicoi	RO	78	G5
Aszód	H	76	B6	Ayvacık	TR	85	E2	Băiculeşti	RO	78	G3
Atalanti	GR	87	H7	Ayvalık	TR	85	F2				

B

Baile Átha Cliath	IRL	4	G2
Baile Átha Luain	IRL	7	J5
Băile Herculane	RO	77	H11
Bailén	E	28	C6
Băileşti	RO	82	C5
Baillargues	F	17	H11
Bailleul	F	10	G3
Bain-de-Bretagne	F	14	F6
Baiona	E	22	D2
Baja	H	76	E5
Bajina Bašta	SRB	81	D10
Bajmok	SRB	76	F6
Bajram Curri	AL	81	G10
Bakırköy	TR	85	C6
Bakum	D	11	C11
Balaguer	E	21	E8
Bălan	RO	78	D5
Balassagyarmat	H	76	A6
Balatonalmádi	H	76	C4
Balatonboglár	H	76	D3
Balatonfüred	H	76	D4
Bălăuşeri	RO	78	E3
Balbriggan	IRL	4	F3
Balcani	RO	79	D7
Bălceşti	RO	82	B6
Balchik	BG	84	D4
Băleni	RO	78	H5
Băleşti	RO	78	G1
Balestrate	I	30	E2
Balikesir	TR	85	E4
Balingen	D	13	E12
Balkány	H	77	B10
Ballainvilliers	F	12	D2
Ballangen	N	57	D5
Ballenstedt	D	43	G7
Ballerup	DK	44	E7
Ballina	IRL	6	G3
Ballinasloe	IRL	7	J4
Ballsh	AL	86	D2
Ballycastle	GB	4	C2
Ballyclare	GB	4	D3
Ballymena	GB	4	D2
Ballymoney	GB	4	C2
Ballynahinch	GB	4	E3
Balmaseda	E	20	B1
Balmazújváros	H	77	B9
Baloteşti	RO	83	B10
Balş	RO	82	B6
Bålsta	S	47	C9
Balsthal	CH	13	G10
Balta	UA	79	B12
Bălţăteşti	RO	78	C6
Bălteni	RO	78	H1
Bălţi	MD	79	B9
Baltiysk	RUS	68	F1
Băluşeni	RO	79	B7
Balvi	LV	67	G9
Bamberg	D	40	D6
Banatski Karlovac	SRB	77	G9
Banatsko Novo Selo	SRB	77	H8
Banbridge	GB	4	E2
Banbury	GB	9	D7
Banca	RO	79	E9
Banchory	GB	3	E7
Band	RO	78	D3
Bandırma	TR	85	D4
Băneasa	RO	83	C10
Băneasa	RO	84	C3
Bangor	GB	4	D3
Bangor	GB	4	G5
Banja	SRB	81	E9
Banja Luka	BIH	80	B5
Bankeryd	S	46	F5
Bankya	BG	82	F5
Bánovce nad Bebravou	SK	75	G9
Banoviči	BIH	81	C8
Banská Bystrica	SK	75	G10
Banská Štiavnica	SK	75	G10
Bansko	BG	82	G5
Banyoles	E	18	G1
Bar	MNE	81	H9
Barakaldo	E	20	B1
Barañain	E	20	C4
Baraolt	RO	78	E5
Barbastro	E	21	E7
Barbate de Franco	E	25	M7
Barberá del Vallès	E	21	F10
Barberino di Mugello	I	35	F7
Bărbuleţu	RO	78	G4
Bărcăneşti	RO	78	H6
Barcellona Pozzo di Gotto	I	30	E6
Barcelona	E	21	F10
Barcin	PL	71	E7
Barcs	H	76	F3
Barczewo	PL	68	H2
Bardejov	SK	73	F2
Barentin	F	15	B10
Barfleur	F	15	B7
Barga	I	34	F6
Bargas	E	26	E4
Bargoed	GB	8	D5
Bargteheide	D	42	C6
Bari	I	31	A9
Bârla	RO	83	B8
Bârlad	RO	79	E8
Bar-le-Duc	F	12	D6
Barletta	I	33	E11
Barlinek	PL	70	E4
Barnard Castle	GB	5	D8
Barnoldswick	GB	5	F8
Barnsley	GB	5	F8
Barnstaple	GB	8	F3
Barnstorf	D	11	C11
Barntrup	D	11	D12
Baronissi	I	30	B6
Barr	F	13	E10
Barrafranca	I	30	F4
Barreiro	P	24	F2
Barrhead	GB	2	H5
Barrow-in-Furness	GB	4	E6
Barry	GB	8	E5
Bârsana	RO	78	B2
Bar-sur-Aube	F	12	E6
Barth	D	43	B9
Barton-upon-Humber	GB	5	F10
Bartoszyce	PL	68	Q3
Basarabeasca	MD	79	E11
Basarabi	RO	84	C4
Basauri	E	23	B12
Bascov	RO	78	H4
Basel	CH	13	F10
Basildon	GB	9	E10
Basingstoke	GB	9	E8
Bassano del Grappa	I	35	B8
Basse-Goulaine	F	14	G6
Bassens	F	16	E4
Bassum	D	11	B11
Bastia	F	19	E12
Bastia	I	32	A5
Batajnica	SRB	77	H8
Batak	BG	83	G7
Batăr	RO	77	D10
Bátaszék	H	76	E5
Bath	GB	8	E6
Bathgate	GB	2	G6
Bátonyterenye	H	77	B7
Battenberg (Eder)	D	40	B3
Battipaglia	I	30	B6
Battle	GB	9	F10
Battonya	H	77	E9
Baume-les-Dames	F	13	G8
Baunatal	D	11	F12
Bauska	LV	69	B7
Bavay	F	10	H4
Bayeux	F	15	C7
Bayonne	F	16	H2
Bayramiç	TR	85	E2
Bayreuth	D	41	D7
Bayston Hill	GB	8	B5
Baza	E	29	D8
Béal an Átha	IRL	6	G3
Béal Átha na Sluaighe	IRL	7	J4
Beasain	E	20	C3
Beas de Segura	E	29	B7
Beaucaire	F	17	G12
Beaumont-lès-Valence	F	18	B5
Beaune	F	12	G6
Beaupréau	F	15	G7
Beauvais	F	12	C2
Bebington	GB	5	G6
Bebra	D	40	B4
Beccles	GB	9	C11
Bečej	SRB	77	F7
Beceni	RO	79	G7
Bechyně	CZ	41	F11
Beclean	RO	78	C3
Bédarieux	F	17	H10
Bédarrides	F	18	C5
Bedford	GB	9	C9
Bedlington	GB	5	C8
Będzin	PL	75	C10
Beelitz	D	43	F9
Beernem	B	10	F4
Beeskow	D	43	F11
Begles	F	16	E4
Beith	GB	2	H5
Beiuş	RO	77	D11
Beja	P	25	H4
Béjar	E	23	H7
Békés	H	77	D9
Békéscsaba	H	77	D9
Bela Crkva	SRB	77	H10
Bela Palanka	SRB	82	E3
Belceşti	RO	79	C7
Bełchatów	PL	71	H9
Belene	BG	83	D8
Belfast	GB	4	D3
Belfort	F	13	F9
Belgrade	SRB	81	B11
Beli Manastir	HR	76	F5
Belišće	HR	76	F5
Bellac	F	16	C6
Bellaria	I	35	F9
Belleville	F	17	C12
Belley	F	36	F3
Bellinzona	CH	34	A4
Bellizzi	I	30	B6
Belluno	I	35	B9
Belmont	GB	3	B12
Belogradchik	BG	82	D4

B

Bois-Guillaume	F	15	C10	Botoşani	RO	79	B7	Brecon	GB	8	D4
Boizenburg	D	42	D6	Botricello	I	31	F9	Breda	NL	10	E6
Bojano	I	33	D8	Boucau	F	16	H2	Bregenz	A	37	C9
Bojnice	SK	75	G9	Bouc-Bel-Air	F	18	D6	Breitenfelde	D	42	C6
Bolaños de Calatrava	E	26	G4	Bouchemaine	F	15	G8	Brekken	N	51	C9
Bolbec	F	15	B9	Bouguenais	F	14	G6	Brekstad	N	54	G2
Boldeşti-Scăeni	RO	78	G6	Bouillargues	F	17	G12	Bremen	D	11	B12
Bolekhiv	UA	73	F6	Boulazac	F	16	E6	Bremerhaven	D	42	C4
Bolesławiec	PL	74	B5	Boulogne-Billancourt	F	12	D2	Bremervörde	D	11	A12
Bolhrad	UA	79	F10	Boulogne-sur-Mer	F	9	F12	Brenes	E	25	J7
Bolintin-Deal	RO	83	B9	Bourbon-Lancy	F	17	B11	Brentwood	GB	9	D10
Bolintin-Vale	RO	83	B9	Bourg-en-Bresse	F	36	E2	Bresalc	RKS	82	F2
Bollène	F	18	C4	Bourges	F	12	G2	Brescia	I	34	C6
Bollnäs	S	52	E4	Bourgoin-Jallieu	F	36	G2	Bressanone	I	37	D12
Bollullos Par del Condado	E	25	J6	Bourg-St-Andéol	F	17	F12	Bressuire	F	15	H8
				Bourg-St-Maurice	F	36	F5	Brest	BY	72	G6
Bologna	I	35	E8	Bourgueil	F	15	G9	Brest	F	14	E2
Bolsover	GB	5	G9	Bourne	GB	5	H10	Brevik	S	47	C9
Bolton	GB	5	F7	Bournemouth	GB	8	F7	Brežice	SLO	39	G11
Bolzano	I	37	E11	Bourron-Marlotte	F	12	E3	Breznik	BG	82	F5
Bompas	F	18	F1	Bovalino	I	31	G8	Brezno	SK	75	F11
Bondeno	I	35	D8	Boves	I	19	C9	Briançon	F	19	A8
Bo'ness	GB	2	G6	Boville Ernica	I	33	D7	Briare	F	12	F3
Bonn	D	11	G9	Boxmeer	NL	11	E7	Bridgend	GB	2	H3
Bonneville	F	36	F4	Božava	HR	80	D2	Bridgend	GB	8	E4
Bonyhád	H	76	E5	Bra	I	19	B10	Bridgnorth	GB	8	C6
Boo	S	47	C9	Bracciano	I	32	C5	Bridgwater	GB	8	E5
Bootle	GB	5	G7	Bräcke	S	52	B3	Bridlington	GB	5	E10
Boppard	D	11	H10	Brackley	GB	9	D8	Bridport	GB	8	F5
Bor	SRB	82	C3	Bracknell	GB	9	E8	Brig	CH	34	A2
Borås	S	45	A7	Brad	RO	77	E12	Brigg	GB	5	F10
Borca	RO	78	C5	Bradford	GB	5	F8	Brightlingsea	GB	9	D11
Borcea	RO	84	B3	Brae	GB	3	B12	Brighton	GB	9	F9
Bordeaux	F	16	E4	Braga	P	22	F2	Brignais	F	36	F2
Bordesholm	D	42	B5	Bragadiru	RO	83	B10	Brignoles	F	19	D7
Bordighera	I	19	D9	Bragadiru	RO	83	D9	Brilon	D	11	E11
Borduşani	RO	84	B3	Bragança	P	22	E5	Brindisi	I	31	B11
Borgholm	S	45	C12	Brăhăşeşti	RO	79	E8	Brioude	F	17	D10
Borgia	I	31	F9	Brăila	RO	79	G9	Brisighella	I	35	E8
Borgo	F	19	E12	Braine-l'Alleud	B	10	G5	Bristol	GB	8	E6
Borgomanero	I	34	C3	Braintree	GB	9	D10	Brive-la-Gaillarde	F	17	E7
Borgo San Dalmazzo	I	19	C9	Brakel	B	10	F4	Briviesca	E	20	D1
Borgo San Lorenzo	I	35	F8	Bramming	DK	44	F2	Brixham	GB	8	G4
Borgosesia	I	34	B2	Bramsche	D	11	C10	Brixworth	GB	9	C8
Borgo Val di Taro	I	34	E5	Bran	RO	78	F5	Brno	CZ	74	F6
Borhaug	N	48	F3	Brande	DK	44	E3	Bro	S	47	C9
Borken	D	11	D9	Brandenburg	D	43	F9	Broadstairs	GB	9	E11
Borkum	D	42	C1	Brandon	GB	9	C10	Brod	MK	86	B4
Borlänge	S	52	G3	Brăneşti	RO	83	B10	Brodick	GB	4	B4
Borna	D	41	B8	Braniewo	PL	68	G1	Brodnica	PL	71	D9
Bornova	TR	85	H3	Braslaw	BY	69	D10	Bromarv	FIN	53	H11
Borovo Selo	HR	76	G5	Braşov	RO	78	F5	Bromma	S	47	C9
Borşa	RO	78	B3	Brastavăţu	RO	83	C7	Bromölla	S	45	E9
Borsbeek	B	10	F5	Bratca	RO	77	D12	Bromsgrove	GB	8	C6
Boryslav	UA	73	F5	Bratislava	SK	75	H7	Bron	F	36	F2
Bosa	I	32	E2	Bratovoeşti	RO	82	C6	Brønderslev	DK	44	B4
Bosanska Dubica	BIH	76	G2	Bratsigovo	BG	83	G7	Bronte	I	30	E5
Bosanska Gradiška	BIH	76	G3	Bratunac	BIH	81	D9	Broşteni	RO	78	C5
Bosanska Krupa	BIH	80	B4	Braunau am Inn	A	39	B7	Brou	F	15	E10
Bosanski Brod	BIH	76	G4	Braunschweig	D	42	F6	Broumov	CZ	74	C6
Bosanski Novi	BIH	76	G1	Braunton	GB	8	E3	Broxburn	GB	2	G6
Bosanski Šamac	BIH	76	G5	Bray	IRL	4	G3	Bruchhausen-Vilsen	D	11	B12
Boscotrecase	I	30	B5	Brbinj	HR	80	D2	Bruchmühlbach	D	13	C10
Bosilegrad	SRB	82	F4	Brčko	BIH	76	H5	Bruck an der Mur	A	39	D10
Boskovice	CZ	74	E6	Bré	IRL	4	G3	Bruges	B	10	F4
Boston	GB	5	H10	Breaza	RO	78	G5	Brugge	B	10	F4
Boteå	S	52	B6	Brebu	RO	78	G5	Brumunddal	N	51	G8
Boteşti	RO	79	C7	Brechin	GB	3	F7	Brunflo	S	51	B12
Botevgrad	BG	82	E6	Brecht	B	10	E6	Brunico	I	38	E5
Botoroaga	RO	83	C9	Břeclav	CZ	75	G7	Brunkeberg	N	48	D5

Brunsbüttel	D	42	C4
Bruntál	CZ	75	D8
Bruravik	N	48	B3
Brussel	B	10	F5
Brusturi-Drăgănești	RO	78	C6
Bruxelles	B	10	F5
Bruz	F	14	E6
Brymbo	GB	4	G6
Bryne	N	48	E2
Bryukhovychi	UA	73	E6
Brzeg	PL	75	B8
Brzeg Dolny	PL	75	B7
Brzesko	PL	73	D1
Brzeszcze	PL	75	D10
Brzeziny	PL	71	G10
Brzozów	PL	73	E3
Buarcos	P	24	B2
Buca	TR	85	H3
Buccino	I	31	B7
Bucecea	RO	78	B6
Bucharest	RO	83	B10
Buchs	CH	37	C8
Bucine	I	35	G8
Buciumeni	RO	78	G5
Bückeburg	D	11	D12
Buckhaven	GB	3	G7
Buckie	GB	3	D7
Buckingham	GB	9	D8
Buckley	GB	4	G6
Bucov	RO	78	H6
Bučovice	CZ	75	F7
Bucureşti	RO	83	B10
Bud	N	50	B4
Budaörs	H	76	C5
Budapest	H	76	C6
Buddusò	I	32	E3
Budeşti	RO	83	C10
Bueu	E	22	D2
Buftea	RO	83	B10
Bugojno	BIH	80	D6
Bugyi	H	76	C6
Buhuşi	RO	79	D7
Builth Wells	GB	8	C4
Bujalance	E	28	C5
Bujanovac	SRB	82	F3
Buk	PL	70	F6
Bullas	E	29	C9
Bulle	CH	36	D5
Bulqizë	AL	86	B3
Bumbeşti-Jiu	RO	78	G1
Buñol	E	27	F9
Bunteşti	RO	77	D11
Burbach	D	11	G10
Burgas	BG	83	F12
Burg bei Magdeburg	D	43	F8
Burgdorf	CH	13	G10
Burghausen	D	39	C7
Burglengenfeld	D	41	F8
Burgos	E	23	D10
Burgstädt	D	41	B9
Burgsvik	S	47	H9
Burgum	NL	11	B8
Burhaniye	TR	85	F3
Burlada	E	20	C4
Burnley	GB	5	F7
Burntisland	GB	2	G6
Burrel	AL	86	B2
Burriana	E	27	E10
Burton Latimer	GB	9	C8
Burton upon Trent	GB	5	H8

Burwell	GB	9	C10
Bury	GB	5	F7
Bury St Edmunds	GB	9	C10
Busalla	I	19	B11
Busca	I	19	B9
Bushtyna	UA	78	A1
Busko-Zdrój	PL	73	C1
Bussolengo	I	35	C7
Buşteni	RO	78	G5
Busto Arsizio	I	34	C3
Büsum	D	42	B4
Butera	I	30	G4
Butzbach	D	11	G11
Bützow	D	43	C8
Buxerolles	F	16	B5
Buxtehude	D	42	D5
Buxton	GB	5	G8
Büyükçekmece	TR	85	B5
Buzău	RO	79	G7
Buziaş	RO	77	F10
Buzoeşti	RO	83	B8
Byahoml'	BY	69	F12
Byala	BG	83	D9
Byala Slatina	BG	82	D6
Byarozawka	BY	69	H8
Bychawa	PL	73	B4
Bydgoszcz	PL	71	D7
Bygland	N	48	E5
Byrum	DK	44	B5
Bystřice nad Pernštejnem			
	CZ	74	E6
Bytča	SK	75	F9
Bytom	PL	75	C10
Bytów	PL	71	B7
Byxelkrok	S	45	B12

C

Cabañaquinta	E	23	B7
Čabar	HR	39	H9
Cabeza del Buey	E	26	G2
Cabezón de la Sal	E	23	B9
Cabra	E	28	D5
Cabras	I	32	F2
Čačak	SRB	81	D11
Caccamo	I	30	E3
Cacém	P	24	F2
Cáceres	E	24	D6
Čadca	SK	75	E9
Cadeo	I	34	D5
Cádiz	E	25	L7
Caen	F	15	C4
Caerdydd	GB	8	E5
Caerfyrddin	GB	8	D3
Caergybi	GB	4	G4
Caernarfon	GB	4	G5
Caerphilly	GB	8	E5
Cagli	I	35	G10
Cagliari	I	32	G3
Cagnano Varano	I	33	D11
Cagnes-sur-Mer	F	19	D8
Cahors	F	17	F7
Cahul	MD	79	F9
Căianu Mic	RO	78	C3
Caiazzo	I	30	A5
Cairo Montenotte	I	19	B10
Caisleán an Bharraigh	IRL	7	H3
Caister-on-Sea	GB	9	B12
Căiuţi	RO	79	E7

Caivano	I	30	B5
Cajvana	RO	78	B6
Čakovec	HR	76	E1
Calafat	RO	82	C5
Calafell	E	21	F9
Calafindeşti	RO	78	B6
Calahorra	E	20	D3
Calais	F	9	F12
Calamonte	E	24	F6
Călan	RO	77	F12
Calañas	E	25	J6
Călăraşi	MD	79	C10
Călăraşi	RO	82	D6
Călăraşi	RO	83	C12
Calascibetta	I	30	F4
Calasetta	I	32	H1
Calasparra	E	29	B9
Calatafimi	I	30	E2
Calatayud	E	20	F4
Calbe (Saale)	D	43	G8
Caldas da Rainha	P	24	D2
Caldas de Reis	E	22	C2
Caldes de Montbui	E	21	E10
Caldicot	GB	8	E5
Calenzano	I	35	F7
Călimăneşti	RO	78	G3
Calimera	I	31	C11
Călineşti	RO	78	H4
Calitri	I	31	B7
Callosa d'En Sarrià	E	27	G10
Calne	GB	8	E6
Calpe	E	27	G11
Caltabellotta	I	30	F3
Caltagirone	I	30	F5
Caltanissetta	I	30	F4
Caltavuturo	I	30	E4
Călugăreni	RO	83	C10
Calvi	F	19	E10
Calzada de Calatrava	E	26	G4
Camariñas	E	22	B1
Camas	E	25	J7
Cambados	E	22	D2
Camborne	GB	8	G2
Cambrai	F	10	H4
Cambridge	GB	9	C9
Cambrils	E	21	G8
Camenca	MD	79	A10
Camerano	I	35	G11
Camerino	I	35	H10
Camerota	I	31	C7
Cammarata	I	30	F3
Campagnano di Roma	I	32	C5
Campanario	E	24	F8
Campbeltown	GB	4	C3
Câmpeni	RO	77	E12
Câmpia Turzii	RO	78	D2
Campi Bisenzio	I	35	F7
Campiglia Marittima	I	32	A2
Campillos	E	28	E4
Câmpina	RO	78	G5
Campi Salentina	I	31	C11
Campli	I	33	B7
Campobasso	I	33	D9
Campobello di Licata	I	30	F4
Campobello di Mazara	I	30	F2
Campo de Criptana	E	26	F5
Campofelice di Roccella	I	30	E4
Campo Maior	P	24	E5
Campomarino	I	33	C9
Campomorone	I	19	B11

C

C

C

Cuéllar	E	23	F9
Cuenca	E	27	E7
Cuers	F	19	E7
Cuevas de Almanzora	E	29	D9
Cugir	RO	78	F1
Cugnaux	F	17	H7
Cuijk	NL	11	E7
Cúllar-Baza	E	29	D8
Cullera	E	27	F10
Cullompton	GB	8	F4
Cumbernauld	GB	2	G5
Cumnock	GB	4	C5
Cumpăna	RO	84	C4
Cuneo	I	19	C9
Cuorgnè	I	34	C1
Cupar	GB	3	G7
Cupcina	MD	79	A8
Čuprija	SRB	82	C2
Curcani	RO	83	C11
Curinga	I	31	F8
Curtea de Argeş	RO	78	G3
Curtici	RO	77	E9
Čurug	SRB	77	G7
Cusset	F	17	C10
Cutro	I	31	E9
Cutrofiano	I	31	C11
Cuxhaven	D	42	C4
Cwmbrân	GB	8	D5
Czaplinek	PL	70	D5
Czarna Białostocka	PL	72	D5
Czarne	PL	70	C6
Czarnków	PL	70	E6
Czersk	PL	71	C7
Czerwionka-Leszczyny	PL	75	D9
Częstochowa	PL	75	B10
Człuchów	PL	71	C7

D

Dabas	H	76	C6
Dąbrowa Białostocka	PL	68	H6
Dąbrowa Górnicza	PL	75	C10
Dąbrowa Tarnowska	PL	73	D2
Dăbuleni	RO	82	D6
Dachau	D	37	A11
Dačice	CZ	74	F5
Dafni	GR	89	B7
Daimiel	E	26	G5
Đakovo	HR	76	G5
Dalarö	S	47	C10
Dalby	S	45	E8
Dalj	HR	76	G5
Dalkeith	GB	3	H7
Dalmine	I	34	C5
Dalsbruk	FIN	53	H11
Dalton-in-Furness	GB	4	E6
Damme	B	10	F4
Damme	D	11	C11
Damwoude	NL	11	B8
Daneţi	RO	82	C6
Dannenberg (Elbe)	D	43	D7
Darabani	RO	79	A7
Dărăşti Ilfov	RO	83	C10
Dar Ben Karricha el Behri	MA	28	H3
Dar Chaoui	MA	28	H3
Darda	HR	76	F5
Dardilly	F	36	F2
Darfo Boario Terme	I	34	B6
Darlington	GB	5	D8

Darłowo	PL	45	H12
Dărmăneşti	RO	78	B6
Dărmăneşti	RO	78	E6
Dărmăneşti	RO	78	H5
Darmstadt	D	13	B11
Darque	P	22	E2
Dartford	GB	9	E10
Dartmouth	GB	8	G4
Daruvar	HR	76	F3
Dassel	D	42	G5
Datça	TR	88	F3
Daugavpils	LV	69	D10
Daventry	GB	9	C8
Davoli	I	31	F8
Davos	CH	37	D9
Davutlar	TR	88	D2
Dawlish	GB	8	G4
Dax	F	16	G3
Deal	GB	9	E11
Debar	MK	86	B3
Debeljača	SRB	77	G8
Dębica	PL	73	D2
Dęblin	PL	72	H4
Dębno	PL	43	E11
Debrecen	H	77	B10
Debrzno	PL	70	D6
Decazeville	F	17	F8
Děčín	CZ	41	C11
Decize	F	12	H4
Dedemsvaart	NL	11	C8
Dedovichi	RUS	67	F12
Degerfors	S	46	C5
Deggendorf	D	39	A7
De Haan	B	10	F3
Deinze	B	10	F4
Dej	RO	78	C2
Delčevo	MK	82	G4
Delémont	CH	13	G9
Deleni	RO	79	C7
Delft	NL	10	D5
Delfzijl	NL	11	A9
Delia	I	30	F4
Delle	F	13	F9
Delmenhorst	D	11	B11
Delsbo	S	52	D4
Deltebre	E	21	G8
Delvinë	AL	86	E3
Demirci	TR	85	F5
Demir Hisar	MK	86	C4
Demirköy	TR	84	G3
Demmin	D	43	C9
Denbigh	GB	4	G6
Den Burg	NL	10	B6
Dendermonde	B	10	F5
Den Haag	NL	10	D5
Den Helder	NL	10	B6
Denia	E	27	G11
Denny	GB	2	G5
Densburen	CH	13	G10
Déols	F	15	H11
Derby	GB	5	H8
Derecske	H	77	C10
Dereham	GB	9	B11
Derry	GB	4	D1
Dersca	RO	78	B6
Derventa	BIH	76	H4
Descartes	F	15	H10
Dessau	D	43	G8
Deta	RO	77	G9
Detmold	D	11	D12

Dettelbach	D	40	D5
Detva	SK	75	G10
Deutschlandsberg	A	39	E10
Deva	RO	77	F12
Dévaványa	H	77	C9
Devecser	H	76	C3
Deventer	NL	11	D8
Devin	BG	83	H7
Devizes	GB	8	E6
Devnya	BG	83	E12
Dewsbury	GB	5	F8
Diamante	I	31	D7
Diano Marina	I	19	C10
Didcot	GB	9	D7
Didymoteicho	GR	85	B2
Diekirch	L	13	B8
Diepholz	D	11	C11
Dieppe	F	9	H11
Dietikon	CH	13	G11
Digne-les-Bains	F	19	C7
Digoin	F	17	B11
Dijon	F	12	G6
Dikili	TR	85	F2
Dilbeek	B	10	F5
Dimitrovgrad	BG	83	G9
Dimitrovgrad	SRB	82	E4
Dinan	F	14	E6
Dinard	F	14	D6
Dingolfing	D	38	B6
Dingwall	GB	2	D5
Dinkelsbühl	D	40	F5
Dinklage	D	11	C11
Diosig	RO	77	C11
Dippoldiswalde	D	41	B10
Diss	GB	9	C11
Ditrău	RO	78	D5
Dives-sur-Mer	F	15	C8
Djurås	S	52	G3
Dnestrovsc	MD	79	D12
Dno	RUS	67	E12
Dobanovci	SRB	81	B11
Dobczyce	PL	75	D11
Dobele	LV	66	H4
Döbeln	D	41	B9
Doberlug-Kirchhain	D	43	G10
Doboj	BIH	81	B7
Dobre Miasto	PL	68	G2
Dobreşti	RO	77	D11
Dobrich	BG	84	D3
Dobříš	CZ	41	E11
Dobroteşti	RO	83	C8
Dobruška	CZ	74	D6
Doetinchem	NL	11	D8
Dofteana	RO	78	E7
Dokkum	NL	11	A7
Dokshytsy	BY	69	F11
Doksy	CZ	41	C11
Dole	F	13	G7
Dolhasca	RO	79	C7
Dolianova	I	32	G3
Dolni Chiflik	BG	84	E3
Dolni Dŭbnik	BG	83	D7
Dolný Kubín	SK	75	F10
Dolyna	UA	73	F6
Domat Ems	CH	37	D8
Domažlice	CZ	41	E9
Dombås	N	50	D6
Dombóvár	H	76	E4
Domérat	F	17	B9
Domneşti	RO	83	B10

D

D

Name	Country	Page	Grid
Domodossola	I	34	B3
Dömsöd	H	76	C6
Domusnovas	I	32	G2
Domžale	SLO	39	G9
Donaghadee	GB	4	D3
Don Benito	E	24	E7
Doncaster	GB	5	F9
Dondușeni	MD	79	A8
Donji Miholjac	HR	76	F4
Donji Vakuf	BIH	80	D6
Donostia/San Sebastián	E	20	B3
Đorče Petrov	MK	82	G2
Dorchester	GB	8	F6
Dordrecht	NL	10	E6
Dorgali	I	32	E3
Dorking	GB	9	E9
Dormagen	D	11	F9
Dor Mărunt	RO	83	B11
Dornbirn	A	37	C9
Dorog	H	76	B5
Dorohoi	RO	78	B6
Dorsten	D	11	E9
Dortmund	D	11	E10
Dörverden	D	11	B12
Dos Hermanas	E	25	K7
Douarnenez	F	14	E2
Doué-la-Fontaine	F	15	G8
Douglas	GBM	4	E5
Douvaine	F	36	E4
Dover	GB	9	E11
Dovhe	UA	73	H5
Downham Market	GB	9	B10
Downpatrick	GB	4	E3
Drachten	NL	11	B8
Dragalina	RO	83	B12
Drăgănești	RO	78	H6
Drăgănești	RO	79	F8
Drăgănești-Olt	RO	83	C7
Drăgănești-Vlașca	RO	83	C9
Drăgășani	RO	83	B7
Dragør	DK	45	F7
Draguignan	F	19	D7
Drajna	RO	78	G6
Drama	GR	87	C9
Drammen	N	49	C7
Dravograd	SLO	39	F10
Drawsko Pomorskie	PL	70	D5
Dresden	D	41	B10
Dreux	F	12	D1
Drevsjø	N	51	E9
Drezdenko	PL	70	E5
Dridu	RO	83	B10
Driffield	GB	5	E10
Drniš	HR	80	D4
Drobeta-Turnu Severin	RO	82	B4
Drochia	MD	79	A9
Drogheda	IRL	4	F2
Drohobych	UA	73	F5
Droichead Átha	IRL	4	F2
Droichead Nua	IRL	4	G2
Droitwich Spa	GB	8	C6
Dronero	I	19	B9
Dronfield	GB	5	G8
Dronten	NL	11	C7
Druskininkai	LT	69	G7
Dryanovo	BG	83	E9
Dryna	N	50	C3
Dubăsari	MD	79	C11
Dublin	IRL	4	G2
Dublyany	UA	73	E6
Dubove	UA	78	A2
Dubrovnik	HR	81	G7
Dudestii Vechi	RO	77	E8
Dudley	GB	8	C6
Dueville	I	35	C8
Duga Resa	HR	39	H11
Dugo Selo	HR	39	G12
Dülgopol	BG	83	E12
Dulovo	BG	83	C12
Dumbarton	GB	2	G5
Dumbrava Roșie	RO	78	D6
Dumbrăveni	RO	78	B6
Dumbrăveni	RO	78	E3
Dumfries	GB	4	C6
Dumitrești	RO	79	F7
Dumnicë e Poshtme	RKS	82	E2
Dunaföldvár	H	76	D5
Dunaharaszti	H	76	C6
Dunajská Streda	SK	76	B3
Dunakeszi	H	76	B6
Dunaújváros	H	76	D5
Dunavarsány	H	76	C6
Dunbar	GB	3	G7
Dunblane	GB	2	G5
Dundalk	IRL	4	E2
Dun Dealgan	IRL	4	E2
Dundee	GB	3	F7
Dunfermline	GB	2	G6
Dungannon	GB	4	D2
Dún Garbhán	IRL	7	M5
Dungarvan	IRL	7	M5
Dunkerque	F	10	F2
Dún Laoghaire	IRL	4	G3
Dunmurry	GB	4	D3
Dunoon	GB	2	G4
Dunstable	GB	9	D8
Dupnitsa	BG	82	G5
Durango	E	20	B2
Durban-Corbières	F	18	E1
Dúrcal	E	28	E6
Đurđevac	HR	76	E2
Düren	D	11	G8
Durham	GB	5	D8
Durlas	IRL	7	L5
Durlești	MD	79	C10
Durrës	AL	86	B1
Dursley	GB	8	D6
Dursunbey	TR	85	E5
Düsseldorf	D	11	F9
Dve Mogili	BG	83	D9
Dvůr Králové	CZ	74	C5
Dyce	GB	3	E8
Dynów	PL	73	E3
Dzhebel	BG	87	B3
Działdowo	PL	71	D10
Dzierzgoń	PL	71	C9
Dzyarzhynsk	BY	69	H10

E

Name	Country	Page	Grid
Eastbourne	GB	9	F10
Eastfield	GB	5	E10
East Grinstead	GB	9	E9
East Kilbride	GB	2	H5
Eastleigh	GB	9	F7
East Wittering	GB	9	F8
Ebbw Vale	GB	8	D5
Ebensee	A	39	C8
Ebensfeld	D	40	D6
Ebenthal	A	39	F9
Eberndorf	A	39	F9
Ebersbach	D	41	B11
Eberswalde-Finow	D	43	E10
Eboli	I	30	B6
Écija	E	28	D4
Ečka	SRB	77	G8
Eckernförde	D	42	B5
Eckington	GB	5	G9
Edelény	H	73	H1
Edemissen	D	42	F6
Edessa	GR	86	C6
Edinburgh	GB	2	G6
Edincik	TR	85	D4
Edineț	MD	79	A8
Edirne	TR	83	H11
Edland	N	48	C4
Edremit	TR	85	E3
Eforie	RO	84	C5
Eger	H	77	B8
Egersund	N	48	F3
Eggesin	D	43	C10
Eghezée	B	10	G6
Egremont	GB	4	E6
Éguilles	F	18	D5
Egyek	H	77	B9
Ehingen (Donau)	D	37	A9
Eibar	E	20	B2
Eibenstock	D	41	C8
Eibergen	NL	11	D8
Eichstätt	D	38	A4
Eidet	N	54	F6
Eidsbugarden	N	50	F5
Eilenburg	D	41	A8
Einbeck	D	42	G5
Eindhoven	NL	11	E7
Einsiedeln	CH	13	G11
Eisenach	D	40	B5
Eisenberg	D	41	B7
Eisenerz	A	39	D10
Eisenhüttenstadt	D	43	F11
Eisenstadt	A	76	B1
Eivissa	E	29	G7
Ejea de los Caballeros	E	20	D4
Ekenäs	FIN	64	G4
Ekerö	S	47	C9
Eksjö	S	45	A10
Elassona	GR	86	E6
El Astillero	E	23	B10
Elbasan	AL	86	C2
Elbeuf	F	15	C10
Elbląg	PL	71	B9
El Burgo de Osma	E	20	F1
Elche/Elx	E	29	B11
Elda	E	27	H9
Elefsina	GR	89	B7
El Ejido	E	29	E7
Elek	H	77	D9
Elektrėnai	LT	69	F7
Elena	BG	83	E9
El Escorial	E	23	H10
El Espinar	E	23	G9
El Fendek	MA	28	H3
Elgin	GB	2	D6
Elin Pelin	BG	82	F6
Elizondo	E	20	B4
Ełk	PL	68	H4
Elkhovo	BG	83	G11
Elland	GB	5	F8
Ellesmere Port	GB	5	G7

F

Filipeştii de Pădure	RO	78	H5
Filipstad	S	46	B5
Filottrano	I	35	G11
Finale Emilia	I	35	D8
Finale Ligure	I	19	C10
Finkenstein	A	39	F8
Finspång	S	47	D7
Finsterwalde	D	43	G10
Fionnphort	GB	2	G2
Fiorenzuola d'Arda	I	34	D5
Firenze	I	35	F7
Fishguard	GB	8	D2
Fisksätra	S	47	C9
Fismes	F	12	C4
Fisterra	E	22	C1
Fiuggi	I	32	D6
Fiumefreddo di Sicilia	I	30	E6
Fivizzano	I	34	E6
Flămânzi	RO	79	B7
Fleet	GB	9	E8
Fleetwood	GB	4	F6
Flekkefjord	N	48	F3
Flen	S	47	D8
Flensburg	D	44	G3
Flers	F	15	D4
Fleurance	F	16	G6
Flint	GB	4	G6
Flix	E	21	F7
Floda	S	44	A7
Flöha	D	41	B9
Floirac	F	16	E4
Florence	I	35	F7
Florenville	B	13	B7
Floreşti	MD	79	B10
Floreşti	RO	78	D2
Floreşti-Stoeneşti	RO	83	B9
Floridia	I	30	G6
Florina	GR	86	D5
Florø	N	50	E1
Flötningen	S	51	E9
Foča	BIH	81	E8
Foça	TR	85	G2
Focşani	RO	79	F8
Focuri	RO	79	C8
Foggia	I	33	D10
Fohnsdorf	A	39	D9
Foix	F	21	C9
Folignano	I	33	B7
Foligno	I	32	A6
Folkestone	GB	9	F11
Folldal	N	51	D7
Follonica	I	32	A2
Fondevila	E	22	E3
Fondi	I	33	E7
Fonsorbes	F	17	H7
Fontaine	F	18	A6
Fontainebleau	F	12	E3
Fontaine le Comte	F	16	B5
Fontanellato	I	34	D6
Fontenay-le-Comte	F	16	B3
Fonyód	H	76	D3
Forăşti	RO	78	C6
Forcalquier	F	18	C6
Forchheim	D	40	E6
Førde	N	50	E2
Fordingbridge	GB	9	F7
Forfar	GB	3	F7
Forio	I	30	B4
Forlì	I	35	E9
Forlimpopoli	I	35	F9
Formby	GB	4	F6
Formello	I	32	C5
Formia	I	30	A4
Formofoss	N	54	F5
Forres	GB	2	D6
Fors	S	52	B4
Forsand	N	48	E3
Forshaga	S	46	C4
Forsmark	S	52	G6
Forsnes	N	50	A5
Forssa	FIN	53	F12
Forst	D	43	G11
Fortuna	E	29	C10
Fort William	GB	2	F4
Fosnavåg	N	50	D2
Fossano	I	19	B9
Fossombrone	I	35	G10
Fót	H	76	B6
Fougères	F	15	E7
Fourmies	F	12	A5
Fourna	GR	86	G5
Fournoi	GR	89	C12
Foz	E	22	B4
Fraga	E	21	F7
Fragagnano	I	31	C10
Francavilla al Mare	I	33	B8
Francavilla di Sicilia	I	30	E6
Francavilla Fontana	I	31	B10
Frânceşti	RO	78	G3
Francofonte	I	30	F5
Frankenberg (Eder)	D	11	F11
Frankfurt am Main	D	11	H11
Frankfurt an der Oder	D	43	F11
Frascati	I	32	D5
Fraserburgh	GB	3	D8
Frasin	RO	78	B5
Frastanz	A	37	C9
Frăteşti	RO	83	C10
Frauenfeld	CH	13	F12
Fredensborg	DK	44	E7
Fredericia	DK	44	F3
Frederiksberg	DK	44	E7
Frederikshavn	DK	44	B4
Frederikssund	DK	44	E6
Frederiksværk	DK	44	E6
Fredrika	S	55	F11
Fredrikstad	N	46	C1
Fregenal de la Sierra	E	24	G6
Freiberg	D	41	B9
Freiburg im Breisgau	D	13	E10
Freilassing	D	39	C7
Freising	D	38	B5
Freistadt	A	39	B9
Freital	D	41	B10
Fréjus	F	19	D8
Freudenstadt	D	13	E11
Freyung	D	39	A8
Fribourg	CH	13	H9
Friedberg	D	38	B4
Friedland	D	43	C10
Friesach	A	39	E9
Friesoythe	D	11	B10
Friitala	FIN	53	E10
Frinton-on-Sea	GB	9	D11
Friol	E	22	C4
Friville-Escarbotin	F	9	H11
Frohnleiten	A	39	D10
Frome	GB	8	E6
Frontignan	F	18	D3
Frosinone	I	33	D7
Frumuşica	RO	79	B7
Frumuşiţa	RO	79	F9
Frunzivka	UA	79	C12
Frutigen	CH	36	E6
Frýdek-Místek	CZ	75	E9
Fucecchio	I	35	F7
Fuengirola	E	28	F4
Fuenlabrada	E	26	D4
Fuensalida	E	26	E3
Fuente de Cantos	E	24	G6
Fuente del Maestre	E	24	F6
Fuente Obejuna	E	24	G8
Fuentes de Andalucía	E	25	J8
Fuglafjørður	FO	2	B9
Fulda	D	40	C4
Fumay	F	12	B6
Fumel	F	16	F6
Fundão	P	24	B5
Fundeni	RO	83	B10
Fundulea	RO	83	B11
Fürstenau	D	11	C10
Fürstenberg	D	43	D9
Fürstenfeld	A	39	E11
Fürstenfeldbruck	D	37	A11
Fürstenzell	D	39	B7
Fürth	D	40	E6
Furudal	S	52	F3
Furusund	S	47	B10
Fuscaldo	I	31	E8
Fushë Kosovë	RKS	81	G12
Fushë-Krujë	AL	86	B2
Füssen	D	37	C10
Futog	SRB	77	G7
Füzesabony	H	77	B8
Füzesgyarmat	H	77	C9

G

Gabicce Mare	I	35	F10
Gabrovo	BG	83	E9
Gadebusch	D	43	C7
Găeşti	RO	83	B9
Gaeta	I	30	A4
Gafanha da Nazaré	P	22	G2
Gagliano da Capo	I	31	D12
Gagnef	S	52	G3
Gaildorf	D	40	F4
Gaillac	F	17	G8
Gaillimh	IRL	7	J3
Gaillon	F	15	C10
Gainsborough	GB	5	G9
Găiseni	RO	83	B9
Gălăneşti	RO	78	B5
Galanta	SK	75	H8
Galashiels	GB	5	B7
Galata	BG	84	E3
Galaţi	RO	79	G9
Galatina	I	31	C11
Galatone	I	31	C11
Gâldău	RO	83	B12
Galicea Mare	RO	82	C5
Gallardon	F	12	D1
Gallipoli	I	31	C11
Gällivare	S	60	D3
Galston	GB	4	B5
Galway	IRL	7	J3
Gamleby	S	47	F8
Gammelstaden	S	56	C4
Gand	B	10	F4

G

Gragnano	I	30	B5	Grums	S	46	C4	Habo	S	46	F5
Grajewo	PL	68	H5	Grünberg	D	11	G12	Haddington	GB	3	G7
Grammichele	I	30	F5	Grybów	PL	73	E2	Haderslev	DK	44	F3
Gramsh	AL	86	C3	Gryfice	PL	43	C12	Hadımköy	TR	85	B5
Granada	E	28	E6	Gryfino	PL	43	D11	Hadleigh	GB	9	D11
Grândola	P	24	G3	Gryt	S	47	E8	Hadsten	DK	44	D4
Grangemouth	GB	2	G6	Guadalajara	E	20	G1	Hagen	D	11	E10
Granollers	E	21	E10	Guadix	E	29	D7	Hagenow	D	43	D7
Gransee	D	43	D9	Gualdo Cattaneo	I	32	B5	Hagfors	S	46	B4
Grantham	GB	5	H9	Gualdo Tadino	I	35	G10	Hagsta	S	52	F5
Granville	F	14	D6	Guarda	P	22	H4	Haguenau	F	13	D10
Grao	E	27	E11	Guardamar del Segura	E	29	C11	Hailsham	GB	9	F10
Grassano	I	31	B8	Guardavalle	I	31	F8	Hainburg an der Donau	A	75	H7
Grasse	F	19	D8	Guardiagrele	I	33	C8	Hainichen	D	41	B9
Gratkorn	A	39	E10	Guardia Sanframondi	I	30	A5	Hajdúböszörmény	H	77	B10
Graulhet	F	17	G8	Guardo	E	23	C8	Hajdúdorog	H	77	B10
Gravelines	F	9	F12	Guareña	E	24	F7	Hajdúhadház	H	77	B10
Gravesend	GB	9	E10	Guastalla	I	34	D6	Hajdúnánás	H	77	B10
Gravina di Catania	I	30	F6	Gubbio	I	35	G10	Hajdúsámson	H	77	B10
Gravina in Puglia	I	31	B8	Guben	D	43	G11	Hajdúszoboszló	H	77	C9
Gray	F	13	G7	Gubin	PL	43	G11	Hajnówka	PL	72	E6
Graz	A	39	E10	Guénange	F	13	C8	Hakkenpää	FIN	53	G10
Grazzanise	I	30	A5	Guer	F	14	F5	Hălăucești	RO	79	C7
Great Dunmow	GB	9	D10	Guérande	F	14	G5	Halberstadt	D	43	G7
Great Gonerby	GB	5	H9	Guéret	F	17	C8	Hălchiu	RO	78	F5
Great Malvern	GB	8	C6	Gueugnon	F	17	B11	Halden	N	46	C2
Great Shelford	GB	9	C9	Gugești	RO	79	F8	Haldensleben	D	43	F7
Great Torrington	GB	8	F3	Guglionesi	I	33	C9	Halesowen	GB	8	C6
Great Yarmouth	GB	9	C12	Guichen	F	14	F6	Halesworth	GB	9	C11
Grebănu	RO	79	G7	Guidel	F	14	F4	Halhjem	N	48	B2
Greenisland	GB	4	D3	Guidonia-Montecelio	I	32	C6	Halifax	GB	5	F8
Greenock	GB	2	G4	Guildford	GB	9	E8	Hälla	S	55	G10
Greifswald	D	43	B10	Guillena	E	25	J7	Halle	B	10	G5
Grenaa	DK	44	D5	Guimarães	P	22	F3	Halle (Saale)	D	41	A7
Grenade	F	17	G7	Guînes	F	9	F12	Hällefors	S	46	B5
Grenchen	CH	13	G10	Guingamp	F	14	D4	Hallein	A	39	D7
Grenoble	F	18	A6	Guipavas	F	14	E2	Hall in Tirol	A	37	C11
Greve in Chianti	I	35	G8	Guisborough	GB	5	D9	Hallsberg	S	46	D6
Greven	D	11	D10	Guitiriz	E	22	B3	Hallstahammar	S	47	B7
Grevena	GR	86	E5	Gujan-Mestras	F	16	F3	Halmeu	RO	77	B12
Grevenmacher	L	13	B8	Gulbene	LV	67	G8	Halmstad	S	45	C7
Greystones	IRL	4	G3	Gullegem	B	10	F4	Halstead	GB	9	D10
Grez-Doiceau	B	10	G6	Gülübovo	BG	83	G9	Halstenbek	D	42	C5
Grigiškès	LT	69	F8	Gunja	HR	76	H5	Haltingen	D	13	F10
Grigoriopol	MD	79	C11	Günzburg	D	38	B3	Ham	F	12	B3
Grimma	D	41	B9	Gunzenhausen	D	40	F6	Hamar	N	49	A8
Grimmen	D	43	B9	Gura Humorului	RO	78	B5	Hamburg	D	42	C5
Grimsby	GB	5	F10	Gurghiu	RO	78	D4	Hämeenlinna	FIN	64	E5
Grimstad	N	48	F5	Gur'yevsk	RUS	68	F2	Hameln	D	11	D12
Grindsted	DK	44	E2	Gusev	RUS	68	F4	Hamilton	GB	2	H5
Grisslehamn	S	47	A10	Guspini	I	32	G2	Hamina	FIN	65	F8
Grivița	RO	83	B12	Gussago	I	34	G2	Hamm	D	11	E10
Grocka	SRB	81	C11	Gustavsberg	S	47	C10	Hammel	DK	44	D3
Grodków	PL	75	C7	Güstrow	D	43	C8	Hammelburg	D	40	D4
Grodzisk Mazowiecki	PL	71	F11	Gütersloh	D	11	D11	Hammerdal	S	55	G8
Grodzisk Wielkopolski	PL	70	F5	Gvardeysk	RUS	68	F3	Hammerfest	N	58	B6
Grójec	PL	71	G11	Gvarv	N	48	D6	Hamminkeln	D	11	E8
Grömitz	D	43	B7	Gyál	H	76	C6	Hanau	D	13	A12
Groningen	NL	11	B8	Gyomaendrőd	H	77	D8	Hanko	FIN	64	H4
Großenhain	D	41	B10	Gyöngyös	H	77	B7	Hannover	D	42	F5
Grosseto	I	32	B4	Győr	H	76	B3	Hannut	B	10	G6
Grosuplje	SLO	39	G9	Gytheio	GR	88	E5	Hansnes	N	58	D3
Grotli	N	50	D4	Gyula	H	77	D9	Haparanda	S	56	B6
Grottaferrata	I	32	D5					Harburg (Schwaben)	D	38	A4
Grottaglie	I	31	B10					Hard	A	37	C9
Grottammare	I	33	A7	**H**				Hardenberg	NL	11	C8
Grotte	I	30	F4					Haren (Ems)	D	11	C9
Grove	GB	9	D7	Haaksbergen	NL	11	D9	Hargshamn	S	47	A10
Grudziądz	PL	71	D8	Haapsalu	EST	66	C4	Harjavalta	FIN	53	E10
Grumo Appula	I	31	A9	Haarlem	NL	10	C6	Hârlău	RO	79	C7

H

K

Krosno	PL	73	E3
Krosno Odrzańskie	PL	70	G4
Krotoszyn	PL	71	G7
Krško	SLO	39	G10
Krujë	AL	86	B2
Krumbach (Schwaben)	D	37	A10
Krumovgrad	BG	87	B12
Krupina	SK	75	G10
Krupka	CZ	41	C10
Kruševac	SRB	82	D2
Kruševo	MK	86	B4
Kruszwica	PL	71	E8
Krutådal	N	55	C7
Krya Vrysi	GR	86	D6
Krylbo	S	47	A7
Krynica	PL	73	E2
Krzyż Wielkopolski	PL	70	E5
Kubrat	BG	83	D10
Kučevo	SRB	82	B2
Kuçovë	AL	86	D2
Küçükçekmece	TR	85	B6
Küçükköy	TR	85	F2
Kufstein	A	38	D6
Kuhmo	FIN	63	E10
Kukës	AL	81	H11
Kula	BG	82	C4
Kula	SRB	76	F6
Kula	TR	85	G5
Kuldīga	LV	66	G2
Kulmbach	D	41	D7
Kulykiv	UA	73	D6
Kumanovo	MK	82	G3
Kumla	S	46	C6
Kunda	EST	67	B8
Kungälv	S	46	F2
Kungsängen	S	47	C9
Kungsbacka	S	44	B6
Kungshamn	S	46	E2
Kungsör	S	47	C7
Kunhegyes	H	77	C8
Kunmadaras	H	77	C8
Kunszentmárton	H	77	D8
Kunszentmiklós	H	76	C6
Künzell	D	40	C4
Künzelsau	D	40	F4
Kuopio	FIN	65	B8
Kupiškis	LT	69	D8
Kŭrdzhali	BG	83	H9
Kuressaare	EST	66	E3
Kurikka	FIN	53	C11
Kuřim	CZ	74	F6
Kurort Schmalkalden	D	40	C5
Kuršėnai	LT	68	C5
Kuršumlija	SRB	82	E2
Kurtzea	E	20	B2
Kuru	FIN	53	D12
Kusadak	SRB	81	C12
Kuşadası	TR	88	D2
Küssnacht	CH	13	G11
Kustavi	FIN	53	G10
Kutina	HR	76	G2
Kutno	PL	71	F9
Kuusamo	FIN	61	F11
Kuusankoski	FIN	65	E7
Kuz'molovskiy	RUS	65	G11
Kuznechnoye	RUS	65	E10
Kvinesdal	N	48	F4
Kvinlog	N	48	F4
Kwidzyn	PL	71	C9
Kybartai	LT	68	F5
Kyjov	CZ	75	F7
Kyllini	GR	88	C3
Kymi	GR	87	H9
Kyritz	D	43	E8
Kysucké Nové Mesto	SK	75	E9
Kythira	GR	88	F6
Kyustendil	BG	82	G4

L

Laage	D	43	C8
La Almunia de Doña Godina	E	20	F4
La Bañeza	E	23	D7
Lábatlan	H	76	B5
La Baule-Escoublac	F	14	G5
Labin	HR	35	D12
La Bisbal d'Empordà	E	18	G2
La Bresse	F	13	E9
La Broque	F	13	E9
Labruguière	F	17	H8
Laç	AL	86	B2
Lacanau-Océan	F	16	E3
Laćarak	SRB	76	G6
La Carlota	E	28	D4
La Carolina	E	28	B6
La Charité-sur-Loire	F	12	G3
La Châtre	F	17	B8
La Ciotat	F	18	E6
La Coruna	E	22	B3
La Côte-St-André	F	36	G2
La Couronne	F	16	D5
La Crau	F	19	E7
Ladispoli	I	32	C4
Lærdalsøyri	N	50	F4
La Fare-les-Oliviers	F	18	D5
La Ferté-Alais	F	12	E2
La Ferté-Bernard	F	15	E9
La Ferté-Gaucher	F	12	D4
La Ferté-Macé	F	15	D8
La Ferté-sous-Jouarre	F	12	D3
La Ferté-St-Aubin	F	12	F2
La Flèche	F	15	F8
La Garde	F	19	E7
Lage	D	11	D11
Lagkadas	GR	87	D7
Lagnieu	F	36	F3
Lagonegro	I	31	C7
Lagord-la-Rochelle	F	16	C3
Lagos	P	25	K3
La Grande-Combe	F	17	F11
Laguna de Duero	E	23	F9
Laholm	S	45	D7
Lahoysk	BY	69	G11
Lahr (Schwarzwald)	D	13	E10
Lahti	FIN	64	E6
L'Aigle	F	15	D9
Laihia	FIN	53	B10
Laitila	FIN	53	F10
Laives	I	37	E11
Lajosmizse	H	76	C6
Lakhdenpokh'ya	RUS	65	D11
Lakki	GR	88	E2
L'Alcora	E	27	E9
Lalín	E	22	C3
La Línea de la Concepción	E	28	G3
La Londe-les-Maures	F	19	E7
La Maddalena	I	32	C3
La Manga del Mar Menor	E	29	D11
La Massana	AND	21	D9
Lamballe	F	14	E5
Lambesc	F	18	D5
Lamborn	S	52	F3
Lamego	P	22	G4
Lamezia	I	31	F8
Lamia	GR	86	G6
La Mure	F	18	A6
Lana	I	37	D11
Lanaken	B	11	F7
Lanark	GB	2	H6
Lancaster	GB	5	E7
Lanciano	I	33	C8
Łańcut	PL	73	D3
Lancy	CH	36	E4
Landeck	A	37	C10
Landerneau	F	14	E2
Landivisiau	F	14	D3
Landsberg am Lech	D	37	B10
Landshut	D	38	B6
Landskrona	S	45	E7
Lanester	F	14	F4
Langedijk	NL	10	C6
Langen	D	42	C4
Langenlois	A	39	B11
Langesund	N	49	E7
Langevåg	N	48	C2
Langgöns	D	11	G11
Langoiran	F	16	E4
Langon	F	16	F4
Langreo	E	23	B7
Langres	F	13	F7
Langwedel	D	11	B12
Lannemezan	F	21	B7
Lannilis	F	14	D2
Lannion	F	14	D4
Lanškroun	CZ	74	D6
La Nucía	E	27	G10
Lanusei	I	32	F3
Laon	F	12	B4
Lapinjärvi	FIN	65	F7
La Pola de Gordón	E	23	C7
La Pommeraye	F	15	G7
Lapovo	SRB	81	D12
Lappeenranta	FIN	65	E9
Lappersdorf	D	41	F8
Lâpseki	TR	85	D2
Lapua	FIN	53	B11
La Puebla de Almoradiel	E	26	F5
La Puebla de Cazalla	E	25	K8
La Puebla de Montalbán	E	26	E3
Łapy	PL	72	E5
L'Aquila	I	33	C7
Laracha	E	22	B2
La Ravoire	F	36	G3
Larbert	GB	2	G6
Lärbro	S	47	F10
Laredo	E	20	B1
La Réole	F	16	F4
Largs	GB	2	H4
Lari	I	34	G6
La Riche	F	15	G9
La Rinconada	E	25	J7
Larino	I	33	D9
Larisa	GR	86	F6
Larkollen	N	49	D8
Larmor-Plage	F	14	F4
Larne	GB	4	D3
La Robla	E	23	C7
La Rochelle	F	16	C3
La Roche-sur-Yon	F	16	B2

L

L

L

Luimneach	IRL	7	L4
Luino	I	34	B3
Luizi Călugăra	RO	79	D7
Lukavac	BIH	81	C8
Lukovit	BG	83	E7
Łuków	PL	72	G4
Luleå	S	56	C4
Lüleburgaz	TR	85	B3
Lumbres	F	9	F12
Lumezzane	I	34	C6
Lumina	RO	84	C4
Lumparland	FIN	47	A12
Lunca	RO	79	B7
Lunca	RO	83	C8
Lunca de Jos	RO	78	D6
Luncavița	RO	79	G9
Lund	S	45	E8
Lüneburg	D	42	D6
Lunel	F	17	H11
Lunéville	F	13	D8
Lunguleţu	RO	83	B9
L'Union	F	17	H7
Lupeni	RO	77	G12
Lure	F	13	F8
Lurgan	GB	4	E2
Lu-Ruchheim	D	13	C11
Lusciano	I	30	B5
Lushnjë	AL	86	C2
Lustenau	A	37	C9
Lutherstadt Wittenberg	D	43	G9
Lütjenburg	D	42	B6
Luton	GB	9	D9
Luxembourg	L	13	B8
Luxeuil-les-Bains	F	13	F8
Luzern	CH	13	G11
Luzzi	I	31	E8
L'viv	UA	73	E6
Lwówek Śląski	PL	74	B5
Lyaskovets	BG	83	E9
Lycksele	S	55	E11
Lydney	GB	8	D6
Lymans'ke	UA	79	D12
Lymington	GB	9	F7
Lyneham	GB	8	E6
Lyon	F	36	F2
Lysekil	S	46	E2
Lyss	CH	13	G9
Lytham St Anne's	GB	4	F6
Lyubashivka	UA	79	B12
Lyubimets	BG	83	G10

M

Maardu	EST	66	B6
Maaseik	B	11	F7
Maastricht	NL	11	F7
Mablethorpe	GB	5	G11
Macclesfield	GB	5	G8
Macea	RO	77	E9
Macerata	I	35	G11
Machecoul	F	14	H6
Măcin	RO	79	G9
Macomer	I	32	E2
Mâcon	F	17	B12
Madan	BG	87	B11
Maddaloni	I	30	A5
Made	NL	10	E6
Madona	LV	67	G7
Madrid	E	23	H10

Madridejos	E	26	F5
Mæl	N	48	C6
Mafra	P	24	E1
Magdeburg	D	43	F7
Magherafelt	GB	4	D2
Magione	I	35	G9
Maglaj	BIH	81	C7
Maglavit	RO	82	C5
Maglie	I	31	C11
Maglód	H	76	C6
Magura	SRB	81	G12
Măgurele	RO	83	B10
Mahmudia	RO	79	G11
Mahón	E	29	E12
Maia	P	22	F2
Măicăneşti	RO	79	G8
Maidenhead	GB	9	E8
Maidstone	GB	9	E10
Maieru	RO	78	C4
Mainburg	D	38	B5
Maintenon	F	12	D1
Mainz	D	13	A11
Maiolati Spontini	I	35	G11
Majadahonda	E	23	H10
Majdanpek	SRB	82	B3
Makarska	HR	80	E5
Makó	H	77	E8
Maków Mazowiecki	PL	71	E11
Maków Podhalański	PL	75	E11
Mala	IRL	7	M4
Malacky	SK	75	G7
Maladzyechna	BY	69	G10
Málaga	E	28	E5
Malagón	E	26	F4
Malahide	IRL	4	G3
Malalbergo	I	35	D8
Malaryta	BY	72	G6
Malbork	PL	71	C9
Malchin	D	43	C9
Malchow	D	43	D8
Măldăeni	RO	83	C8
Maldon	GB	9	D10
Malemort-sur-Corrèze	F	17	E7
Malente	D	42	B6
Malesherbes	F	12	E2
Mali Idoš	SRB	77	F7
Mali Lošinj	HR	80	C1
Malines	B	10	F5
Malkara	TR	85	C3
Mallaig	GB	2	E3
Mallorca	E	29	F9
Mallow	IRL	7	M4
Malmberget	S	60	D3
Malmesbury	GB	8	E6
Malmö	S	45	F7
Malmslätt	S	46	E6
Malnaş	RO	78	E5
Måløy	N	50	D2
Malpica	E	22	B2
Malton	GB	5	E9
Malu Mare	RO	82	C6
Malung	S	49	A11
Mamers	F	15	E9
Mamonovo	RUS	68	F1
Mamuras	AL	86	B2
Manacor	E	29	F10
Mănăstirea	RO	83	C11
Mănăstirea Caşin	RO	79	E7
Mancha Real	E	28	C6
Manchester	GB	5	G7

Manciano	I	32	B4
Mandal	N	48	G4
Mandelieu-la-Napoule	F	19	D8
Mandello del Lario	I	34	B4
Mandra	GR	89	B7
Manduria	I	31	C10
Măneciu	RO	78	G6
Manerbio	I	34	C6
Măneşti	RO	78	H5
Manfredonia	I	33	D11
Mangalia	RO	84	C4
Mangualde	P	22	G4
Maniago	I	35	B10
Manisa	TR	85	G3
Manlleu	E	21	E10
Mannheim	D	13	C11
Manningtree	GB	9	D11
Manno	CH	34	B4
Manoppello	I	33	C8
Manosque	F	18	D6
Manresa	E	21	E9
Mansfield	GB	5	G9
Mantes-la-Ville	F	12	D1
Mantova	I	35	D7
Mäntsälä	FIN	64	F6
Mänttä	FIN	64	C5
Mäntyluoto	FIN	53	E10
Manyas	TR	85	D4
Manzanares	E	26	G5
Manziana	I	32	C5
Maracena	E	28	D6
Mărăcineni	RO	79	G7
Maranello	I	35	E7
Marano di Napoli	I	30	B5
Mărăşeşti	RO	79	F8
Maratea	I	31	D7
Marbella	E	28	F4
Marburg an der Lahn	D	11	G11
Marby	S	51	B12
Marcali	H	76	D3
March	GB	9	C9
Marche-en-Famenne	B	11	H7
Marchena	E	25	J8
Marchtrenk	A	39	C9
Marcianise	I	30	A5
Marciano della Chiana	I	35	G8
Marennes	F	16	C3
Margate	GB	9	E11
Margherita di Savoia	I	33	E11
Marghita	RO	77	C11
Marginea	RO	78	B5
Mărgineni	RO	79	D7
Mariánské Lázně	CZ	41	D8
Maribo	DK	44	G5
Maribor	SLO	39	F11
Mariehamn	FIN	47	A11
Marienberg	D	41	C9
Mariestad	S	46	D5
Marigliano	I	30	B5
Marignane	F	18	D5
Marijampolė	LT	68	F6
Marín	E	22	D2
Marina di Gioiosa Ionica	I	31	G8
Marineo	I	30	E3
Marinha Grande	P	24	C2
Marino	I	32	D5
Markdorf	D	37	B8
Market Deeping	GB	9	B9
Market Drayton	GB	5	H7
Market Harborough	GB	9	C8

Marki	PL	71	F11	Mažeikiai	LT	68	C4	Mesoraca	I	31	E9
Markkleeberg	D	41	B8	Mazzarino	I	30	F4	Messina	I	31	E7
Markopoulo	GR	89	C7	Meadela	P	22	E2	Messini	GR	88	D4
Marktoberdorf	D	37	B10	Meaux	F	12	D3	Meta	I	30	B5
Marktredwitz	D	41	D8	Mechelen	B	10	F5	Metallostroy	RUS	65	H11
Marl	D	11	E9	Medemblik	NL	10	C6	Metković	HR	80	F6
Marlborough	GB	9	E7	Medgidia	RO	84	C4	Metlika	SLO	39	H10
Marly	CH	13	H9	Mediaş	RO	78	E3	Metz	F	13	C8
Marmande	F	16	F5	Medicina	I	35	E8	Meximieux	F	36	F2
Marmaraereğlisi	TR	85	C4	Medieşu Aurit	RO	77	B12	Meylan	F	18	A6
Marmari	GR	89	B8	Medina del Campo	E	23	F8	Mezdra	BG	82	E6
Marmolejo	E	28	C5	Medina de Pomar	E	23	C11	Mèze	F	18	D3
Marne	D	42	C4	Medina-Sidonia	E	25	M7	Mezőberény	H	77	D9
Marne-la-Vallée	F	12	D3	Medzilaborce	SK	73	F3	Mezőcsát	H	77	B9
Maromme	F	15	C10	Megara	GR	88	B6	Mezőhegyes	H	77	E9
Marousi	GR	89	B8	Mehadia	RO	77	H11	Mezőkeresztes	H	77	B8
Marquise	F	9	F12	Meilen	CH	13	G11	Mezőkovácsháza	H	77	E9
Marsala	I	30	E1	Meinerzhagen	D	11	F10	Mezőkövesd	H	77	B8
Mârşani	RO	82	C6	Meiningen	D	40	C5	Mezőtúr	H	77	D8
Marsberg	D	11	E12	Meißen	D	41	B10	Mezzolombardo	I	35	A7
Marsciano	I	32	A5	Mejorada del Campo	E	23	H11	Miajadas	E	24	E7
Marseillan	F	18	E2	Meldola	I	35	F9	Miastko	PL	70	C6
Marseille	F	18	E5	Meldorf	D	42	B4	Michalovce	SK	73	G3
Marsillargues	F	17	H11	Melenci	SRB	77	F8	Middelburg	NL	10	E4
Märsta	S	47	B8	Melendugno	I	31	C12	Middelfart	DK	44	F3
Marstrand	S	46	F2	Melfi	I	31	B7	Middelharnis	NL	10	E5
Martano	I	31	C12	Melicucco	I	31	G8	Middlesbrough	GB	5	D9
Martfű	H	77	C8	Melide	E	22	C3	Middleton	GB	5	F7
Martigny	CH	34	B1	Melilli	I	30	G6	Middlewich	GB	5	G7
Martil	MA	28	H3	Melissano	I	31	D11	Midhurst	GB	9	F8
Martin	SK	75	F10	Melito di Porto Salvo	I	31	H7	Midleton	IRL	7	M4
Martina Franca	I	31	B10	Melk	A	39	B10	Miðvágur	FO	3	B8
Martinsicuro	I	33	B8	Melksham	GB	8	E6	Miechów	PL	75	C11
Martorell	E	21	F10	Melle	F	16	B4	Międzychód	PL	70	E5
Martos	E	28	C6	Mellrichstadt	D	40	C5	Międzyrzec Podlaski	PL	72	G5
Maruggio	I	31	C10	Mělník	CZ	41	C11	Międzyrzecz	PL	70	F4
Marvejols	F	17	F10	Mels	CH	37	D8	Międzyzdroje	PL	43	C11
Maryport	GB	4	D6	Melton Mowbray	GB	5	H9	Mielec	PL	73	D2
Marzabotto	I	35	E7	Melun	F	12	D3	Miercurea-Ciuc	RO	78	E5
Mascali	I	30	E6	Mélykút	H	76	E6	Mieres	E	23	B7
Mascalucia	I	30	F6	Memaliaj	AL	86	D2	Miesbach	D	37	B12
Massa	I	34	F6	Memmingen	D	37	B9	Migennes	F	12	F4
Massafra	I	31	B10	Mende	F	17	F10	Migné-Auxances	F	16	B5
Massa Lombarda	I	35	E8	Menemen	TR	85	G3	Miguelturra	E	26	G4
Massamagrell	E	27	F10	Menfi	I	30	F2	Mihăeşti	RO	78	G3
Massa Marittimo	I	32	A2	Mengeš	SLO	39	G9	Mihăeşti	RO	78	G4
Massarosa	I	34	F6	Mengíbar	E	28	C6	Mihăileşti	RO	83	B10
Măstăcani	RO	79	F9	Mennecy	F	12	D2	Mihail Kogălniceanu	RO	84	B4
Matala	GR	89	G9	Mentana	I	32	C5	Mihai Viteazu	RO	78	D2
Mataró	E	21	F10	Menton	F	19	D9	Mijas	E	28	F4
Mătăsari	RO	82	A5	Meppel	NL	11	C8	Mikkeli	FIN	65	D8
Matca	RO	79	F8	Meppen	D	11	C9	Milan	I	34	C4
Matelica	I	35	G10	Mer	F	12	F1	Milano	I	34	C4
Matera	I	31	B9	Merag	HR	80	B1	Milas	TR	88	E3
Mátészalka	H	77	B11	Merano	I	37	D11	Milazzo	I	30	D6
Matino	I	31	C11	Mercato San Severino	I	30	B6	Milcovul	RO	79	F8
Matlock	GB	5	G8	Mercato Saraceno	I	35	F9	Mildenhall	GB	9	C10
Mattersburg	A	39	C12	Mercogliano	I	30	B6	Mileto	I	31	F8
Mattinata	I	33	D11	Merei	RO	79	G7	Milevsko	CZ	41	E11
Maubeuge	F	10	H5	Meriç	TR	85	B2	Milford Haven	GB	8	D2
Mauguio	F	17	H11	Merichas	GR	89	D8	Milicz	PL	70	H6
Mauléon	F	15	H7	Mérida	E	24	E6	Militello in Val di Catania	I	30	F5
Mauléon-Licharre	F	20	B5	Merseburg (Saale)	D	41	A7	Millau	F	17	G10
Maurset	N	48	B4	Merthyr Tydfil	GB	8	D4	Millom	GB	4	E6
Mavrodin	RO	83	C8	Méru	F	12	C2	Milly-la-Forêt	F	12	E2
Mayen	D	11	G9	Merzig	D	13	C8	Milna	HR	80	E4
Mayenne	F	15	E8	Mesagne	I	31	B11	Milton Keynes	GB	9	D8
Mazamet	F	21	B10	Mesimeri	GR	87	D7	Mimizan	F	16	F2
Mazara del Vallo	I	30	F2	Mesola	I	35	D9	Mimoň	CZ	41	C11
Mazarrón	E	29	D10	Mesolongi	GR	88	B3	Minas de Riotinto	E	25	H6

Mindelheim	D	37	B10	Mölle	S	44	D7	Monte San Giovanni Campano	I	33	D7
Minden	D	11	D12	Mollerussa	E	21	E8	Montesano sulla Marcellana	I	31	C7
Mindszent	H	77	D7	Mölln	D	42	C6	Monte San Savino	I	35	G8
Minehead	GB	8	E4	Mölndal	S	46	F3	Monte Sant'Angelo	I	33	D11
Mineo	I	30	F5	Mölnlycke	S	44	A6	Montesarchio	I	30	A5
Minervino Murge	I	31	A8	Molpe	FIN	53	B10	Montescaglioso	I	31	B9
Minsk	BY	69	H11	Momchilgrad	BG	87	B11	Montesilvano	I	33	B8
Minturno	I	30	A4	Monaghan	IRL	4	E2	Montespertoli	I	35	G7
Mira	I	35	C9	Moncada	E	27	F10	Montevarchi	I	35	G8
Mirabella Eclano	I	30	A6	Moncalieri	I	19	A9	Monthey	CH	36	E5
Mirabella Imbaccari	I	30	F5	Monchaltorf	CH	37	C7	Montignoso	I	34	F6
Miramas	F	18	D5	Mondolfo	I	35	F10	Montijo	E	24	E6
Miramont-de-Guyenne	F	16	F5	Mondoñedo	E	22	B4	Montilla	E	28	D4
Miranda de Ebro	E	20	C1	Mondovì	I	19	C10	Montivilliers	F	15	B9
Mirandela	P	22	F5	Mondragone	I	30	A4	Montluçon	F	17	B9
Mirandola	I	35	D7	Monemvasia	GR	88	G6	Montmélian	F	36	G4
Mircea Vodă	RO	84	C4	Monesterio	E	25	H7	Montmorillon	F	16	B6
Mirceşti	RO	79	C7	Monfalcone	I	35	B11	Montorio al Vomano	I	33	B7
Mirecourt	F	13	E8	Monforte de Lemos	E	22	D4	Montoro	E	28	C5
Mireşu Mare	RO	77	C12	Monifieth	GB	3	F7	Montpellier	F	17	H11
Miroslaveşti	RO	79	C7	Mońki	PL	72	D5	Montpon-Ménestérol	F	16	E5
Misano Adriatico	I	35	F10	Monmouth	GB	8	D5	Montreuil-Juigné	F	15	F8
Misilmeri	I	30	E3	Monolithos	GR	88	G3	Montreux	CH	36	E5
Miskolc	H	73	H1	Monopoli	I	31	B10	Montrichard	F	15	G10
Mistelbach	A	39	B12	Monor	H	76	C6	Montrond-les-Bains	F	17	D12
Misterbianco	I	30	F6	Monóvar	E	27	H9	Montrose	GB	3	F7
Mistretta	I	30	E5	Monreale	I	30	E3	Monts	F	15	G9
Mitreni	RO	83	C11	Mons	B	10	G5	Mont-St-Aignan	F	15	C10
Mitrovicë	RKS	81	F12	Monselice	I	35	C8	Monza	I	34	C4
Mittersill	A	38	D6	Monster	NL	10	D5	Monzón	E	21	E7
Mittweida	D	41	B9	Monsummano Terme	I	35	F7	Moorbad Lobenstein	D	41	C7
Mizhhir''ya	UA	73	G5	Montalbano Jonico	I	31	C9	Moordorf (Südbrookmerland)	D	11	A9
Mizil	RO	78	G6	Montalcino	I	32	A3	Mór	H	76	C4
Miziya	BG	82	D6	Montale	I	35	F7	Mora	E	26	E4
Mjölby	S	46	E6	Montalto di Castro	I	32	C4	Mora	S	51	F12
Mjøndalen	N	49	C7	Montalto Uffugo	I	31	E8	Morąg	PL	68	G1
Mladá Boleslav	CZ	41	C12	Montana	BG	82	D5	Mórahalom	H	77	E7
Mladenovac	SRB	81	C11	Montargis	F	12	F3	Moraleja	E	24	C6
Mława	PL	71	D10	Montataire	F	12	C2	Morano Calabro	I	31	D8
Mnichovo Hradiště	CZ	41	C12	Montauban	F	17	G7	Moratalla	E	29	B9
Moaña	E	22	D2	Montauroux	F	19	D8	Moravská Třebová	CZ	74	E6
Moara Vlăsiei	RO	83	B10	Montbard	F	12	F5	Moravské Budějovice	CZ	74	F5
Modena	I	35	E7	Montbéliard	F	13	F9	Morbach	D	13	B9
Modica	I	30	G5	Montbrison	F	17	D11	Morbegno	I	34	B5
Modra	SK	75	G7	Montceau-les-Mines	F	17	B12	Morciano di Romagna	I	35	F10
Modriča	BIH	76	H4	Montchanin	F	12	H5	Morcone	I	33	E9
Modugno	I	31	A9	Mont-de-Marsan	F	16	G4	Morecambe	GB	5	E7
Moers	D	11	E8	Montdidier	F	12	B3	Moreni	RO	78	H5
Mogilno	PL	71	E7	Montebello Ionico	I	31	H7	Morestel	F	36	F3
Moguer	E	25	K6	Monte-Carlo	MC	19	D9	Morez	F	36	E4
Mohács	H	76	F5	Montechiarugolo	I	34	E6	Morges	CH	36	E4
Mohelnice	CZ	75	E7	Montefalco	I	32	B5	Morlaix	F	14	D3
Moieciu	RO	78	G5	Montefiascone	I	32	B4	Moroeni	RO	78	G5
Moineşti	RO	78	E6	Montefrío	E	28	D5	Morón de la Frontera	E	25	K8
Mo i Rana	N	55	B7	Montegiorgio	I	35	H11	Morpeth	GB	5	C8
Moirans	F	36	G3	Montegranaro	I	35	G11	Morshyn	UA	73	F6
Moisei	RO	78	B3	Montehermoso	E	24	C6	Mortagne-au-Perche	F	15	D9
Moissac	F	16	G6	Monteiasi	I	31	C10	Mortagne-sur-Sèvre	F	15	G7
Mojkovac	MNE	81	F9	Montelepre	I	30	E3	Morteau	F	13	G8
Mokrin	SRB	77	F8	Montelibretti	I	32	C6	Mosbach	D	13	C12
Mol	SRB	77	F7	Montélimar	F	18	B4	Moscavide	P	24	F2
Mola di Bari	I	31	A9	Montella	I	30	B6	Mosina	PL	70	F6
Moldava nad Bodvou	SK	73	G2	Montellano	E	25	K8	Mosjøen	N	54	C6
Molde	N	50	C4	Montelupo Fiorentino	I	35	F7	Mosonmagyaróvár	H	76	B3
Moldova Nouă	RO	82	B2	Montemor-o-Novo	P	24	F3	Moss	N	49	D8
Moldoviţa	RO	78	B5	Montepulciano	I	32	A4	Most	CZ	41	C10
Molêtai	LT	69	E8	Monteriggioni	I	35	G7	Mostar	BIH	81	E7
Molfetta	I	31	A9	Monteroni d'Arbia	I	35	G8	Mosterhamn	N	48	C2
Molina de Segura	E	29	C10	Monteroni di Lecce	I	31	C11	Móstoles	E	26	D4
Moliterno	I	31	C7	Monterotondo	I	32	C5	Mostys'ka	UA	73	E5

Mota del Cuervo	E	26	F6
Motala	S	46	E6
Moţăţei	RO	82	C5
Motherwell	GB	2	H5
Motril	E	28	E6
Motru	RO	82	A5
Motta San Giovanni	I	31	G7
Mottola	I	31	B9
Mougins	F	19	D8
Moulins	F	17	B10
Moulins-les Metz	F	13	C8
Moura	P	24	G5
Mourenx	F	20	B5
Mouscron	B	10	G4
Moutier	CH	13	G9
Moûtiers	F	36	G4
Moyenmoutier	F	13	E9
Mozirje	SLO	39	F10
Mrągowo	PL	68	H3
Mrkonjić-Grad	BIH	80	C5
Mszana Dolna	PL	75	E11
Mszczonów	PL	71	G11
Much	D	11	F9
Mudanya	TR	85	D6
Mugeni	RO	78	E4
Muggia	I	35	C12
Mühlhausen (Thüringen)	D	40	B5
Muineachán	IRL	4	E2
Mukacheve	UA	73	G4
Mula	E	29	C10
Mulhouse	F	13	F9
Müllheim	D	13	F10
Mullingar	IRL	4	F1
Mullsjö	S	46	F5
Mulsanne	F	15	F9
Münchberg	D	41	D7
München	D	38	C5
Munchingen	D	13	D12
Mundolsheim	F	13	D10
Munich	D	38	C5
Munkebo	DK	44	F4
Münnerstadt	D	40	D5
Münsingen	D	38	B2
Münsingen	CH	13	H10
Munster	F	13	E9
Münster	D	11	D10
Münster	D	42	E6
Munteni	RO	79	F8
Muradiye	TR	85	G3
Muratlı	TR	85	B3
Murcia	E	29	C10
Muret	F	21	B9
Murgeni	RO	79	E9
Muriedas	E	23	B10
Murnau am Staffelsee	D	37	B11
Muro	E	29	F10
Muro Lucano	I	31	B7
Muros	E	22	C1
Murowana Goślina	PL	70	F6
Mûrs-Erigné	F	15	G8
Murska Sobota	SLO	39	F11
Mürzzuschlag	A	39	D11
Musselburgh	GB	3	G7
Musselkanaal	NL	11	B9
Mussidan	F	16	E5
Mussomeli	I	30	F4
Mustafakemalpaşa	TR	85	D5
Muxia	E	22	B1
Myadzyel	BY	69	F10
Mykolayiv	UA	73	E6

Mykonos	GR	89	D10
Myllykoski	FIN	65	F7
Myory	BY	69	D11
Myrina	GR	87	E11
Myślenice	PL	75	D11
Myślibórz	PL	43	E11
Myszków	PL	75	C10
Mytilini	GR	85	F2

N

Naantali	FIN	53	G10
Naas	IRL	4	G2
Nabburg	D	41	E8
Náchod	CZ	74	C6
Nădlac	RO	77	E8
Nádudvar	H	77	C9
Næstved	DK	44	F6
Nafpaktos	GR	88	B4
Nafplio	GR	88	C6
Nagold	D	13	D11
Nagyatád	H	76	E3
Nagyecsed	H	77	B11
Nagyhalász	H	73	H3
Nagykálló	H	77	B10
Nagykanizsa	H	76	E2
Nagykáta	H	77	C7
Nagykőrös	H	77	C7
Nagyszénás	H	77	D8
Naintré	F	16	A5
Nairn	GB	2	D6
Nájera	E	20	D2
Nakło nad Notecią	PL	71	D7
Nakskov	DK	44	G5
Náměšť nad Oslavou	CZ	74	F6
Namsos	N	54	F4
Namur	B	10	G6
Namysłów	PL	75	B8
Nancy	F	13	D8
Nantes	F	14	G6
Nantwich	GB	5	G7
Naousa	GR	86	D6
Naples	I	30	B5
Napoli	I	30	B5
Narbonne	F	18	E2
Nardò	I	31	C11
Narni	I	32	B5
Naro	I	30	F4
Närpes	FIN	53	C10
Narva	EST	67	B10
Narvik	N	57	D5
Năsăud	RO	78	C3
Našice	HR	76	G4
Nasielsk	PL	71	F11
Naso	I	30	E5
Nässjö	S	45	A10
Nastola	FIN	65	E7
Naujoji Akmenė	LT	68	C5
Naumburg (Saale)	D	41	B7
Navalcarnero	E	26	D4
Navalmoral de la Mata	E	24	C8
Navalvillar de Pela	E	24	E8
Navan	IRL	4	F2
Navarcles	E	21	E10
Navàs	E	21	E9
Navia	E	22	B5
Năvodari	RO	84	B5
Naxos	GR	89	D10
Nazaré	P	24	D2

Nea Alikarnassos	GR	89	G10
Nea Artaki	GR	89	A7
Nea Filadelfeia	GR	89	B7
Nea Ionia	GR	87	F7
Nea Liosia	GR	89	B7
Nea Makri	GR	89	B7
Neapoli	GR	88	E6
Nea Styra	GR	89	B8
Neath	GB	8	D4
Neckartenzlingen	D	38	B2
Nedelino	BG	87	B11
Nedstrand	N	48	D2
Negotin	SRB	82	C4
Negotino	MK	86	C6
Negreşti	RO	79	D8
Negreşti-Oaş	RO	78	B1
Negru Vodă	RO	84	C4
Nehoiu	RO	78	G6
Neksø	DK	45	G10
Neman	RUS	68	E4
Nemenčinė	LT	69	F8
Nemours	F	12	E3
Nenagh	IRL	7	K4
Nepi	I	32	C5
Nérac	F	16	G5
Neratovice	CZ	41	D11
Nerja	E	28	E6
Nerva	E	25	H6
Nes	N	49	B7
Nesna	N	54	B5
Neston	GB	4	G6
Nettuno	I	32	D5
Neuageri	CH	37	C7
Neubrandenburg	D	43	C9
Neuburg an der Donau	D	38	A4
Neuchâtel	CH	13	H9
Neuenhaus	D	11	C9
Neuenkirchen	D	42	D5
Neufchâteau	B	13	B7
Neufchâteau	F	13	E7
Neufchâtel-en-Bray	F	12	B1
Neufchâtel-Hardelot	F	9	F12
Neuhof	D	40	C4
Neumarkt in der Oberpfalz	D	41	F7
Neumünster	D	42	B5
Neunkirchen	A	39	C11
Neunkirchen	D	13	C9
Neuruppin	D	43	E9
Neustadt an der Aisch	D	40	E6
Neustadt an der Weinstraße	D	13	C11
Neustrelitz	D	43	D9
Neutraubling	D	41	F8
Neuville-lès-Dieppe	F	9	H11
Neuwied	D	11	G10
Neviano	I	31	C11
New Alresford	GB	9	F8
Newark-on-Trent	GB	5	G9
Newbridge	IRL	4	G2
Newbury	GB	9	E7
Newcastle	GB	4	E3
Newcastle-under-Lyme	GB	5	G7
Newcastle upon Tyne	GB	5	D8
Newhaven	GB	9	F9
Newmarket	GB	9	C10
Newport	GB	5	H7
Newport	GB	8	E5
Newport	GB	9	F7
Newport Pagnell	GB	9	D8
Newquay	GB	8	G2
New Romney	GB	9	F11

N

Name	Country	Pg	Grid
New Ross	IRL	7	L6
Newry	GB	4	E2
Newton Abbot	GB	8	G4
Newton Aycliffe	GB	5	D8
Newtown	GB	8	C4
Newtownabbey	GB	4	D3
Newtownards	GB	4	D3
Nicastro	I	31	F8
Nice	F	19	D9
Nichelino	I	19	A9
Nicolae Bălcescu	RO	79	E7
Nicolae Bălcescu	RO	84	B4
Nicolosi	I	30	F6
Nicorești	RO	79	F8
Nicosia	I	30	E5
Nicotera	I	31	F8
Niculițel	RO	79	G10
Nidda	D	11	G12
Nidzica	PL	71	D10
Niebüll	D	44	G2
Niederbronn-les-Bains	F	13	D10
Nieder Reisbach	D	41	G8
Niemodlin	PL	75	C8
Nienburg (Saale)	D	43	G8
Nienburg (Weser)	D	11	C12
Niesky	D	41	B12
Nigrita	GR	87	C8
Nijar	E	29	E8
Nijmegen	NL	11	D7
Nijverdal	NL	11	C8
Nikel'	RUS	59	E11
Nikopol	BG	83	D8
Nikšić	MNE	81	F8
Nîmes	F	17	G12
Nimigea	RO	78	C3
Niort	F	16	B4
Niš	SRB	82	D3
Niscemi	I	30	E5
Nisko	PL	73	C3
Nisporeni	MD	79	C9
Nitra	SK	75	G8
Nittenau	D	41	F8
Nittendorf	D	41	F7
Nivala	FIN	62	F5
Nizza Monferrato	I	19	B10
Nocera Terinese	I	31	E8
Nocera Umbra	I	32	A6
Noci	I	31	B10
Nogent-le-Roi	F	12	D1
Nogent-le-Rotrou	F	15	D2
Noia	E	22	C2
Noicattaro	I	31	A9
Noirmoutier-en-l'Île	F	14	G5
Nokia	FIN	53	E12
Nomeland	N	48	D4
Nonancourt	F	15	D10
None	I	19	A9
Noordwijk-Binnen	NL	10	D5
Nora	S	46	C6
Norberg	S	47	B7
Nordborg	DK	44	G3
Norden	D	42	C2
Norderney	D	42	C2
Norderstedt	D	42	C5
Nordfjordeid	N	50	D2
Nordhausen	D	40	A6
Nordholz	D	42	C4
Nordhorn	D	11	C9
Nördlingen	D	38	A3
Noreikiškės	LT	68	F6
Norheimsund	N	48	B3
Nørresundby	DK	44	C4
Nørre Vorupør	DK	44	C2
Norrköping	S	47	E7
Norrtälje	S	47	B10
Northallerton	GB	5	E8
Northam	GB	8	F3
Northampton	GB	9	C8
North Berwick	GB	3	G7
Northeim	D	42	G5
North Walsham	GB	9	B11
Northwich	GB	5	G7
Norton	GB	5	E9
Nortorf	D	42	B5
Nort-sur-Erdre	F	14	G6
Norwich	GB	9	B11
Noto	I	30	G6
Notodden	N	48	D6
Notre-Dame-de-Gravenchon	F	15	C9
Nottingham	GB	5	H9
Nottuln	D	11	D9
Nouzonville	F	12	B6
Nová Baňa	SK	75	G9
Novaci	RO	78	G2
Nová Dubnica	SK	75	F9
Novafeltria	I	35	F9
Nova Gorica	SLO	35	B11
Nova Gradiška	HR	76	G3
Nova Pazova	SRB	77	H8
Novara	I	34	C3
Nova Siri	I	31	C9
Nova Varoš	SRB	81	E10
Nova Zagora	BG	83	F10
Novelda	E	27	H9
Novellara	I	35	D7
Nové Mesto nad Váhom	SK	75	G8
Nové Město na Moravé	CZ	74	E6
Nové Zámky	SK	76	B4
Novi Bečej	SRB	77	F7
Novi Iskŭr	BG	82	F5
Novi Kneževac	SRB	77	E7
Novi Ligure	I	19	B11
Novi Pazar	BG	83	D12
Novi Pazar	SRB	81	F11
Novi Sad	SRB	77	G7
Novi Travnik	BIH	80	D6
Novo Beograd	SRB	81	B11
Novo Mesto	SLO	39	G10
Novo Miloševo	SRB	77	F8
Novorzhev	RUS	67	G11
Novoselytsya	UA	78	A6
Novovolyns'k	UA	73	C6
Novoyavorivs'ke	UA	73	D5
Novska	HR	76	G2
Nový Bor	CZ	41	C11
Nový Bydžov	CZ	74	D5
Nový Jičín	CZ	75	E8
Novyy Rozdil	UA	73	E6
Nowa Dęba	PL	73	C3
Nowa Ruda	PL	74	C6
Nowa Sarzyna	PL	73	D4
Nowa Sól	PL	70	G5
Nowe	PL	71	C8
Nowe Miasto Lubawskie	PL	71	D9
Nowogard	PL	43	C12
Nowy Dwór Gdański	PL	71	B9
Nowy Dwór Mazowiecki	PL	71	F11
Nowy Sącz	PL	73	E1
Nowy Targ	PL	75	E11
Nowy Tomyśl	PL	70	F5
Noyon	F	12	B3
Nubledo	E	23	B7
Nuenen	NL	11	E7
Nuits-St-Georges	F	12	G6
Nules	E	27	E10
Nummela	FIN	64	G5
Nuneaton	GB	9	C7
Nunspeet	NL	11	C7
Nuoro	I	32	E3
Nurmes	FIN	63	G10
Nurmo	FIN	53	B11
Nürnberg	D	40	E6
Nusco	I	30	B6
Nușfalău	RO	77	C12
Nybergsund	N	51	F10
Nyborg	DK	44	F5
Nyborg	N	48	B2
Nybro	S	45	C11
Nyby	FIN	53	B10
Nyergesújfalu	H	76	B5
Nyíradony	H	77	B10
Nyírbátor	H	77	B11
Nyíregyháza	H	77	B10
Nyírtelek	H	77	A10
Nykøbing	DK	44	G6
Nykøbing Mors	DK	44	C2
Nykøbing Sjælland	DK	44	E6
Nyköping	S	47	D8
Nykvarn	S	47	C9
Nymburk	CZ	41	D12
Nynäshamn	S	47	D9
Nyon	CH	36	E4
Nyons	F	18	C5
Nýřany	CZ	41	E9
Nýrsko	CZ	41	F9
Nysa	PL	75	C7

O

Name	Country	Pg	Grid
Oadby	GB	9	B8
Oakham	GB	9	B8
Oban	GB	2	F4
O Barco	E	22	D5
Oberammergau	D	37	B11
Obernai	F	13	E10
Oberriet	CH	37	C9
Oberstdorf	D	37	C10
Obiliq	RKS	81	G12
Obrenovac	SRB	81	C11
Ocaña	E	26	E5
O Carballiño	E	22	D3
O Castelo	E	22	C2
Occhiobello	I	35	D8
Ochsenfurt	D	40	E5
Ocna Mureş	RO	78	E2
O Convento	E	22	D2
O Corgo	E	22	C4
Ócsa	H	76	C6
Odda	N	48	C3
Odder	DK	44	E4
Odense	DK	44	F4
Oderzo	I	35	B9
Odivelas	P	24	F2
Odobeşti	RO	79	F7
Odobeşti	RO	83	B9
Odorheiu Secuiesc	RO	78	E5
Odry	CZ	75	E8
Odžaci	SRB	76	F6
Oebisfelde	D	43	F7

Oelsnitz	D	41	C8
Offenbach am Main	D	11	H11
Offenburg	D	13	E10
Ogre	LV	66	G5
Ogrezeni	RO	83	B9
Ogulin	HR	80	A2
Ohrid	MK	86	C4
Oia	GR	89	F10
Oituz	RO	79	E7
Okehampton	GB	8	F3
Øksfjord	N	58	C5
Olaine	LV	66	H5
Oława	PL	75	B7
Olbia	I	32	D3
Oldenburg	D	11	B11
Oldham	GB	5	F8
Olecko	PL	68	G5
Oleśnica	PL	75	B7
Olesno	PL	75	B9
Olevano Romano	I	32	D6
Olhão	P	25	K4
Oliva	E	27	G10
Oliva de la Frontera	E	24	G5
Oliveira de Azeméis	P	22	G2
Olivenza	E	24	F5
Olivet	F	12	F2
Olkusz	PL	75	D11
Ollioules	F	18	E6
Ollon	CH	36	E5
Olney	GB	9	C8
Olofsfors	S	55	G12
Olofström	S	45	D9
Olomouc	CZ	75	E7
Olonne-sur-Mer	F	16	B2
Oloron-Ste-Marie	F	20	B5
Olot	E	21	D10
Olsberg	D	11	E11
Ølstykke	DK	44	E6
Olsztyn	PL	68	H2
Olsztynek	PL	68	H2
Oltenița	RO	83	C11
Olula del Río	E	29	D8
Olvera	E	28	E3
Omagh	GB	4	D1
Omegna	I	34	B3
Omiš	HR	80	E5
Ommen	NL	11	C8
O Mosteiro	E	22	D2
Omurtag	BG	83	E10
Onchan	GBM	4	E5
Onda	E	27	E10
Ondarroa	E	20	B2
Onești	RO	79	E7
Onet-le-Château	F	17	F9
Ontinyent	E	27	G10
Onzain	F	15	F10
Oostende	B	10	F3
Oosterhout	NL	10	E6
Opalenica	PL	70	F5
Opatija	HR	35	C12
Opatów	PL	73	C2
Opava	CZ	75	D8
O Pedrouzo	E	22	C3
Opochka	RUS	67	H10
Opoczno	PL	71	H10
Opole	PL	75	C8
Opole Lubelskie	PL	73	B3
O Porriño	E	22	D2
Oppido Mamertina	I	31	G8
Oradea	RO	77	C10
Orange	F	18	C5
Oranienburg	D	43	E9
Orăștie	RO	77	F12
Orașu Nou	RO	77	B12
Oravița	RO	77	G10
Orbassano	I	19	A9
Orbeasca	RO	83	C9
Orbetello	I	32	B3
Orchomenos	GR	88	B6
Ordes	E	22	C3
O Real	E	22	B3
Orebić	HR	80	F5
Örebro	S	46	C6
Orense	E	22	D3
Orestiada	GR	85	B2
Orgiva	E	28	E6
Orhei	MD	79	C10
Oria	I	31	C10
Orihuela	E	29	C11
Orimattila	FIN	64	F6
Oristano	I	32	F2
Orivesi	FIN	64	D5
Orkanger	N	51	B7
Orlea	RO	83	D7
Orléans	F	12	F2
Ormes	F	12	C5
Ormož	SLO	39	F11
Ormskirk	GB	5	F7
Orneta	PL	68	G2
Örnsköldsvik	S	53	A7
Orosei	I	32	E4
Orosháza	H	77	D8
Oroszlány	H	76	C4
Orșova	RO	82	B4
Ørsta	N	50	D3
Orta Nova	I	33	E11
Orte	I	32	B5
Orthez	F	20	B5
Ortigueira	E	22	A3
Ortona	I	33	C8
Orvault	F	14	G6
Orvieto	I	32	B5
Oryakhovo	BG	82	D6
Orzinuovi	I	34	C5
Orzysz	PL	68	H4
Os	N	51	C8
Osby	S	45	D9
Oschatz	D	41	B9
Oschersleben (Bode)	D	43	F7
O Seixo (Tomiño)	E	22	E2
Osen	N	54	F3
Osica de Sus	RO	83	C7
Osijek	HR	76	F5
Osimo	I	35	G11
Osipaonica	SRB	81	C12
Oskarshamn	S	45	B12
Oslo	N	46	B1
Osnabrück	D	11	D10
Osor	HR	80	C1
Oșorhei	RO	77	C11
Osøyri	N	48	B2
Oss	NL	11	E7
Ostend	B	10	F3
Osterburg (Altmark)	D	43	E8
Osterhofen	D	39	A7
Ostermundigen	CH	13	H10
Östersund	S	51	B12
Ostiglia	I	35	D7
Ostrava	CZ	75	D9
Ostróda	PL	68	H1
Ostrov	CZ	41	C9
Ostrov	RO	83	C12
Ostrov	RUS	67	F10
Ostroveni	RO	82	D6
Ostrowiec Świętokrzyski	PL	73	B2
Ostrów Mazowiecka	PL	72	E4
Ostrów Wielkopolski	PL	71	G7
Ostrzeszów	PL	71	H7
Ostuni	I	31	B10
Osuna	E	28	D4
Oswestry	GB	4	H6
Oświęcim	PL	75	D10
Oțelu Roșu	RO	77	F11
Otley	GB	5	F8
Otmuchów	PL	75	C7
Otočac	HR	80	B2
Otok	HR	76	G5
Otopeni	RO	83	B10
O Toural	E	22	D2
Otranto	I	31	C12
Ottaviano	I	30	B5
Ottenby	S	45	D12
Otterndorf	D	42	C4
Ouistreham	F	15	C8
Oulainen	FIN	62	E5
Oullins	F	17	C12
Oulu	FIN	62	D6
Oulunsalo	FIN	62	D6
Oundle	GB	9	C9
Oupeye	B	11	G7
Ouranoupoli	GR	87	D9
Ourense	E	22	D3
Outokumpu	FIN	65	B10
Outreau	F	9	F11
Ovada	I	19	B11
Ovar	P	22	G2
Överammer	S	52	A4
Ovidiu	RO	84	C4
Oviedo	E	23	B7
Oxelösund	S	47	D8
Oxford	GB	9	D7
Oxie	S	45	F8
Oxted	GB	9	E9
Oyonnax	F	36	E3
Ożarów	PL	73	C3
Özbaşı	TR	88	D3
Özd	H	73	H1
Ozersk	RUS	68	F4
Ozieri	I	32	E2
Ozimek	PL	75	C9
Ozorków	PL	71	G9

P

Pabianice	PL	71	G9
Pabradė	LT	69	E9
Paceco	I	30	E2
Pachino	I	30	G6
Pacy-sur-Eure	F	12	C1
Paczków	PL	75	C7
Paderborn	D	11	E11
Padeș	RO	77	G12
Padina	RO	79	H8
Padina	SRB	77	G8
Padinska Skela	SRB	77	H8
Padova	I	35	C8
Padrón	E	22	C2
Padsvillye	BY	69	E11
Padul	E	28	E6

P

Padula	I	31	C7	Partanna	I	30	E2	Periam	RO	77	E9
Paide	EST	67	C7	Parthenay	F	16	B4	Périgueux	F	16	E6
Paignton	GB	8	G4	Partinico	I	30	E3	Periş	RO	83	B10
Paimio	FIN	53	G11	Partizánske	SK	75	G9	Perişoru	RO	83	B12
Paimpol	F	14	D4	Paşcani	RO	79	C7	Peristeri	GR	89	B7
Paisley	GB	2	H5	Pasewalk	D	43	C10	Perleberg	D	43	D8
Pajęczno	PL	75	B10	Pasłęk	PL	68	G1	Përmet	AL	86	E3
Pakrac	HR	76	G2	Passau	D	39	B8	Pernik	BG	82	F5
Pakruojis	LT	68	C6	Pastavy	BY	69	E10	Péronnas	F	36	E2
Paks	H	76	D5	Pasvalys	LT	69	C7	Péronne	F	12	B3
Palafrugell	E	18	G2	Pásztó	H	77	B7	Perpignan	F	18	F1
Palagiano	I	31	B9	Pătârlagele	RO	78	G6	Perros-Guirec	F	14	D4
Palagonia	I	30	F5	Paterna	E	27	F10	Pershore	GB	8	C6
Palaikastro	GR	89	G11	Paternion	A	39	E8	Perstorp	S	45	D8
Palaiochora	GR	89	G7	Paternò	I	30	F6	Perth	GB	2	G6
Palaiokastritsa	GR	86	F2	Patos	AL	86	D2	Pertuis	F	18	D6
Palamas	GR	86	F6	Patra	GR	88	B4	Perugia	I	35	H9
Palamós	E	18	H2	Pattensen	D	42	F5	Perushtitsa	BG	83	G7
Palanga	LT	68	C3	Patti	I	30	E6	Pervomaisc	MD	79	D12
Palas de Rei	E	22	C3	Pau	F	20	B6	Pesaro	I	35	F10
Palau	I	32	C3	Pauillac	F	16	E3	Pescara	I	33	B8
Palavas-les-Flots	F	17	H11	Păuneşti	RO	79	E8	Pescia	I	35	F6
Palazzolo Acreide	I	30	G6	Pavia	I	34	C4	Peshkopi	AL	86	B3
Paldiski	EST	66	B5	Pavilly	F	15	B10	Peshtera	BG	83	G7
Palencia	E	23	C7	Pavlikeni	BG	83	E9	Pesnica	SLO	39	F11
Palermo	I	30	E3	Pavlovsk	RUS	65	H11	Pesochnyy	RUS	65	G11
Palestrina	I	32	D6	Pavullo nel Frignano	I	35	E7	Peso da Régua	P	22	F4
Palić	SRB	77	E11	Payerne	CH	13	H9	Pessac	F	16	E3
Palma Campania	I	30	B5	Pazardzhik	BG	83	G7	Peterborough	GB	9	C9
Palma del Río	E	28	C3	Pazin	HR	35	C12	Peterhead	GB	3	D8
Palma de Mallorca	E	29	F9	Peal de Becerro	E	29	C7	Peterlee	GB	5	D9
Palma di Montechiaro	I	30	G4	Peccioli	I	35	G7	Petersfield	GB	9	F8
Palmi	I	31	D7	Pécel	H	76	C6	Petilia Policastro	I	31	E9
Palombara Sabina	I	32	C6	Pechea	RO	79	F9	Petreşti	RO	83	B9
Păltinoasa	RO	78	B6	Pechory	RUS	67	E9	Petrich	BG	87	B8
Pamiers	F	21	B9	Pecica	RO	77	E9	Petrila	RO	78	G1
Pamplona/Iruña	E	20	C4	Pécs	H	76	E4	Petrinja	HR	76	G1
Panagyurishte	BG	83	F7	Pedro Muñoz	E	26	F6	Petrodvorets	RUS	65	H10
Panazol	F	17	C7	Pedroso	P	22	G2	Petroşani	RO	78	G1
Pančevo	SRB	77	H8	Peebles	GB	4	B6	Petrovac	SRB	82	B2
Panciu	RO	79	F7	Peer	B	11	F7	Petrovaradin	SRB	77	G7
Pâncota	RO	77	E10	Pegnitz	D	41	E7	Peyrehorade	F	16	H3
Pănet	RO	78	D3	Pego	E	27	G10	Pézenas	F	18	D2
Panevėžys	LT	69	D7	Peiraias	GR	89	C7	Pezinok	SK	75	H7
Pantelimon	RO	83	B10	Peitz	D	43	G11	Pfaffenhoffen	F	13	D10
Paola	I	31	E8	Pejë	RKS	81	G11	Pfarrkirchen	D	39	B7
Pápa	H	76	C3	Pelago	I	35	F8	Pforzheim	D	13	D11
Papenburg	D	11	B10	Pelhřimov	CZ	74	E4	Piacenza	I	34	D5
Parabita	I	31	C11	Pelplin	PL	71	C8	Piana degli Albanesi	I	30	E3
Paracín	SRB	82	C2	Pembroke	GB	8	D2	Pianella	I	33	C8
Paralia	GR	88	E6	Pembroke Dock	GB	8	D2	Pianoro	I	35	E8
Paralia Avdiron	GR	87	C11	Peñafiel	E	23	E10	Piaseczno	PL	71	G11
Paralia Saranti	GR	88	B6	Peñaranda de Bracamonte	E	23	G8	Piatra Neamţ	RO	78	D6
Paray-le-Monial	F	17	B11	Peñarroya-Pueblonuevo	E	24	G8	Piatra Olt	RO	83	B7
Parchim	D	43	D8	Penarth	GB	8	E5	Piazza Armerina	I	30	F5
Parczew	PL	72	G5	Peniche	P	24	D1	Picassent	E	27	F10
Pardubice	CZ	74	D5	Penicuik	GB	2	H6	Pickering	GB	5	E9
Parempuyre	F	16	E3	Peñíscola	E	21	H7	Piedimonte Matese	I	33	E8
Parets del Vallès	E	21	F10	Penmarch	F	14	F2	Piedrabuena	E	26	G4
Parga	GR	86	G3	Penne	I	33	B8	Piedras Blancas	E	23	B7
Pargas	FIN	53	G11	Penrith	GB	5	D7	Pieksämäki	FIN	65	C8
Pargolovo	RUS	65	G11	Penzance	GB	8	G1	Pieńsk	PL	41	B12
Paris	F	12	D2	Penzberg	D	37	B11	Piera	E	21	F9
Pârjol	RO	79	D7	Pëqin	AL	86	C2	Pierrelatte	F	17	F12
Parkano	FIN	53	D11	Perama	GR	89	C7	Piešťany	SK	75	G8
Parma	I	34	D6	Perechyn	UA	73	G4	Pietarsaari	FIN	56	G5
Pärnu	EST	66	D5	Peretu	RO	83	C8	Pietraperzia	I	30	F4
Paroikia	GR	89	D9	Perg	A	39	B9	Pietrasanta	I	34	F6
Parsberg	D	41	F7	Pergine Valsugana	I	35	B7	Pihlava	FIN	53	E10
Pârscov	RO	78	G7	Pergola	I	35	G10	Piła	PL	70	D6

P

Name	Country		
Potenza Picena	I	35	G11
Potlogi	RO	83	B9
Potsdam	D	43	F9
Pottendorf	A	39	C12
Poulton-le-Fylde	GB	5	F7
Pouzauges	F	15	H7
Považská Bystrica	SK	75	F9
Póvoa de Varzim	P	22	F2
Poyrazcık	TR	85	F3
Požarevac	SRB	81	C12
Požega	HR	76	G3
Požega	SRB	81	D10
Poznań	PL	70	F6
Pozo Alcón	E	29	C7
Pozoblanco	E	26	H2
Pozuelo de Alarcón	E	23	H10
Pozzallo	I	30	G5
Pozzuoli	I	30	B5
Prabuty	PL	71	C9
Prachatice	CZ	41	F10
Prades	F	21	C10
Prado del Rey	E	25	L8
Prague	CZ	41	D11
Praha	CZ	41	D11
Praia a Mare	I	31	D7
Praia da Tocha	P	24	B2
Praid	RO	78	D4
Praszka	PL	75	B9
Prato	I	35	F7
Pravia	E	22	B6
Predappio	I	35	F9
Predeal	RO	78	F5
Preetz	D	42	B6
Preiļi	LV	69	C10
Prejmer	RO	78	F5
Preko	HR	80	D2
Premià de Mar	E	21	F10
Premnitz	D	43	E8
Prenzlau	D	43	D10
Přerov	CZ	75	E8
Preševo	SRB	82	G2
Presicce	I	31	D11
Prešov	SK	73	F2
Pressbaum	A	39	C11
Prestatyn	GB	4	G6
Přeštice	CZ	41	E9
Preston	GB	5	F7
Prestwick	GB	4	C4
Preuteşti	RO	78	C6
Preveza	GR	86	G4
Priboj	SRB	81	E9
Příbram	CZ	41	E10
Priego de Córdoba	E	28	D5
Prienai	LT	68	F6
Prievidza	SK	75	G9
Prijedor	BIH	76	H2
Prijepolje	SRB	81	E10
Prilep	MK	86	B5
Primorsk	RUS	65	G9
Priolo Gargallo	I	30	G6
Priozersk	RUS	65	E11
Prishtinë	RKS	82	F2
Priština	RKS	82	F2
Pritzwalk	D	43	D8
Privas	F	17	E12
Priverno	I	32	D6
Prizren	RKS	81	G11
Prizzi	I	30	E3
Prnjavor	BIH	76	H3
Probištip	MK	82	G3
Prokuplje	SRB	82	E2
Prostějov	CZ	75	E7
Proszowice	PL	73	D1
Provadiya	BG	83	E12
Provins	F	12	D4
Prudhoe	GB	5	D8
Prudnik	PL	75	C8
Prüm	D	11	H8
Prundeni	RO	83	B7
Prundu	RO	83	C10
Prundu Bârgăului	RO	78	C4
Pruszcz Gdański	PL	71	B8
Pruszków	PL	71	F11
Przasnysz	PL	71	E11
Przemków	PL	70	H5
Przemyśl	PL	73	E4
Przeworsk	PL	73	D4
Przysucha	PL	71	H11
Psachna	GR	89	A7
Psarades	GR	86	C4
Pskov	RUS	67	E10
Ptolemaïda	GR	86	D5
Ptuj	SLO	39	F11
Puchenii Mari	RO	83	A10
Puchheim	D	38	C5
Púchov	SK	75	F9
Pucioasa	RO	78	G5
Puck	PL	71	A8
Puçol	E	27	E10
Puente-Genil	E	28	D4
Puerto de Santa Maria	E	25	L7
Puertollano	E	26	G4
Puerto Lumbreras	E	29	D9
Puerto Real	E	25	L7
Pui	RO	77	F12
Puigcerdà	E	21	D10
Puig-reig	E	21	E9
Pula	HR	35	D12
Pula	I	32	H2
Puławy	PL	72	H4
Pulsano	I	31	C10
Puttusk	PL	71	E11
Punta Umbría	E	25	K5
Purgstall an der Erlauf	A	39	C10
Pürvomay	BG	83	G8
Pushkin	RUS	65	H11
Pushkinskiye Gory	RUS	67	G11
Püspökladány	H	77	C9
Pustomyty	UA	73	E6
Puszczykowo	PL	70	F6
Pusztaszabolcs	H	76	C5
Putignano	I	31	B10
Putnok	H	73	H1
Puttgarden	D	43	A7
Pyle	GB	8	E4
Pyrgos	GR	88	C3
Pyrzyce	PL	43	D11
Pyskowice	PL	75	C9
Pytalovo	RUS	67	G10
Pythagoreio	GR	88	D2

Q

Name	Country		
Quakenbrück	D	11	C10
Qualiano	I	30	B5
Quarrata	I	35	F7
Quarteira	P	25	K3
Quartu Sant'Elena	I	32	G3
Quedlinburg	D	43	G7
Querfurt	D	41	A7
Quiberon	F	14	G4
Quiliano	I	19	C11
Quimper	F	14	F3
Quimperlé	F	14	F3
Quintana de la Serena	E	24	F8
Quintanar de la Orden	E	26	F5
Quiroga	E	22	D4

R

Name	Country		
Raahe	FIN	56	E6
Raalte	NL	11	C8
Rabastens	F	17	G7
Rabka	PL	75	E11
Răcăciuni	RO	79	E7
Racale	I	31	D11
Racalmuto	I	30	F4
Răcari	RO	83	B9
Racconigi	I	19	B9
Răchitoasa	RO	79	E8
Racibórz	PL	75	D9
Ráckeve	H	76	C5
Radashkovichy	BY	69	G11
Rădăuţi	RO	78	B6
Radebeul	D	41	B10
Radenthein	A	39	E8
Radlje ob Dravi	SLO	39	F10
Radnevo	BG	83	G10
Radom	PL	72	H3
Radomir	BG	82	F5
Radomsko	PL	75	B10
Radovanu	RO	83	C11
Radoviš	MK	82	H4
Radovljica	SLO	39	F9
Radstock	GB	8	E6
Răducăneni	RO	79	D9
Radviliškis	LT	68	D6
Radymno	PL	73	D4
Radziejów	PL	71	E8
Radzyń Podlaski	PL	72	G5
Raffadali	I	30	F3
Ragunda	S	52	B4
Ragusa	I	30	G5
Rahden	D	11	C11
Rahovec	RKS	81	G11
Rain	D	38	B4
Raisio	FIN	53	G10
Rakamaz	H	73	H2
Rakhiv	UA	78	A3
Rakitovo	BG	82	G6
Rákóczifalva	H	77	C8
Rakovník	CZ	41	D10
Rakovski	BG	83	G8
Rakvere	EST	67	B8
Ramacca	I	30	F5
Rambervillers	F	13	E8
Rambouillet	F	12	D2
Râmnicu Sărat	RO	79	G7
Râmnicu Vâlcea	RO	78	G3
Ramonville-St-Agne	F	17	H7
Ramsey	GBM	4	E5
Ramsgate	GB	9	E11
Ramsjö	S	52	D3
Rånåsfoss	N	46	B2
Randazzo	I	30	E6
Randers	DK	44	D4
Randsjö	S	51	D11
Randsverk	N	50	E6

R

Seville	E	25	J7	Simeonovgrad	BG	83	G9	Skopje	MK	82	G2
Sevlievo	BG	83	E8	Simeria	RO	77	F12	Skorovatn	N	54	E5
Sevnica	SLO	39	G10	Şimian	RO	82	B4	Skövde	S	46	E5
Sevojno	SRB	81	D10	Simitli	BG	82	G5	Skråmestø	N	48	B1
Sevrey	F	36	F4	Şimleu Silvaniei	RO	77	C12	Skrunda	LV	66	H2
Seynod	F	36	F4	Simmerath	D	11	G8	Skuodas	LT	68	C3
Seysses	F	21	B9	Simrishamn	S	45	F9	Skurup	S	45	F8
Sežana	SLO	35	B12	Sinaia	RO	78	G5	Skutskär	S	52	G5
Sézanne	F	12	D4	Sinalunga	I	35	G8	Skwierzyna	PL	70	F4
Sezze	I	32	D6	Sindelfingen	D	40	G3	Slagelse	DK	44	F5
Sfântu Gheorghe	RO	78	F5	Sındırgı	TR	85	F5	Slangerup	DK	44	E6
's-Gravenhage	NL	10	D5	Sindos	GR	87	D7	Slănic	RO	78	G6
's-Gravenzande	NL	10	D5	Sines	P	25	H2	Slantsy	RUS	67	C10
Shaftesbury	GB	8	F6	Sîngera	MD	79	D11	Slaný	CZ	41	D10
Shanklin	GB	9	F8	Sîngerei	MD	79	B9	Slatina	HR	76	F3
Sharkawshchyna	BY	69	E11	Siniscola	I	32	E3	Slatina	RO	78	C6
Shats'k	UA	72	H6	Sinj	HR	80	D5	Slatina	RO	83	B7
Shchyrets'	UA	73	E6	Sinnai	I	32	G3	Slättberg	S	51	F12
Sheerness	GB	9	E10	Sinnes	N	48	E3	Slavičín	CZ	75	F8
Sheffield	GB	5	G8	Sintra	P	24	F1	Slavonski Brod	HR	76	G4
Shefford	GB	9	D9	Sint-Truiden	B	10	F6	Slavyanovo	BG	83	D8
Shepton Mallet	GB	8	E6	Siófok	H	76	D4	Sławno	PL	70	B6
Sherborne	GB	8	F6	Sion	CH	34	A1	Sleaford	GB	5	H10
Sherburn in Elmet	GB	5	F9	Şipote	RO	79	C8	Sligeach	IRL	6	G4
Sheringham	GB	5	H12	Sira	N	48	F3	Sligo	IRL	6	G4
's-Hertogenbosch	NL	11	E7	Siracusa	I	30	G6	Sliven	BG	83	F10
Shijak	AL	86	B2	Siret	RO	78	B6	Slivnitsa	BG	82	E5
Shkodër	AL	81	H9	Şiria	RO	77	E10	Slobozia	MD	79	D12
Shrewsbury	GB	8	B5	Širvintos	LT	69	E8	Slobozia	RO	83	B8
Shtime	RKS	81	G12	Sisak	HR	76	G1	Slobozia	RO	83	B12
Shumen	BG	83	E11	Şişeşti	RO	78	B2	Slough	GB	9	E8
Shyryayeve	UA	79	C12	Sisteron	F	18	C6	Sløvåg	N	50	G1
Siatista	GR	86	E5	Siteia	GR	89	G11	Slovenj Gradec	SLO	39	F10
Šiauliai	LT	68	C6	Sitges	E	21	F9	Slovenska Bistrica	SLO	39	F11
Šibenik	HR	80	D3	Sittard	NL	11	F7	Slovenske Konjice	SLO	39	F10
Sibiu	RO	78	F3	Sivac	SRB	76	F6	Słubice	PL	43	F11
Sibo	S	52	E4	Siverskiy	RUS	67	B12	Słupca	PL	71	F7
Siculeni	RO	78	E5	Six-Fours-les-Plages	F	18	E6	Słupsk	PL	70	B6
Šid	SRB	76	G6	Sjenica	SRB	81	E10	Smalyavichy	BY	69	G12
Sidari	GR	86	F2	Sjöbo	S	45	E8	Smarhon'	BY	69	F10
Siderno	I	31	G8	Sjonbotn	N	54	B6	Smederevo	SRB	81	C12
Sidirokastro	GR	87	C6	Skælsør	DK	44	F5	Smederevska Palanka	SRB	81	C12
Sidmouth	GB	8	F5	Skagen	DK	44	A4	Smedjebacken	S	46	A6
Siedlce	PL	72	F4	Skala	GR	89	D12	Smeeni	RO	79	G7
Siegen	D	11	F10	Skalica	SK	75	F7	Śmigiel	PL	70	G6
Siegsdorf	D	38	C6	Skanderborg	DK	44	E3	Smilavichy	BY	69	H12
Siemiatycze	PL	72	F5	Skanör med Falsterbo	S	45	F7	Smiltene	LV	67	F7
Siena	I	35	G8	Skara	S	46	E4	Smolyan	BG	87	B10
Sieradz	PL	71	H8	Skarszewy	PL	71	C8	Smyadovo	BG	83	E11
Sieraków	PL	70	E5	Skarżysko-Kamienna	PL	73	B1	Snagov	RO	83	B10
Sierpc	PL	71	E9	Skawina	PL	75	D11	Sneek	NL	11	B7
Sierre	CH	34	A1	Skegness	GB	5	G11	Snina	SK	73	F3
Sighetu Marmaţiei	RO	78	B2	Skei	N	50	E3	Soběslav	CZ	41	F11
Sighişoara	RO	78	E4	Skellefteå	S	56	E3	Sobra	HR	80	F6
Sigmaringen	D	37	B8	Skerries	IRL	4	F3	Sobrance	SK	73	G3
Signa	I	35	F7	Ski	N	46	B1	Sochaczew	PL	71	F10
Sigüenza	E	20	G2	Skiathos	GR	87	G8	Socuéllamos	E	26	F6
Sigulda	LV	66	G6	Skidal'	BY	72	D7	Sodankylä	FIN	61	C8
Siilinjärvi	FIN	63	H8	Skien	N	49	D7	Söderfors	S	52	G5
Siklós	H	76	F4	Skierniewice	PL	71	G10	Söderhamn	S	52	E5
Šilalė	LT	68	D4	Skipton	GB	5	F8	Söderköping	S	47	E7
Silandro	I	37	D10	Skive	DK	44	D2	Södertälje	S	47	C9
Silistra	BG	83	C12	Skjærhalden	N	46	D1	Södra Sandby	S	45	E8
Silivri	TR	85	B5	Skjern	DK	44	E2	Soest	D	11	E11
Silkeborg	DK	44	D3	Skjervøy	N	58	D4	Sofades	GR	86	F6
Silla	E	27	F10	Škofja Loka	SLO	39	G9	Sofia	BG	82	F5
Sillamäe	EST	67	B9	Skoghall	S	46	C4	Sögel	D	11	B10
Silleda	E	22	C3	Skogmo	N	54	E4	Søgne	N	48	G5
Šilutė	LT	68	E3	Skole	UA	73	F5	Soham	GB	9	C10
Silvi	I	33	B8	Skopelos	GR	87	G9	Soignies	B	10	G5

Torre Annunziata	I	30	B5	Trebujena	E	25	L7	Tržič	SLO	39	F9
Torre del Greco	I	30	B5	Trecastagni	I	30	F6	Tsebrykove	UA	79	C12
Torredonjimeno	E	28	C6	Trefynwy	GB	8	D5	Tuam	IRL	7	H3
Torrejón de Ardoz	E	23	H11	Tréguier	F	14	D4	Tübingen	D	13	D12
Torrelaguna	E	23	G11	Trélazé	F	15	G8	Tubize	B	10	G5
Torrelavega	E	23	B10	Trelleborg	S	45	F8	Tuchola	PL	71	D7
Torremaggiore	I	33	D10	Tremp	E	21	D8	Tuchów	PL	73	E2
Torremolinos	E	28	F5	Trenčín	SK	75	F8	Tudela	E	20	E4
Torrent	E	27	F10	Trento	I	35	B7	Tudora	RO	79	B7
Torre-Pacheco	E	29	C11	Treorchy	GB	8	D4	Tudor Vladimirescu	RO	79	F8
Torre Santa Susanna	I	31	C11	Trepuzzi	I	31	C11	Tufeşti	RO	79	H9
Torres Novas	P	24	D3	Třešť	CZ	74	F5	Tui	E	22	E2
Torres Vedras	P	24	E2	Trets	F	18	D6	Tukums	LV	66	G4
Torrevieja	E	29	C11	Treuchtlingen	D	40	F6	Tulach Mhór	IRL	7	J5
Torrijos	E	26	E3	Trevi	I	32	B6	Tulcea	RO	79	G10
Torrita di Siena	I	35	H8	Treviglio	I	34	C5	Tullamore	IRL	7	J5
Torroella de Montgrí	E	18	G2	Treviso	I	35	B9	Tulle	F	17	D7
Torrox	E	28	E6	Trévoux	F	17	C12	Tulnici	RO	79	F7
Torsås	S	45	D11	Trianta	GR	88	G4	Tuluceşti	RO	79	F9
Torshälla	S	47	C7	Tricarico	I	31	B8	Tumba	S	47	C9
Tórshavn	FO	3	B9	Tricase	I	31	D12	Tunbridge Wells, Royal	GB	9	E10
Torslanda	S	44	A6	Trier	D	13	B8	Tura	H	77	B6
Tortolì	I	32	F3	Trieste	I	35	C12	Turceni	RO	82	B5
Tortona	I	19	B11	Trifeşti	RO	79	D7	Turčianske Teplice	SK	75	F10
Tortora	I	31	D7	Triggiano	I	31	A9	Turda	RO	78	D2
Tortoreto	I	33	B8	Trignac	F	14	G5	Turek	PL	71	G8
Tortorici	I	30	E5	Trigueros	E	25	J6	Turenki	FIN	64	E5
Tortosa	E	21	G7	Trikala	GR	86	F5	Türgovishte	BG	83	E11
Toruń	PL	71	E8	Trim	IRL	4	F2	Turgutalp	TR	85	F4
Tostedt	D	42	D5	Třinec	CZ	75	E9	Turgutlu	TR	85	H4
Totana	E	29	C10	Tring	GB	9	D8	Türi	EST	66	C6
Tótkomlós	H	77	E8	Trino	I	19	A10	Turi	I	31	B9
Totnes	GB	8	G4	Tripoli	GR	88	C5	Turin	I	19	A9
Totton	GB	9	F7	Tritenii de Jos	RO	78	D2	Turka	UA	73	F5
Toul	F	13	D7	Trittau	D	42	C6	Túrkeve	H	77	C8
Toulon	F	18	E6	Trivento	I	33	D9	Turku	FIN	53	G11
Toulouges	F	18	F1	Trnava	SK	75	G8	Turnhout	B	10	E6
Toulouse	F	17	H7	Trofa	P	22	F2	Turnov	CZ	41	C12
Tourcoing	F	10	G3	Trofaiach	A	39	D10	Turnu Măgurele	RO	83	D8
Tourlaville	F	14	B6	Trofors	N	54	C6	Tursi	I	31	C8
Tournai	B	10	G4	Trogir	HR	80	E4	Turţ	RO	77	B12
Tournefeuille	F	17	H7	Troia	I	33	E10	Tuscania	I	32	B4
Tournon-sur-Rhône	F	18	A5	Troina	I	30	E5	Tuszyn	PL	71	G9
Tournus	F	36	E2	Troisdorf	D	11	F9	Tutrakan	BG	83	C11
Tours	F	15	G9	Trollhättan	S	46	E3	Tuttlingen	D	13	F12
Towcester	GB	9	C8	Tromsdalen	N	58	D2	Tuusula	FIN	64	F6
Trabotivište	MK	82	G4	Tromsø	N	58	D2	Tuve	S	44	A6
Traian	RO	79	D7	Trondheim	N	51	A7	Tuzla	BIH	81	C8
Trakai	LT	69	F8	Troon	GB	4	B4	Tuzla	RO	84	C5
Tralee	IRL	7	M2	Tropea	I	31	F8	Tveit	N	48	D3
Trá Li	IRL	7	M2	Trosa	S	47	D9	Tvøroyri	FO	3	C9
Tramariglio	I	32	E1	Trostberg	D	38	C6	Tvürditsa	BG	83	F9
Trá Mhór	IRL	7	M6	Trouville-sur-Mer	F	15	C9	Twardogóra	PL	75	A8
Tramore	IRL	7	M6	Trowbridge	GB	8	E6	Twist	D	11	C9
Tranås	S	46	F6	Troyan	BG	83	E7	Twistringen	D	11	B11
Tranbjerg	DK	44	E4	Troyes	F	12	E5	Tyachiv	UA	78	A2
Trani	I	31	A8	Trpanj	HR	80	F6	Tychy	PL	75	D10
Trapani	I	30	E2	Trstená	SK	75	E11	Tyfors	S	46	A5
Trasacco	I	33	C7	Trstenik	SRB	81	E12	Tynset	N	51	D8
Traun	A	39	B9	Trujillo	E	24	D7	Tyrnavos	GR	86	F6
Traunreut	D	38	C6	Truro	GB	8	G2	Tysse	N	48	B2
Traunstein	D	38	C6	Truşeşti	RO	79	B7				
Travnik	BIH	80	C6	Truskavets'	UA	73	F5				
Trbovlje	SLO	39	G10	Trüstenik	BG	83	D7	**U**			
Třebíč	CZ	74	F5	Trutnov	CZ	74	C5				
Trebinje	BIH	81	F7	Tryavna	BG	83	E9	Úbeda	E	29	C7
Trebisacce	I	31	D9	Trzcianka	PL	70	E5	Ubli	HR	80	F5
Trebišov	SK	73	G3	Trzebiatów	PL	70	C4	Ubrique	E	25	L8
Trebnje	SLO	39	G10	Trzebnica	PL	75	A7	Uchte	D	11	C12
Třeboň	CZ	41	F11	Trzemeszno	PL	71	F7	Uckfield	GB	9	F9

U

V

Ø

Øksfjord	N	58	C5
Ølstykke	DK	44	E6
Ørsta	N	50	D3

Å

Åbo	FIN	53	G11
Åby	S	47	D7
Åfjord	N	54	G3
Ågskaret	N	57	G2
Åhus	S	45	E9
Åkarp	S	45	E8
Åkersberga	S	47	C10
Åkerstrømmen	N	51	E8
Åkrehamn	N	48	D2
Ålesund	N	50	C3

Åmot	N	48	D5
Åmål	S	46	D3
Åndalsnes	N	50	C4
Åre	S	51	A10
Århus	DK	44	D4
Ås	N	51	B9
Åsele	S	55	F10
Åseral	N	48	E4
Åstorp	S	45	D7
Åtvidaberg	S	47	E7

Ä

Älmhult	S	45	D9
Älta	S	47	C9
Älvros	S	51	D12
Älvsbyn	S	56	C3
Ängelholm	S	45	D7
Äänekoski	FIN	64	B6

Ö

Örebro	S	46	C6
Örnsköldsvik	S	53	A7
Östersund	S	51	B12
Överammer	S	52	A4

MIX
Paper from
responsible sources

FSC
www.fsc.org

FSC® C007454

FSC™ is a non-profit international organisation established to promote
the responsible management of the world's forests. Products carrying the
FSC label are independently certified to assure consumers that they come
from forests that are managed to meet the social, economic and
ecological needs of present and future generations,
and other controlled sources.

Find out more about HarperCollins and the environment at
www.harpercollins.co.uk/green

Spring H Praise

2005/06

C000214137

SPRING HARVEST

Equipping the Church for action

Copyright and photocopying

No part of this publication may be reproduced in any form without the permission of the copyright holder of the songs and the publisher of the songbook. Exceptions to this rule are made for holders of licences issued by Christian Copyright Licensing International as follows:

Church Copyright Licence:

> churches and organisations holding this licence may reproduce the words of the songs within the terms of their licence.

Music Reproduction Licence:

> churches and organisations holding this licence may reproduce the music of the songs within the terms of their licence.

For information about the above licences, contact:

For UK and Europe – Christian Copyright Licensing (Europe) Ltd,
P.O. Box 1339, Eastbourne, East Sussex, BN21 1AD.

For USA and Canada – Christian Copyright Licensing Inc,
17201 NE Sacramento Street, Portland, Oregon 97230, USA

Australasia – Christian Copyright Licensing Asia Pacific Pty Ltd, P.O. Box 664,
Baulkham Hills Business Centre, Sydney, NSW 2153, Australia

Africa – Christian Copyright Licensing Africa Pty Ltd, P.O. Box 2347,
Durbanville 7551, South Africa

UNAUTHORISED PHOTOCOPYING IS ILLEGAL and detrimental to the work and ministry of the songwriters and publishers.

All rights reserved. All songs are reproduced by kind permission of the copyright holders – details of which are shown beneath each song/hymn. Any omission of acknowledgement to composer or publisher will be corrected in future editions.

Acknowledgements

Scripture quotations taken from the HOLY BIBLE, NEW INTERNATIONAL VERSION. Copyright ©1973, 1978, 1984 by International Bible Society. Used by permission of Hodder and Stoughton Limited. All rights reserved. "NIV" is a registered trade mark of International Bible Society. UK trademark number 1448790

Music type setting and new arrangements by David Ball, davidoxon@aol.com
Cover design by Adept Design
Printed in England by Halcyon

Published by Spring Harvest, 14 Horsted Square, Uckfield, East Sussex, TN22 1QG, UK.
Spring Harvest. A Registered Charity.
Distributed by ICC, Silverdale Road, Eastbourne, East Sussex, BN20 7AB, UK.

Spring Harvest wishes to acknowledge and thank the following people for their help in the compilation and production of this songbook:
Andrew Crookall, Malc Garda, Mel Holden, Cheryl Jenkinson, David Peacock, Gareth Robinson, Tre Sheppard, Kate Silber, and Spring Harvest Head Office staff.
Thank you to Marie Birkinshaw, Mark Earey, Nick Harding, Mel Holden, Northumbria Community, Lesley Parker, Joel Payne, Ruth Sermon, Jackie Sheppard, Paul Sheppy, Joy Townhill, Allister Walker, Richard Williamson and The Archbishops Council for liturgy and worship tips.

ISBN 1 899 78851 4

Contents

Songs are listed in order of first line, not title. In a few cases,
alphabetical ordering of songs has been changed slightly, in
order to ensure that page turns are not needed in any
two-page songs.

The words edition of this songbook is also available in Braille and Giant print

Index

Song titles differing from first lines are in italics

5

1

After I've done everything
(I will stand)

Capo 3 (D)

Godfrey Birtill

1. Af-ter I've done e-v'ry-thing,— I will stand, with my eyes on my
dark-est days,— I will stand, and bring a sa-cri-fice—

King of kings, I will stand. I will stand: I will stand in con-
— of praise, I will stand. I will stand: no mat-ter what is thrown—

— fi-dence— to see the Lord's de-li—ve-rance, yes I will stand. I will
— at me, I'll stand a-gainst the de—vil's schemes,— yes I will stand. I will

stand: of this I'm ab-so-lute—ly sure,— I'll see the good-ness of—
stand: up-right— and un—di-sturbed,— un-a-fraid I'm stand-

— the Lord,— yes I will stand. Be-cause I'm stand—ing with
ing firm,— yes I will stand.

Copyright © 2004 Thankyou Music/Adm. by worshiptogether.com songs excl. UK & Europe, adm. by Kingsway Music
tym@kingsway.co.uk Used by permission

All I want is to know you, Jesus
(Nothing is as wonderful)

Scott Underwood

1. 3. All I want is to know you, Je-sus. All I want is to know
2. All I want is to know you, Je-sus, and the po-wer that raised

I be-long to you. Show me all of the things that are worth-less,
you from the dead. Help me for-get all the things that I've done:

that I thought were so va-lua-ble to you. No-things is as love-ly,
set my heart on what lies a head.

no-thing is as wor-thy, no-thing is as won-der-ful as know-ing you.

Copyright © 1996 Mercy/Vineyard Publishing adm. CopyCare, P.O. Box 77, Hailsham, East Sussex, BN27 3EF, UK.
music@copycare.com Used by permission

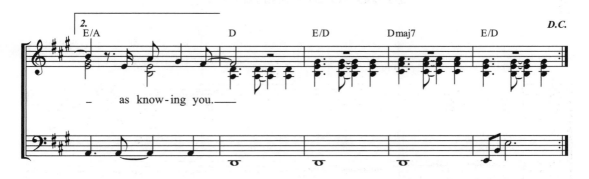

as know-ing you.

Coda

2a   In every place and in every age

Praise the name of the living God,
in every place and in every age.

God is the source of wisdom and power
in every place and in every age.

God determines times and seasons
in every place and in every age.

God brings light to search the darkness
in every place and in every age.

God gives knowledge and understanding
in every place and in every age.

Praise the name of the living God,
in every place and in every age.

Copyright © 2005 Mark Earey

A love so amazing

Paul Oakley

1. A love so a - maz - ing has come to save — me,
2. Your ways are faith - ful, your works are beau - ti - ful,

and this love chan - ges e - v'ry - thing.—
your word sets the cap - tives free.—

Fa - ther, you found me, your good - ness sur - rounds me;
Your hand up - on me heals and re - stores me,

This song is recorded on the Spring Harvest 2004 Live Worship Album

Copyright © 2003 Thankyou Music/Adm. by worshiptogether.com songs excl. UK & Europe, adm. by Kingsway Music
tym@kingsway.co.uk Used by permission.

(continued over...)

3a   Prayer for blessing

Go before us, Lord, through the many changes of this world.
As each new day dawns, may we truly abide in you and know your
abiding in us.
May we grow and flourish, rooted at all times in the one true vine.
To the glory of your Holy Name. Amen.

Copyright © 2005 Marie Birkinshaw

As high as the heavens
(The voice of hope)

Lara Martin

(continued over...)

Lara Martin (Abundant Life Ministries, Bradford, England). Copyright © 2002 Thankyou Music/Adm. by worshiptogether.com songs excl. UK & Europe, adm. by Kingsway Music tym@kingsway.co.uk Used by permission.

high!

2. You were the one___ be - fore time___ be - gan;___ there's

no - thing be - yond___ your con - trol.___ My con - fi - dence,___ my as -

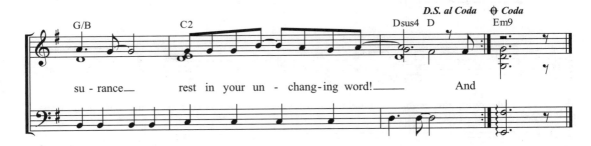

su - rance___ rest in your un - chang-ing word!___ And

4a   I rest in you

From 2 Timothy 4:18

Lord, in you I rest; sure that you will rescue me from all evil

and will lead me safely to your heavenly kingdom.

5

As the light of the sun
(Lord of the harvest)

Words: Andy Bromley & Chris Bowater
Music: Andy Bromley

As the light of the sun— in the earth,— let sal-va-tion be known.—

As the wa-ters co-ver the sea,— let your glo-ry fill— the earth.—

E-v'ry tribe,— e-v'ry tongue,— e-v'ry peo-ple on— the earth— would hear of your fame, hear the sound of your name.—

Lord of the har-vest, send out the wor-kers,

This song is recorded on the Spring Harvest 2005 New Songs Album

Copyright © 2004 Thankyou Music/Adm. by worshiptogether.com songs excl. UK & Europe, adm. by Kingsway Music tym@kingsway.co.uk
and © 2003 Sovereign Lifestyle Music Ltd. P.O. Box 356, Leighton Buzzard, LU7 3WP, UK. sovereignmusic@aol.com Used by permission

6

As we bring our songs of love today
(How long?)

Graham Kendrick

Copyright © 2002 Make Way Music, P.O. Box 263, Croydon, CR9 5AP, UK.
International copyright secured. All rights reserved. Used by permission.

7

As we gather
(Gathering song)

Eoghan Heaslip

As we ga - ther here to - ge - ther in your pre - sence,
as your peo - ple we ac-know - ledge and re - mem - ber

the works of your hands, your pur-pose and plans,

your word through the a - ges___ like an an - chor for___ all time;___

___ as one___ we sing:___ he who has pro - mised___

Copyright © 2004 Vertical Worship Songs/Sovereign Music UK, P.O. Box 356, Leighton Buzzard, LU7 3WP, UK. sovereignmusic@aol.com

8

At the foot of the cross
(Ashes to beauty)

Steadily, with strength

Kathryn Scott

1. At the foot of the cross_____ where grace_____ and suf - f'ring meet,_
_____ where I_____ am made__ com - plete,_

_____ you have shown me your love_____ through__ the judge-
_____ you have gi - ven me life_____ through__ the death__

- ment you__ re - ceived._____ And you've won_____ my_____ heart,_
_ you bore__ for me._____

yes, you've won_____ my_____ heart.__ Now I can

This song is recorded on the Spring Harvest 2004 Live Worship Album

Copyright © 2003 Vertical Worship Songs/Sovereign Music UK. P.O. Box 356, Leighton Buzzard, LU7 3WP, UK. sovereignmusic@aol.com

trade these a-shes in for beau-ty, and wear for-give-ness like a crown.

Com-ing to kiss the feet of mer-cy, I lay

e - v'ry bur - den down,_____ at - the foot of the cross._____

2. At the foot of the cross___ — I trade these a-shes in for —

Last time to Coda

D.C.

D.S.

3. Instrumental Bridge

(continued over...)

23

Yes, you've won‿

I lay e‿v'ry bur‑den down,‿‿‿ I lay e‑v'ry bur‑den down‿

‿ at the foot of the cross.‿‿

8a   Prayer of release

God says, 'I love you my little ones,
you may love yourselves.
Be free from your past.
I release you.
The burdens you have carried
are now dissolved by my love.
You have my word as a lamp to guide you –
take it, use it, share it.'

Copyright © 2000 Ruth Sermon

9 Be still for the presence of the Lord

David Evans
Arr. Geoff Baker

1. Be still, for the presence of the Lord, the Holy One is here;
2. Be still, for the glory of the Lord is shining all around;
3. Be still, for the power of the Lord is moving in this place;

come bow before him now with reverence and fear:
he burns with holy fire, with splendour he is crowned:
he comes to cleanse and heal, to minister his grace:

in him no sin is found - we stand on holy ground.
how awesome is the sight - our radiant King of light!
no work too hard for him, in faith receive from him.

Be still, for the presence of the Lord, the Holy One is here.
Be still, for the glory of the Lord is shining all around.
Be still, for the power of the Lord is moving in this place.

Copyright © 1986 Thankyou Music/Adm. by worshiptogether.com songs excl. UK & Europe, adm. by Kingsway Music
tym@kingsway.co.uk Used by permission

10 Bigger than the air I breathe
(You)

Tim Hughes, Rob Hill
& Jon Mannson

Copyright © 2004 Thankyou Music/adm. by worshiptogether.com songs excl. UK & Europe, adm. by Kingsway Music
tym@kingsway.co.uk Used by permission

(continued over...)

10a Reservoir

You place my feet upon a larger place, Lord,
you give my hands a greater task for you.
You set my eyes upon the far horizon
and in my heart I know your word is true.

You place a reservoir within my heart, Lord,
that all my tears would come from a different place:
that all my ways would minister your grace
to those who long to see your face.

Copyright © Northumbria Community Trust Ltd, Hetton Hall, Chatton, Northumberland, NE66 5SD.

Bless the Lord

Capo 3 (D)

Emma Pears

Driving

Chorus

Bless the Lord,___ O___ my soul,___ bless___ the Lord,___ O___ my soul,_ ___ my heart will re - joice___ in___ his good - ness, for - giv - ing my sins and show - ing me kind - ness. Bless the Lord,___ O___ my soul,_ ___ bless___ the Lord,___ O___ my soul,___ all___ my in - most be - ing,

(continued over...)

This song is recorded on the Spring Harvest 2005 New Songs Album

Copyright © Daybreak Music Ltd. PO Box 2848, Eastbourne, BN20 7XP. All rights reserved. info@daybreakmusic.co.uk
International copyright secured. Used by permission.

30

11a Rejoice in God
From Luke 1:46–47

My soul glorifies the Lord
My spirit rejoices in God my Saviour

12 Blessed be your name

Beth & Matt Redman

Copyright © 2002 Thankyou Music/Adm. by worshiptogether.com songs excl. UK & Europe, adm. by Kingsway Music
tym@kingsway.co.uk Used by permission.

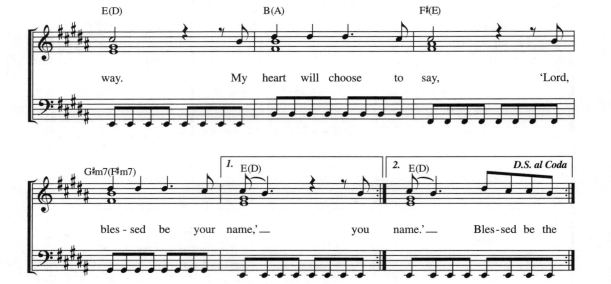

way.   My heart will choose   to say,   'Lord,

bles-sed   be   your name,'—   you   name.'—   Bles-sed be the

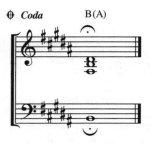

12a Be faithful

A meditation on Acts 11:23

Be faithful as each new day starts.
Be true to God with all your heart.
Let Christ be your guide and know him at your side.
Be true to God with all your heart.
Be faithful though the day seems long.
Be true to God, in Christ be strong.
When life's trials get tough, when storms become too rough,
be true to God, in Christ be strong.
Be faithful till your journey's done.
Be true to God through Christ his Son.
May your heart and mind find peace and deep joy that will not cease.
Be true to God through Christ his Son.

Copyright © 2005 Marie Birkinshaw

13 By the Babylonian rivers

Capo 3 (Dm)

Words: from Psalm 137, Ewald Bash
Music: Latvian melody
arr. Geoff Weaver

With expression ♩ = 86

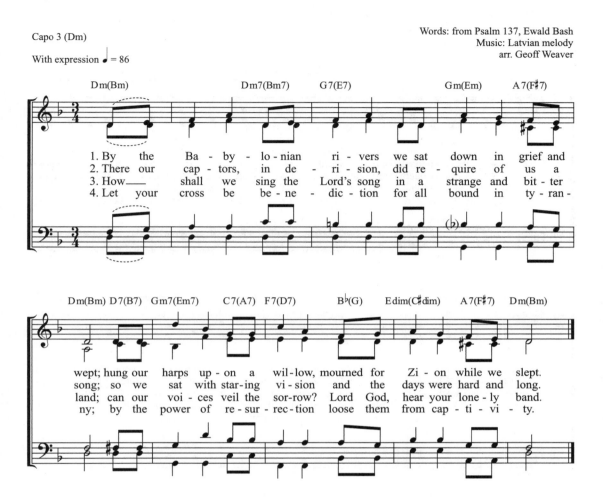

1. By the Ba - by - lo - nian ri - vers we sat down in grief and
2. There our cap - tors, in de - ri - sion, did re - quire of us a
3. How___ shall we sing the Lord's song in a strange and bit - ter
4. Let your cross be be - ne - dic - tion for all bound in ty - ran -

wept; hung our harps up - on a wil - low, mourned for Zi - on while we slept.
song; so we sat with star - ing vi - sion and the days were hard and long.
land; can our voi - ces veil the sor - row? Lord God, hear your lone - ly band.
ny; by the power of re - sur - rec - tion loose them from cap - ti - vi - ty.

This melancholy Latvian folk melody reflects beautifully the desolation of the exiles.
This is very effective when sung unaccompanied or with simple guitar accompaniment

---

13a The faithfulness of the Lord
Psalm 117

Praise the Lord, all you nations,
extol him, all you peoples.
For great is his love towards us,
and the faithfulness of the Lord
endures for ever.

Music arrangement: © Geoff Weaver/Jubilate Hymns, 4 Thorne Park Road, Torquay, TQ2 6RX. www.jubilate.co.uk Used by permission.
Words: © Ewald Bash/copyright control.

14 Christ the eternal Lord

Words: Timothy Dudley-Smith
Music: George Elvey (1816-93)

With strength ♩ = 120

1. Christ the e - ter - nal Lord whose mise here we claim, whose
2. Christ the unchang - ing Word to e - v'ry pass - ing age, whose
3. Christ the re-deem - ing Son who shares our hu - man birth, and
4. Christ the un-fad - ing light of e - ver - last - ing day, our
5. Christ the as-cen - ded King ex - al - ted high a - bove, whose

gifts of grace are free - ly — poured on all who name your Name; with
time - less teach-ings still are — heard set forth on Scrip - ture's page; trans -
by his death sal - va - tion — won for e - v'ry child of earth; in -
morn - ing star in splen - dour — bright, the Life, the Truth, the Way; that
praise un - end - ing a - ges — sing, whom yet un - seen we love; when

thank - ful - ness and praise we stand be - fore your throne, in -
form our thought and mind, en - ligh - ten all who read, with -
spire our hearts, we pray, to tell your love a - broad, that
light of truth you give to ser - vants as to friends, your
mor - tal life is past your voice from hea - ven's throne shall

Words © copyright Timothy Dudley-Smith, 9 Ashlands, Ford, Salisbury, Wilts., England SP4 6DY
in the countries of Europe (including Great Britain and Ireland) and of Africa

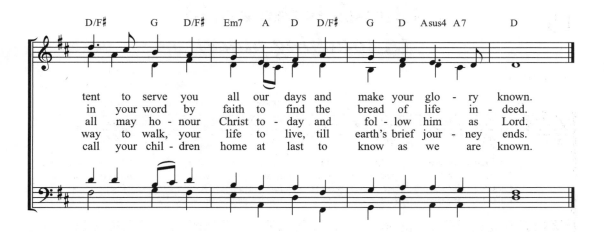

| D/F# | | G | D/F# | Em7 | A | D | D/F# | | G | D | Asus4 | A7 | | D |

tent   to   serve   you   all   our   days   and   make   your   glo - ry   known.
in   your   word   by   faith   to   find   the   bread   of   life   in - deed.
all   may   ho - nour   Christ   to - day   and   fol - low   him   as   Lord.
way   to   walk,   your   life   to   live,   till   earth's   brief   jour - ney   ends.
call   your   chil - dren   home   at   last   to   know   as   we   are   known.

14a Profession of faith: the God who made the world

From Acts 17:24–31

Let us declare our faith in God the Creator:
in God we live and move and have our being.

The God who made the world is Lord of heaven and earth.
He does not live in buildings we have made,
nor does he need anything we can give,
for he himself gives life and breath to all things.

From one ancestor he made all the nations:
he set their times and places,
so they would search and find him
though he is not far from each of us.

God has set a day to judge the world with justice.
He has appointed Jesus Christ to be the judge,
and has proved this by raising him from the dead.

This is our faith.
In God we live and move and have our being. Amen.

Copyright © 2005 Mark Earey

15

Christ's is the world
(A touching place)

Gently but firmly

Words: John L. Bell & Graham Maule
Music: Scottish trad. arr. John L. Bell

1. Christ's is the world in which we move, Christ's are the
2. Feel for the peo-ple we most a-void: strange, or be-
3. Feel for the par-ents who've lost their child. Feel for the
4. Feel for the lives by life con-fused, rid-dled with

folk we're sum-moned to love, Christ's is the voice that
reaved, or ne-ver em-ployed. Feel for the wo-men and
wo-men whom men have de-filed. Feel for the ba-by for
doubt, in lov-ing a-bused. Feel for the lone-ly heart,

calls us to care, and Christ is the one who meets us here.
feel for the men who fear that their liv-ing is all in vain.
whom there's no breast, and feel for the wea-ry who find no rest.
con-scious of sin, which longs to be pure but fears to be-gin.

Chorus (Harmony)

To the lost Christ shows his face. To the un-loved he

Words: John L Bell and Graham Maule. Music: Scottish traditional melody 'Dream Angus' arr. John L Bell.
From 'Love from below' (Wild Goose Publications, 1989). Copyright © 1989 WGRG, Iona Community, Glasgow, G2 3DH, Scotland.

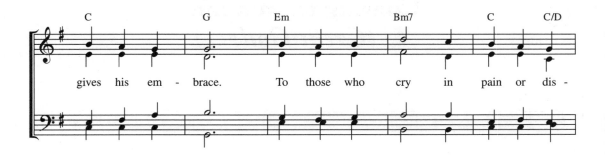

gives his em - brace. To those who cry in pain or dis-

grace,— Christ makes, with his friends, a touch - ing place.

15a A general intercession for those in trouble

We hold before God:
those for whom life is very difficult;
those who have difficult decisions to make,
and who honestly do not know what is the right thing to do.
We hold before God:
those who have difficult tasks to do and to face,
and who fear they may fail in them;
those who have difficult temptations to face,
and who know only too well that they may fall to them,
if they try to meet them alone.
We hold before God:
those who know that they can be their own worst enemies.
We hold before God:
those who have difficult people to work with:
those who have to suffer unjust treatment, unfair criticism,
unappreciated work.
We hold before God:
those who are sad because someone they loved has died;
and any who are disappointed in something for which they hoped
very much.

William Barclay
Copyright © Northumbria Community Trust Ltd, Hetton Hall, Chatton, Northumberland, NE66 5SD

16

Coming to worship
(Great God)

Capo 3 (D)

Joyfully

Carey Luce
& Geraldine Latty

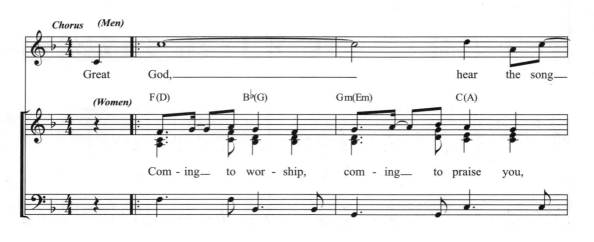

Chorus *(Men)*

Great God,_____ hear the song_____

(Women)

Com - ing__ to wor - ship, com - ing__ to praise you,

_ that we sing.____ Great God,_____

com - ing__ to say that you are__ God.____ Com - ing__ to wor - ship,

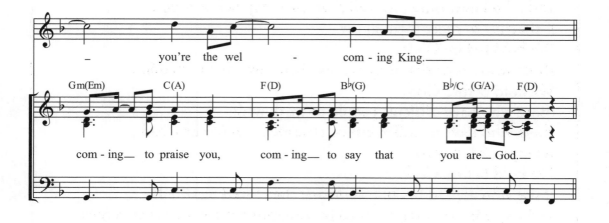

_ you're the wel - com - ing King.____

com - ing__ to praise you, com - ing__ to say that you are__ God.____

Copyright © 2004 Thankyou Music/Adm. by worshiptogether.com songs excl. UK & Europe, adm. by Kingsway Music
tym@kingsway.co.uk Used by permission

Verse

1. You have called us to your ta - ble, young and old, to -
2. Thank you for the gifts you give us, thank you for your
3. May our sto - ry be your sto - ry, may our lives be

ge - ther_ here._ What a fa - mi - ly you make us,
pre - sence_ here._ By the Spi - rit work - ing in us
whol - ly_ yours,_ so that o - thers come to wor - ship

as you call us we draw_ near._ Great
we will wor - ship with - out_ fear._
Je - sus Christ the Lord of_ all._

16a The song of the Lord

Sing the song of the Lord
Sing the song in a hard land
Sing the song of the Lord
Sing the song in an easy land
Sing the song of the Lord
Sing the song in a war-torn land
Sing the song of the Lord
Sing the song in a peaceful land
Sing the song of the Lord
Sing the song in our land
Sing the song of the Lord

Copyright © 2005 Nick Harding

17 Dance, dance
(Joy is in this place)

Words: John Newton (1725-1807)
Music & words adaption: Tim Hughes

With a strong rhythm

This song is recorded on the Spring Harvest Distinctive Sounds – Glory Album

Copyright © 2003 Thankyou Music/Adm. by worshiptogether.com songs excl. UK & Europe, adm. by Kingsway Music
tym@kingsway.co.uk Used by permission.

And e -
Yeah, joy—

- v'ry - bo - dy dance now._____
- is in this place now._____

A - ma - zing grace, how sweet the sound, to save a wretch like

me;_____ I once was lost, but now I'm found, was blind, but now I

see._____

43

Dwell in the midst of us
(Dwell)

18

Casey Corum

Dwell in the midst of us, come and dwell
Dwell in the midst of us, wipe all the tears

in this place. Dwell in the midst of us,
from our fa - ces. Dwell in the midst of us,

come and have your way.
you can have your way.

You can have your way, you can have your way,

Copyright © 2003 Mercy/Vineyard Publishing adm. CopyCare, P.O. Box 77, Hailsham, East Sussex, BN27 3EF, UK.
music@copycare.com Used by permission

you can have your way.

Not our will, but yours be done: come and

change us. Not our will, but yours be done: come, sus-

2nd time D.C.

To end

tain us.

19

Everlasting God
(Yesterday, today, forever)

Capo 3 (D)

Vicky Beeching

Rock style

1. E - ver - last - ing God,____ the years go by but you're____
2. Un - cre - a - ted One,____ you have no end and no____

_ un - chan - ging. In this fra - gile world,____ you
_ be - gin - ning. Earth - ly pow - ers fade,____ but

are the on - ly firm____ foun - da - tion.
there is no end to____ your king - dom.

Al - ways lov -

- ing, al - ways____ true,

al - ways mer -

Copyright © 2002 Thankyou Music/Adm. by worshiptogether.com songs excl. UK & Europe, adm. by Kingsway Music
tym@kingsway.co.uk Used by permission.

(continued over...)

we will trust__ in you,__   in you.__

Yah - weh,__   God un - chan - ging. Yah - weh,__

firm foun - da - tion. You are da - tion.

19a God of gods

From Daniel 2:47

**Come let us worship the living God! God of gods; Lord of kings;
revealer of mysteries; we worship and adore you.**

© Copyright 2005 Mark Earey

Guidelines for presenting song words on screen

DO choose strong colours for your background and your text. For example, strong yellow works well on a blue background. Don't mix colours that are close together in the colour spectrum, e.g. yellow/green; blue/red. Consult with dyslexic and colour-blind members of the congregation for possible problems to avoid.

DO use a point size for your font of at least 36 and bold. You can get away with a 32 point font size but generally 36 is best.

DO use a font that is easy to read. This is not the time for experimenting with fancy text. My personal preference is for Arial. (Times Roman is too fussy and narrow with a very slanted italic form.)

DO use the same font throughout.

DO make sure there are no spelling mistakes.

DO check versions of songs are the same as the ones your church uses whether you get them on a song package or type them in yourself.

DO give each song its own separate file. Save the song with its full title and be particularly wary of those that have similar, or even the same, titles (Eg: Holy holy holy). It is always worth adding a blank slide at the end of a song. The congregation should never see the 'nuts and bolts'; only the end result.

DON'T overfill each slide with text. As a rough guide you should only fill the top two-thirds of the slide with text. This will depend upon the height of your screen. But remember if your screen is fairly low, when people stand up to sing, those sitting at the back of the church may find the lower part of the screen obscured by heads.

DON'T use ALL CAPITAL LETTERS – it actually decreases readability.

DON'T use the feature of lines flying in from left and right.

DON'T use the random transitions to move from slide to slide, in fact don't use any transitions at all!

Taken from 'Beyond the OHP: A practical guide to using technology in worship' by Jackie Shepherd.
Published 2002 by Spring Harvest Publishing Division.

20 Everything I have comes from you
(Acknowledge you)

Andy Bromley

Copyright © 2004 Thankyou Music/Adm. by worshiptogether.com songs excl. UK & Europe, adm. by Kingsway Music
tym@kingsway.co.uk Used by permission.

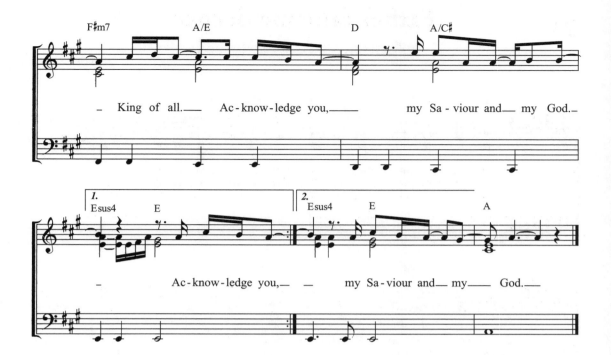

King of all.___ Ac-know-ledge you,_____ my Sa-viour and___ my God.___

1.
Ac-know-ledge you,___ ___ my Sa-viour and___ my___ God.___

20a A prayer in brokenness

O God, I cannot undo the past,
or make it never to have happened! – neither can you.
There are some things that are not possible even for you
– but not many!

I ask you, humbly, and from the bottom of my heart:
please, God,
would you write straight with my crooked lines?
Out of the serious mistakes of my life
will you make something beautiful for you?

Teach me to live at peace with you,
to make peace with others and even with myself.

Give me fresh vision.
Let me experience your love so deeply
that I am free to face the future with a steady eye,
forgiven, and strong in hope.

Copyright © Northumbria Community Trust Ltd, Hetton Hall, Chatton, Northumberland, NE66 5SD.

21 Father take me deeper

Leigh Barnard

Steadily

1. Fa-ther take me deep-er still, that I may know you more,
2. Fa-ther take me deep-er still, that I may serve you more,
3. Fa-ther take me deep-er still, that I may love you more,

through your word and teach-ing may I al-ways hold your
keep me stead-fast in your will and guide me through the
though my faith be wea-kened, may I learn to trust you

truth. For all your ways a-bound in love, your
storm. For you a-lone can guard my steps, your
more. How awe-some are your ways, O Lord, how

thoughts are not my own. Fa-ther take me deep-er with you, that
pre-sence shel-ters me. Fa-ther take me deep-er with you, that
faith-ful is our God. Fa-ther take me deep-er with you, that

This song is recorded on the Spring Harvest 2005 New Songs Album

Copyright © 2004 Daybreak Music Ltd, P.O. Box 2848, Eastbourne, BN20 7XP. All rights reserved. info@daybreakmusic.co.uk
International copyright secured. Used by permission.

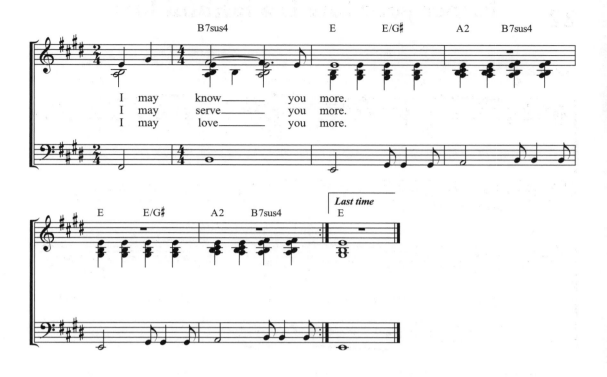

I may know——— you more.
I may serve——— you more.
I may love——— you more.

21a Prayer of abandonment to God

Father, I abandon myself into your hands.
Do with me what you will, whatever you do, I will thank you,
I am ready for all, I accept all.
Let only your will be done in me, as in all your creatures,
and I'll ask nothing else, my Lord.

Into your hands I commend my spirit;
I give it to you with all the love of my heart, for I love you, Lord,
and so need to give myself, to surrender myself into your hands
with a trust beyond all measure, because you are my Father.

Charles de Foucauld
Copyright © Northumbria Community Trust Ltd, Hetton Hall, Chatton, Northumberland, NE66 5SD.

22 Father your love is a faithful love

Robert Critchley

Ballad style

Fa - ther, your love— is a faith - ful love, en - du-ring and ne - ver fail-

ing love.— Through-out the a - ges, stea-dy and true,— and the

dawn of each day— brings your mer - cies new.— And I will put— my trust—

- in— you,— Fa - ther, your love— is faith - ful.— - ful.— So

keep me in— your love— to - day,— take my hand— and lead—

Copyright © 2002 Thankyou Music/Adm. by worshiptogether.com songs excl. UK & Europe, adm. by Kingsway Music
tym@kingsway.co.uk Used by permission.

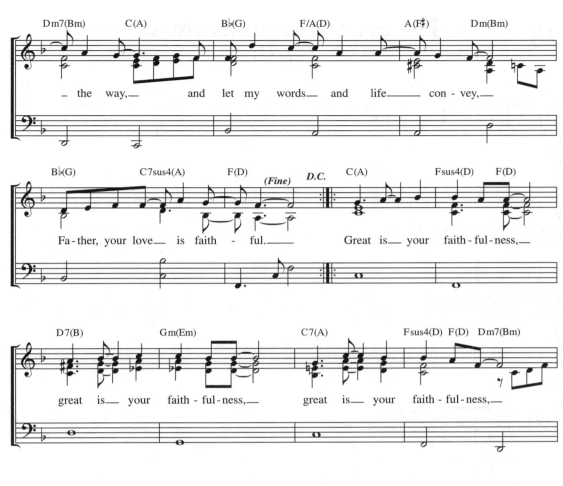

22a Faith in a faithful God

Habakkuk 3: 17–19

Though the fig-tree does not bud and there are no grapes on the vines,
though the olive crop fails and the fields produce no food,
though there are no sheep in the pen and no cattle in the stalls,
yet I will rejoice in the Lord, I will be joyful in God my Saviour.
The Sovereign Lord is my strength;
he makes my feet like the feet of a deer,
he enables me to go on the heights.

23 For every disappointment
(Still)

Copyright © 2003 Authentic Publishing/Admin. by CopyCare, P.O. Box 77, Hailsham, East Sussex, BN27 3EF, UK
music@copycare.com Used by permission.

57

24 From everlasting to everlasting

Copyright © 2001 Thankyou Music/Adm. by worshiptogether.com songs excl. UK & Europe, adm. by Kingsway Music
tym@kingsway.co.uk Used by permission

God. Your lov-ing kind-ness__ en-dures for - e - ver,__ high King of

hea - ven,__ you reign e-ter - nal-ly.__ As - sur-ing peace and__ up-hold-ing

jus-tice, al-ways true, al-ways faith - ful, you will be.__ For you are God,__

God.__ Your love en-dures for - ev-er,

your mer-cy with-out end.__ Your love en-dures for-e - ver, your mer-cy with-out end.__

25 From every corner of the earth
(Calling all nations)

Mark Tedder

Slightly driving

From ev-'ry cor - ner— of— the earth— we will de-clare— your— worth,— your splen-dour— is re - nowned— through all you've— done.— From sea to shin - ing sea— your glo-ry will— be seen,— through

CCLI No: 3042737 Copyright © 1999 Mark Tedder

those that_ you_ have called___ to bear your_ word.__

Chorus We're call-ing all na - tions to_ your side,__ ev-'ry peo-

ple, tongue_ and tribe,__ this ge-ne-ra - tion shall_ de-clare_

_ that you are God.__ All of the na-

tions will_ re - joice__ and we will be_ your voice__

(continued over...)

as we spread___ the awe - some news___ that you're a -

live!

From ev - 'ry cor -

25a Collect for the third Sunday of Easter

Almighty God who in your great mercy gladdened the disciples with
the sight of the risen Lord:
give us such knowledge of his presence with us, that we may be
strengthened and sustained by his risen life and serve you continually
in righteousness and truth: through Jesus Christ your Son our Lord,
who is alive and reigns with you, in the unity of the Holy Spirit,
one God, now and for ever.
Amen

From Common Worship: Services and Prayers for the Church of England. Copyright © The Archbishops' Council 2000

Giver of life

Tim Hughes

(continued over...)

This song is recorded on the Spring Harvest 2005 New Songs Album and the Spring Harvest Distinctive Sounds – Glory Album

Copyright © 2004 Thankyou Music/Adm. by worshiptogether.com songs excl. UK & Europe, adm. by Kingsway Music
tym@kingsway.co.uk Used by permission

You de-light to pour your good-ness down.

Bridge

You de-light to pour your good-ness down. For you are good

D.SS. al fine

26a Creed

From Ephesians 3

Let us declare our faith in God.

We believe in God the Father,
from whom every family in heaven and on earth is named.

We believe in God the Son,
who lives in our hearts through faith,
and fills us with his love.

We believe in God the Holy Spirit,
who strengthens us
with power from on high.

We believe in one God;
Father, Son and Holy Spirit.
Amen

From Common Worship: Services and Prayers for the Church of England. Copyright © The Archbishops' Council 2000

27

Give thanks to the Lord

Sam Hargreaves

1. Give thanks to the Lord, (give thanks to the Lord.) He's been good to us,
2. Give thanks to the Lord, (give thanks to the Lord.) He's been good to us,
3. Give thanks to the Lord, (give thanks to the Lord.) He's been good to us,

(he's been good to us.) He for - gave our sin, (he for - gave our sin).
(he's been good to us.) Lis - tens when we call, (lis - tens when we call.)
(he's been good to us.) Sa - tis - fies our needs, (sa - tis - fies our needs.)

So we sing to him, (so we sing to him.) Died, so we can live,
Faith - ful when we fall, (faith - ful when we fall.) Mer - cy from your throne,
Di - sci - plines and feeds, (di - sci - plines and feeds.) He's our e - v'ry - thing,

(died, so we can live.) Praise is what we give, (praise is what we give.)
(mer - cy from your throne.) Hope in Christ a - lone,
(he's our e - v'ry - thing.) Wor - ship Christ the King!

Copyright © Sam Hargreaves/Jubilate Hymns, 4 Thorne Park Road, Torquay, TQ2 6RX www.jubilate.co.uk Used by permission

(hope in Christ a - lone.) Great is— the Lord and— most wor - thy— of praise,
(Wor - ship Christ the King!)

great is— the Lord most— high.—— Great is— the Lord and— most

wor - thy— of praise, great is— the Lord most— high.——

28

Glory to God,
the source of all our mission

LORD OF THE YEARS

Words: Chris Idle
Music: Michael Baughen

1. Glo - ry to God, the source of all our mis - sion; Je - sus be
2. Proud in our wealth, or de - sti - tute and bro - ken, we can - not
3. East - ward or west - ward, north-ward, south-ward mov - ing, find - ing new
4. Linked by the cross at which we are for - gi - ven, joined by the
5. Send us, Lord Christ, to serve at your di - rec - tion, dy - ing and

praised, the Sa - viour, Lord and Son! Praise to the Spi - rit who con-firms the
live by earth - ly bread a - lone; but by the word that God him-self has
fields, new pat - terns and new role, Christ's fel - low - wor - kers, all his good - ness
love that came to find and save, one in the hope of God's new earth and
liv - ing, yours in loss and gain, true to the Go - spel of your re - sur-

vi - sion; in all the world the will of God be done!
spo - ken, we are set free to make our Ma - ster known.
prov - ing, see how our God is mak - ing peo - ple whole!
hea - ven, we love and give since he first loved and gave.
rec - tion, work - ing and pray - ing till you come to reign.

Words: © Christopher Idle/Jubilate Hymns. Music: © Michael Baughen/Jubilate Hymns
4 Thorne Park Road, Torquay, TQ2 6RX. www.jubilate.co.uk Used by permission

29

God, you are my God
(Glory)

Johnny Parks

1. God, you are— my God,— there's no-one else— like— you;—
2. Death is o - ver - come,— for - gi - ven is— my— sin.—

— you glad - ly gave— your blood,— to bring me back— to you..
— Hea - ven is— my home,— you've wel-comed— me in.—

I will sing— your praise,— I will lift— your— name,-
I can't wait— to hear— the saints join in— one— song;—

(continued over...)

This song is recorded on the Spring Harvest Distinctive Sounds – Glory Album

Copyright © 2001 Thankyou Music/Adm. by worshiptogether.com songs excl. UK & Europe, adm. by Kingsway Music
tym@kingsway.co.uk Used by permission

71

30 God of mercy
(*In your mercy*)

Capo 3 (Em)
Slowly building

Calvin Hollingworth

God of mer - cy, Fa-ther in hea - ven, we con-fess that we have sinned. In our thoughts, our words and our deeds, we have not loved you with our whole heart, we have not loved our neigh - bours as our - selves. In your mer - cy, Lord, for-give what we have been. In your mer - cy, Lord, change what we are. In your

Copyright © Calvin Hollingworth

31

God, you're amazing

Capo 3 (D)
With an African township feel

Richard Swan

God, you're a-maz-ing and I want to sing, lift up my hands, giv-ing praise to the King. You've been so good to me, so I will say: 'Thank you, my God, for your bless-ings to-day!' Hal-le-lu-jah, hal-le-lu-jah, hal-le-lu-jah, hal-le-lu-jah to you. Hal-le-lu-jah, hal-le-lu-jah, hal-le-lu-jah, hal-le-lu-jah to you!

Chorus

Copyright © 2004 Golden Pen Music, 25 Manwood Road, Crofton Park, London, SE4 1AA. All rights reserved. Used by permission

32

Good and gracious

Gareth Robinson

Steadily

Verse

1. Good and gra - cious, att - ri - butes of a
2. Death and hell are now no lon - ger

lo - ving Fath - er, you're high and migh - ty, but
things I fear be - cause you have saved me and I'm

hum - ble all the same. You have made the hea - vens and
grate - ful to the core. I'm your child be - cause of Je -

Chorus

_ the earth, and you made us in your im - age, Lord. Ho - ly,
sus' blood, and your Spi - rit leads me, guides me, fills me.

(continued over...)

Copyright © 2001 Thankyou Music/Adm. by worshiptogether.com songs excl. UK & Europe, adm. by Kingsway Music
tym@kingsway.co.uk Used by permission.

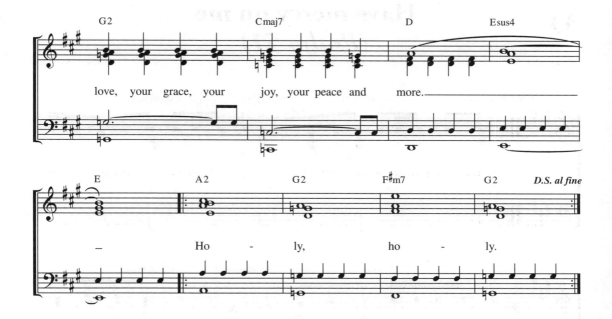

love, your grace, your   joy, your peace and   more._____

Ho - ly,   ho - ly.

32a A prayer for strength

Glorious and ever loving God,
you alone can bring order into our world of chaos.
So challenge the unruly passions of humankind
for the sake of truth and justice,
support us in our frailty and help us to stand upright;
that we may love your commandments and desire to fulfil your will,
until the great day comes when you will receive the whole of creation
into your complete joy.
Through Jesus Christ our Lord,
who is alive and reigns with you,
in the unity of the Holy Spirit, one God,
now and for ever.
Amen.

Copyright © 2005 Marie Birkinshaw

33

Have mercy on me
(Psalm 51)

Capo 2 (G)

Graham Kendrick

Copyright © 2005 Make Way Music, PO Box 263, Croydon, Surrey, CR9 5AP, UK
International copyright secured. All rights reserved. Used by permission.

(continued over...)

The role of the backing vocalist in worship

The character of a backing singer

* Secure in God – knowing what our role is as a part of the worship team and seeing the bigger picture.
* Secure in our gifting – not easily offended if we aren't asked to sing. Knowing that we have a gift from God and looking after it.
* Worshippers – not performers. We want to add our contribution without being distracting in the way we dress and in the way we sound.
* Having a professional manner – turning up on time and ready to sing. Having an encouraging, supportive attitude.
* Being a servant – going the extra mile, not just doing what suits you. Be prepared to serve in the small things as well as the big.
* Worship is a lifestyle, not a career!

Technique

* Most contemporary bands and worship music would require 3 parts – soprano (melody)/alto/tenor.
* The role of a BV is to add colour and emphasis in a song. Don't sing all the time!
* Before the worship time discuss with each other what part of the song should be harmonised. Arrange your parts and go over any parts of the song where phrasing is tricky.
* It is vital to listen to each other so that voices blend – it is not a solo performance. Backing singing requires a great measure of self-discipline.
* Remember to listen to what the other instruments are playing.
* Watch the worship leader closely – this helps you follow the song and to come off at the end of phrases at the same time.
* Extend your repertoire – make sure you are familiar with the old as well as the new songs.
* Be careful of adlibbing too much.

During the worship time

* Be alert – although you are worshipping God, you also need to watch the worship leader.
* Don't be inhibited in your worship – one of the most important things you do is model a worshipper to the congregation. This can really encourage them to participate and to direct their focus to the Lord.
* Be open to the gifts of the Holy Spirit – able to follow the flow of the worship time and bring prophetic input at the right time.

Lesley Parker is a worship school course director, vocalist and prophetic singer who arranges for and conducts choirs. Lesley has sung with Robin Mark, Stoneleigh band, Matt Redman, Paul Oakley and Kate Simmonds.

Here I am
(Majesty)

Stuart Garrard
& Martin Smith

Worshipfully, with strength

1. Here I am, hum-bled by your ma - je - sty,___
   hum - bled by the love that you give,___

   _ cov - ered by your grace___ so free.___
   _ for - gi - ven so that I can for - give.___

   Here I am, know - ing I'm a sin - ful man,___
   Here I stand, know - ing that I'm your de - sire,___

   cov - ered by the blood of the Lamb.___
   sanc - ti - fied by glo - ry and fire.___

   Now I've

This song is recorded on the Spring Harvest 2004 Live Worship Album

Copyright © 2003 Curious? Music. Rights administered by Bucks Music Group Ltd., 11 Uxbridge Street, London, W8 7TQ. Used by permission.

35

Hide me now
(Still)

Reuben Morgan

1. Hide me now under your wings. Cover me within your mighty hand.
2. rest, my soul in Christ alone. Know his pow'r in quietness and trust.

When the oceans rise and thunders roar, I will soar with you above the storm. Father, you are King over the flood;

Copyright © 2002 Reuben Morgan/Hillsong Publishing/Kingsway Music. tym@kingsway.co.uk For the UK. Used by permission.

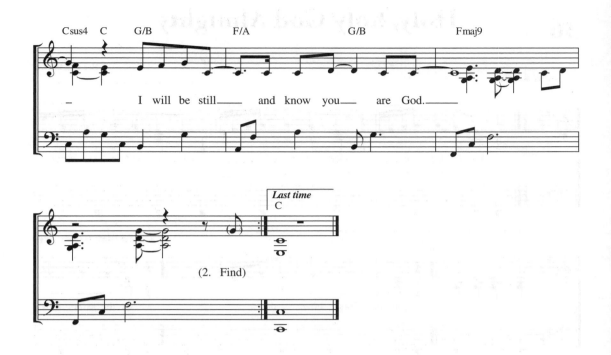

I will be still and know you are God.

(2. Find)

35a I cling to the cross

I cling to the cross
though strong winds try to blow me away.
I cling to the cross
though clever arguments attempt to prise me off.
I cling to the cross
and determine to stay close to my Saviour
– whatever may happen.

I will not be distracted.
I will not be deceived.
I will not be robbed of my security in Christ.

I will stand behind the cross, if necessary.
Christ will take the full force of the hurricane
while I hold tight to the foot of the cross
and take shelter until the storm has passed.

Copyright © 2004 Ruth Sermon

36

Holy, holy God Almighty

Brenton Brown

Copyright © 2001 Vineyard Songs (UK/Eire) admin. by CopyCare, P.O. Box 77, Hailsham, East Sussex, BN27 3EF, UK
music@copycare.com Used by permission.

(continued over...)

Coda

down. God of glo — ry,___ you're so wor - thy,___

1.2.3. all the saints bow___ down.___

4. ___ down.___

36a Prayer of humble access

We do not presume to come to this your table,
merciful Lord, trusting in our own righteousness,
but in your manifold and great mercies.
We are not worthy so much as to
gather up the crumbs under your table.
But you are the same Lord
whose nature is always to have mercy.
Grant us therefore, gracious Lord,
so to eat the flesh of your dear Son Jesus Christ
and to drink his blood,
that we may evermore dwell in him
and he in us.
Amen

From Common Worship: Services and Prayers for the Church of England. Copyright © The Archbishops' Council 2000

37

Holy Spirit, Breath of heaven

Geraldine Latty

Worshipfully

Ho - ly Spi - rit, Breath of hea - ven, Ho - ly
Spi - rit, breathe on us. Breathe us to a
qui - et still - ness

where we trust your love for us.
where we find your place for us.
where we know that you are God.

37a Breath of Jesus
John 20: 21–22

Jesus said, 'Peace be with you! As the Father has sent me, I am
sending you,' and with that he breathed on them and said, 'Receive
the Holy Spirit.'

This song is recorded on the Spring Harvest 2005 New Songs Album

Copyright © 2004 Thankyou Music/adm. by worshiptogether.com songs excl. UK & Europe, adm. by Kingsway Music
tym@kingsway.co.uk Used by permission

38

How easy we forget
(Break our hearts again)

Noel & Tricia Richards

1. How ea-sy we— for-get— that cross of shame,— where One who did— no wrong— took all the blame,— be-cause of love.

2. How ea-sy we— for-get— the love you show.— How wel-com-ing— you are— to e-v'ry-one— who cries to you.

(3.) wea-ry we— be-come— of do-ing good.— How deaf and blind— we are— to those who hurt,— who cry for help.

Chorus

Break our hearts a-gain.—

This song is recorded on the Spring Harvest 2005 New Songs Album

Copyright © 2004 Thankyou Music/Adm. by worshiptogether.com songs excl. UK & Europe, adm. by Kingsway Music
tym@kingsway.co.uk Used by permission

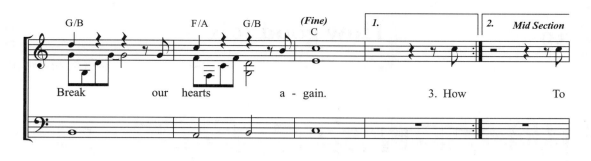

Break our hearts a - gain.   3. How   To

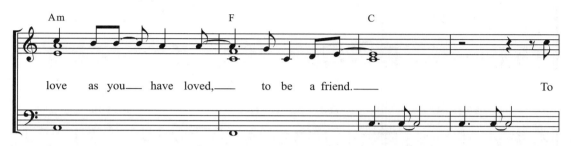

love as you___ have loved,___ to be a friend.___   To

com - fort those___ who mourn,___ and___ dry their tears.

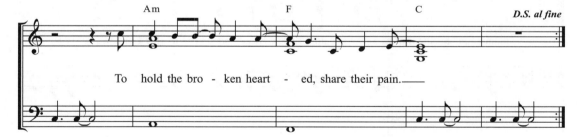

To hold the bro - ken heart - ed, share their pain.___

38a Call to worship and confession

As we join together for worship, let us come honestly before
Almighty God and acknowledge our shortcomings and the way we
have compromised our faith. May the springs of living water well up
within us, that we might be cleansed and renewed through our inner
being. May we be filled afresh with God's love and blessing that we
might serve others and the whole of the created order aright.
In the name of Christ. Amen.

Copyright © 2005 Marie Birkinshaw

How good it is

Keith & Kristyn Getty

39

How good it is, to give thanks un-to the Lord. How good it

is, to sing his prais-es. How good it is, to give

thanks un-to the Lord, sing-ing sweet prais-es to the Lord. *(Fine)*

Be thank-ful, e-v'ry boy and girl; sing it out, be thank-ful e-v'ry-

Copyright © 2002 Thankyou Music/Adm. by worshiptogether.com songs excl. UK & Europe, adm. by Kingsway Music
tym@kingsway.co.uk Used by permission.

one.   He's faith-ful___ to those who___ call___ up - on his

He's faith-ful, he can make you___ clean___ deep down in-

name,   Christ, the Lord of___ all.___ } How good it

side,   no mat - ter where you've___ been.___ }

39a   Sing praises

Psalm 47: 1–6

Clap your hands, all you nations;
shout to God with cries of joy.
How awesome is the Lord Most High,
the great King over all the earth!

He subdued nations under us,
peoples under our feet.
He chose our inheritance for us,
the pride of Jacob, whom he loved.

God has ascended amid shouts of joy,
the Lord amid the sounding of trumpets.
Sing praises to God, sing praises;
sing praises to our King, sing praises.

40

I am not alone
(God is watching)

Capo 2 (D)
Gently

Dave Bilbrough

Copyright © 2005 Dave Bilbrough Songs, PO Box 2612, Romford, RM2 5YB

I can only imagine

41

Bart Millard

(continued over...)

Copyright © 2001 Simpleville Music/Fun Attic Music Admin. by CopyCare, P.O. Box 77, Hailsham, East Sussex, BN27 3EF, UK. music@copycare. com Used by permission.

41a Blessing

May the blessing of the Father who created us,
the Son who died for us, and the Spirit that fills us,
be living in us now and for all time. Amen

Copyright © 2005 Nick Harding

42 I belong to you

Simply

Dave Bilbrough

I be-long to you, King of hea - ven.

Your pro-mi-ses— are true, e - ter-nal is your reign.

E - v'ry-thing— on earth is yours to give— you plea - sure.—

Cen-tered on— your will I am com-

This song is recorded on the Spring Harvest 2005 New Songs Album

Copyright © 2005 Dave Bilbrough Songs, PO Box 2612, Romford, RM2 5YB

43

I don't care what they say
(All day)

Capo 2 (A)

Marty Sampson

♩ = 122

1. I don't care what they say a - bout me,___ it's al -
2. I don't care what it costs a - ny more,___ 'cause

right, al - right. I don't care what they
you gave it all,_ and I'm fol - low - ing you. I don't care what it

think a - bout me,___ it's al - right,___ they'll get it one day.
takes a - ny - more,_ no mat - ter what hap - pens I'm go - ing your way.

I love you,___ I'll fol - low you,___ you are my,___ my___ life.

Copyright © 1999 Marty Sampson/Hillsongs Publishing/Kingsway Music tym@kingsway.co.uk For the UK. Used by permission

I lay my life down
(One way)

Capo 2 (A)

Joel Houston
& Jonathon Douglass

1. I lay my life down at your feet, you're the only
In troubled times it's you I seek, I put you first, that's

2. You are always, always there, e - v'ry how and
You will never, ever change; ye - ster - day, to -

one I need. I turn to you, and you are al - ways there.
all I need
e - v'ry-where, your grace a-bounds so deep - ly with - in me.
day the same,

I hum - ble all I am,
for - e - ver, 'till for - e -

all to you. Here we go.
- ver meets no end.

(continued over...)

Copyright © 2003 Joel Houston & Jonathon Douglass/Hillsong Publishing/Kingsway Music. tym@kingsway.co.uk. For the UK. Used by permission.

104

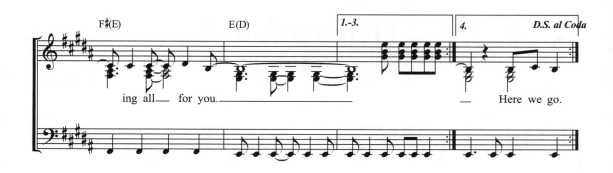

ing all— for you.＿＿＿＿＿

Here we go.

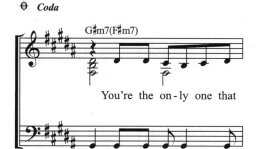

✠ *Coda*

You're the on-ly one that

I could live for.＿＿＿＿＿

44a Open our hearts
Based on Daniel 4:37

Let us open our hearts to the God who lives in light
and reveals all that is hidden.
Lord, all your works are truth;
forgive us when our lives are based on lies.

Lord, all your ways are justice;
forgive us when we are content with unfairness.

Lord, you bring low all who walk in pride;
grant us the humility to recognise our faults,
the strength to change our lives,
and the peace that your love brings. Amen.

Copyright © 2005 Mark Earey

45

I love you Lord

Gareth Robinson

With feeling

Verse

1. I love you,— Lord,— with all of my heart,— with
   love you,— Lord,— with all of my mind,— with

all my e - mo - tions and feel - ings and dreams.— I
e - ve - ry thought— now made cap - tive to you.— I

love you,— Lord,— with all of my soul,— with
love you,— Lord,— with all of my strength,— by

all of my will— and my con - sious in - tent.— With e-v'ry-thing— with-
put-ting to ac - tion the faith— I pro-fess.—

Chorus

This song is recorded on the Spring Harvest 2005 New Songs Album

Copyright © 2004 Thankyou Music/Adm. by worshiptogether.com songs excl. UK & Europe, adm. by Kingsway Music
tym@kingsway.co.uk Used by permission

(continued over...)

in me,— Lord,— be glo - ri - fied.— I love you, for you

first loved— me.— I love you, for you

first loved— me.

45a Trust and confidence

Lord, your servant Daniel showed complete trust and confidence
in your sovereign power, despite oppression and persecution in a
foreign land. May we too find courage to stand against all pressure
to compromise and conform our beliefs to what we know is not in
accordance with your will. Show your power at work among your
people, and develop your gifts within us to help others to reach their
God-given potential.
In the name of Christ
Amen.

Copyright © 2005 Marie Birkinshaw

Small Group worship – singing to a CD

How do we turn singing to a CD in a small group from a self-conscious mumble to a liberated, God-centred experience? Here are some pointers for getting your small group singing:

Stand up – this frees all of the physiological singing apparatus to work properly and also encourages everyone to join in fully. Acoustically you are nearer the ceiling than the carpet so the sound will be much fuller than if you were sitting. Choosing to sit when everyone is standing is much easier than standing when everyone else is sitting!

Turn in up – ten voices in a lounge will be a lot louder than the volume at which you might normally listen to a CD for pleasure. You need to turn the CD up to match the voices otherwise the group will sing as quietly as the CD and will also struggle to keep in step with the recording.

Plan – plan your worship songs and if possible let them flow so that there isn't too much stopping to shuffle CD cases between songs.

Praise » thanksgiving » response
Begin with a song about who God is, helping us to give him praise and glory simply because he is worthy. This should be the easiest song for others to join in with because it doesn't depend on how we are feeling, or what we are experiencing. Then move into thanksgiving for what God has done which is more subjective and is based around our lives with God.

It is from here that we begin to respond from our hearts. This could be with a prepared song or more spontaneous. Maybe you could sing one or two songs of praise and thanksgiving and then have an open time of prayer as you respond to God and the things you have been singing about. You could then find another song, which encapsulates that response, and sing it at the end. Of course we don't want to stop with 'what we think' but to listen to God too.

Develop the spontaneous – if you have the CD at a reasonable volume you could try singing spontaneously at any point during the songs and particularly when the recorded singers do so. Encourage your group to choose a single line eg: 'Jesus is Lord' or 'I love you' and sing it gently over the accompaniment, inventing their own tune as they go. Keep it simple and repetitive.

Some people may like to sing in tongues, or speak out scripture verses, or maybe God will inspire someone to sing prophetically. The key in helping people have the confidence to experiment is to keep it gentle and simple, almost under your breath, as you develop confidence.

Taken from 'Cell worship Leaders Guide' by Joel Payne,
Music Co-ordinator, St Michael le Belfrey, York.

46
I'm here to meet with you
(Meet with me)

Lamont Hiebert

With energy
♩ = 100 *Verse*

I'm here —— to meet —— with you, —— come —— and meet —— with me. —— I'm here —— to find —— you, —— re-veal —— your-self —— to me. As I wait —— you make —— me strong. —— As I long, —— you draw me to —— your —— arms. —— As I stand ——

Copyright © 1999 Maranatha! Music admin. by CopyCare, P.O. Box 77, Hailsham, East Sussex, BN27 3EF, UK
music@copycare.com Used by permission.

and sing—— your praise,—— you come, you come—— and you fill——

— this—— place. Won't you come, won't you come and fill—— this——place?——

As I wait—

47

I'm trading my sorrows
(Yes, Lord)

Darrell Evans

Copyright © 1998 Integrity's Hosanna! Music/Sovereign Music UK. PO Box 356, Leighton Buzzard, LU7 3WP, UK. sovereignmusic@aol.com

48

I need you like the rain
(Beautiful)

Samuel Lane

Capo 3(C)

1. I need you like the rain, come to me
2. I need you to be here, come to me,

and sing a - gain. I long for
I can feel you near. I love you,

your love so much, I've wan - ted
you are my hope: you love me

Copyright 2002 Vineyard Songs (UK/Eire) adm. CopyCare, P.O. Box 77, Hailsham, East Sussex, BN27 3EF, UK
music@copycare.com Used by permission

115

In Christ alone

49

Capo 1 (D)
Steadily

Stuart Townend
& Keith Getty

1. In Christ a - lone my hope is found, he is my light, my strength, my
2. In Christ a - lone - who took on flesh, ful - ness of God in help - less
3. There in the ground his bo - dy lay; light of the world by dark - ness
4. No guilt in life, no fear in death, this is the pow'r of Christ in

song; this cor - ner - stone, this so - lid ground, firm through the
babe! This gift of love and right-eous - ness, scorned by the
slain. Then burst - ing forth in glo - rious day up from the
me; from life's first cry to fi - nal breath, Je - sus com-

fier - cest drought and storm. What heights of love, what depths of
ones he came to save. Till on that cross as Je - sus
grave he rose a - gain! And as he stands in vic - to -
mands my de - sti - ny. No pow'r of hell, no scheme of

Copyright © 2001 Thankyou Music/Adm. by worshiptogether.com songs excl. UK & Europe, adm. by Kingsway Music
tym@kingsway.co.uk Used by permission.

peace,   when fears are   stilled,   when striv - ings   cease!   My com - for-
died,   the wrath of   God   was sa - tis - fied   -   for e - v'ry
ry   sin's curse has   lost   its grip on   me,   for I am
man   can e - ver   pluck   me from his   hand;   till he re-

ter,   my all in   all,   here in the   love of Christ I   stand.
sin   on him was   laid;   here in the   death of Christ I   live.
his   and he is   mine - bought with the   pre - cious blood of   Christ.
turns   or calls me   home,   here in the   pow'r of Christ I'll   stand!

49a Your church

Gracious God, we are your church.
May your church be filled with your vision, and clear in our message.
May your church be a light in the darkness,
and show love in hard places.
May your church be bold in mission, and motivated by change.
Gracious God, we are your church.
May we be all these things and more. **Amen.**

Copyright © 2005 Nick Harding

117

50

In heaven and earth
(Praise the Lord in all the earth)

Noel Richards

Strong rock style

In heav'n and earth,___ there is none like him;___
the Lord of lords,___ the___ King of kings.___
vic - to - ri - ous.___ Praise the Lord___ in all___ the earth,___
___ praise the Lord.___ Praise the Lord___ in all___ the earth,___

He came to earth___ to___ die for us:___
God raised him up___

This song is recorded on the Spring Harvest 2005 New Songs Album

Copyright © 2004 Thankyou Music/Adm. by worshiptogether.com songs excl. UK & Europe, adm. by Kingsway Music
tym@kingsway.co.uk Used by permission

praise the Lord._____ We will wor -

ship with___ one voice,___ in our King___ we will___ re - joice._

We will make___ his glo - ry___ known.___

E - v'ry na - tion, tribe___ and tongue,___ they will know___ what he___ has done,_

when we make___ his glo - ry___ known.___

D.S. al fine

51 In him I have believed

Capo 3 (D)

Kate Simmonds

Brightly

1. In him I have be-lieved, on this my hope now rests, that
2. A peo-ple born of God, u-ni-ted by your call, one
3. What-e-ver trials may come, in faith, Lord, help us stand for
4. And on that fi-nal day, the ci-ti-zens of heav'n, called

Je-sus Christ is ri-sen from the dead! The
faith, one Lord, one Fa-ther of us all. Joined
righ-teous-ness and jus-tice in our land. What
out to be the new Je-ru-sa-lem, in

all-sur-pas-sing joy of know-ing Christ my Lord, the
with the bonds of love, and plan-ted in your house, we
fear can hold us now? We run to-ward the prize, our
mul-ti-tudes will bow down be-fore the throne of God: one

for-mer things, I count them all as loss. Called out of
wor-ship you with hearts and lives poured out. Let us go
lives al-rea-dy cru-ci-fied with Christ! Through e-v'ry
na-tion called from e-v'ry tribe and tongue. Great ce-le-

Copyright © 2004 Thankyou Music/Adm. by worshiptogether.com songs excl. UK & Europe, adm. by Kingsway Music
tym@kingsway.co.uk Used by permission

Bb(G) F(D) C/E(A) F(D) F/A(D) Bb(G) F(D)

dark - ness in - to your good - ness, we are your chil - dren,
on in the pow'r of your Spi - rit, tak - ing your go - spel
nat - ion your king - dom ad - van - ces; who can ex - tin - guish
bra - tion! The glo - ri - ous u - nion: The Li - on of Ju - dah

C(A) F/A(D) Bb(G) F(D)

cho - sen in___ Christ.___ Now in your fa - mily,
to all the___ world,___ de - clar - ing your wis - dom,
this spread - ing___ flame?___ Through tri - bu - la - tions
and the pure, spot - less___ bride!___ All of cre - a - tion

C/E(A) F(D) Gm7(Em7)

heirs of the pro - mise, to your pur - pose on the
our great com - mis - sion, that Je - sus Christ has
we'll stand on your pro - mise: 'I will build my church and
waits for this mo - ment, all your pro - mi - ses ful -

(v.2)

Csus4 (Asus4) C(A) F(D)

earth I give my life.
come to save the lost.
hell will not pre - vail!'
filled in Je - sus Christ!

In the shadow of the cross

52

Ken Riley

1. In the sha-dow of the cross, by the my-ste-ry of grace
2. In the sha-dow of the cross, by the po-wer of your blood

I am saved. In the mi-ra-cle of hope,
I am saved. In your gift of sa-cri-fice,

where our sins are washed a-way, we give you praise.
where the guil-ty are set free, we give you praise.

Chorus

Bles-sed be your name in all the earth, bles-sed be your

Copyright © 2004 McKenzie Music

In you we live

53

Graham Kendrick
Arr. R. Lewis

Steadily

In you__ we live, Je-sus, in you__ we move.

In you__ we breathe, Je-sus, in you__ we love. And we are

your bo-dy here, we are your bo-dy here.

Copyright © 2002 Make Way Music, P.O. Box 263, Croydon, CR9 5AP, UK. International copyright secured. All rights reserved. Used by permission.

Your touch - our hands, your words - our voice, your way - our feet,
You give - we share, you lead - we go, you send - we serve,

your tears— in our eyes, } your Spi-rit is here.
you build— and we grow, }

Verse

1. A - cross— the world you're mov-ing; the sound— of prayer
2. You are— the light that's dawn-ing, you are— the hope

is grow-ing strong - er, from e - v'ry tribe
trans-form-ing all things; free - ing— the whole

1st time through repeat v 1 only
2nd time sing both verses.

and na-tion join-ing— in one sal - va-tion song._____
cre - a-tion to join— in one sal - va-tion

(continued over...)

song,_____ one song.

(One song.) In you__ we live, Je-sus, in you__ we move.
In you__ we breathe, Je-sus, in you__ we love.

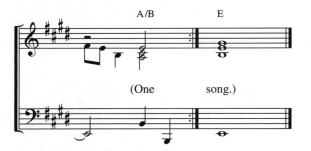

(One song.)

53a Open-hearted God

From Acts 11

Open-hearted God,
let us never close our hearts to those for whom Christ died.
God of all creation,
let us call nothing unclean that your love has embraced.
God of new horizons,
send your Holy Spirit to guide and direct us,
now and always.
Amen.

Copyright © 2005 Mark Earey

54 Into your hands I commit again
(With all I am)

Reuben Morgan

1. In - to your hands_____ I com-mit a - gain,
2. I'll walk with you_____ wher - e - ver you go,

_____ all I am for you, Lord._____ You hold my world_____
_ through tears and_ joy,_____ I'll trust in_ you. And I will live_____

_ in the palm of your_ hand,_____ and I am_ yours_____ for - e - ver.
_ in_ all of your_ ways,_____ and your pro - mi - ses_____ for - e - ver.

_
_

Je - sus, I_ be - lieve_____ in you._

(continued over...)

This song is recorded on the Spring Harvest 2005 New Songs Album

Copyright © 2003 Reuben Morgan/Hillsong Publishing/Kingsway Music. tym@kingsway.co.uk For the UK. Used by permission

128

I will wor - ship,— I will wor - ship— you.—

1. I will wor - 2. Je-sus, I— be-lieve— with all— I— am.

54a Nan's Blessing

I'll never understand the love
the Lord Jesus has for you,
I'll never understand how much he loves you.
But this much I know:
that he loves you,
he loves you with all of his heart,
and you are so precious to him.

Copyright © Northumbria Community Trust Ltd, Hetton Hall, Chatton, Northumberland, NE66 5SD.

It is by your mighty power

Copyright © 2003 Thankyou Music/Adm. by worshiptogether.com songs excl. UK & Europe, adm. by Kingsway Music
tym@kingsway.co.uk Used by permission.

a-bove all rule_ and reign_ and all_ au-tho-ri-ty._ Yet you_

have come to live_ in us,_ and it is by_ your migh-ty pow-er we be-lieve._

1.,2.   3.

2. You en - a -
3. When the clouds_

55a Let's go to God

Let's go to God together,
and feel his welcoming embrace.

Let's go to God together,
and know his overwhelming generosity.

Let's go to God together,
and receive.

Let's go to God together,
and be blessed.

As we marvel at God's generosity and overflow with his joy,
so we are eager to share this most holy and devoted God
with others who are empty. Amen.

Copyright © 2004 Ruth Sermon

56 It's time to make a declaration
(Declaration)

Unhurried ♩ = 130

Dave Bilbrough

1. It's time to make a de-cla - ra-tion, that I will live my life for you. The fields are white for har-vest, the la-bou-rers are few, yes, what-ever, Lord, you ask me I will__ do.

2. It's time to make a de-cla - ra-tion, that I will live my life for you. Free-ly you have gi-ven, free-ly I've re-ceived, so where-ever, Lord, you send me I will__

3. It's time to make a de-cla - ra-tion, that I will live my life for you. I'm rea-dy to see vi-sions, I'm rea-dy to see dreams, your will find ex-pres-sion in my__

Copyright © 2005 Dave Bilbrough Songs, PO Box 2612, Romford, RM2 5YB

133

57

I've been made rich
(Everybody)

Jonathan James

I've been made rich____ by his___ love for me, a child of the Most___ High, the One who res - cued me.___ I've been made strong____ by his___ Spi - rit in me, filled with his po - wer to see a na - tion changed.____ He is my Fa - ther,

Jonathan James (Abundant Life Ministries, Bradford, England). Copyright © 2003 Thankyou Music/Adm. by worshiptogether.com songs
excl. UK & Europe, adm. by Kingsway Music tym@kingsway.co.uk Used by permission

(continued over...)

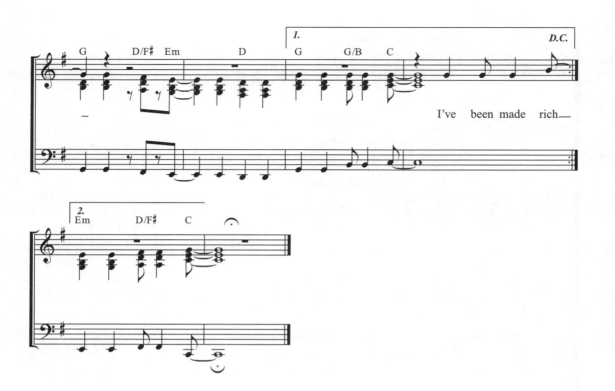

I've been made rich—

57a Prayer for power for living in the present

Now is the time for us to live as kingdom people,
called out of darkness into marvellous light.
Share the Spirit's gifts for the glory of Jesus,
receive the riches of God's love and mercy.

Blow mighty winds of heaven,
come holy fire, return,
renew your truth in us,
come, Holy Spirit, burn.
Release our tongues to speak out
that all may hear of you,
make us true witnesses of Christ the living Lord.
Amen

Copyright © 2005 Marie Birkinshaw

58

I've had questions
(When the tears fall)

Tim Hughes

1. I've had ques - tions with-out an - swers, I've known sor - row,
2. In the lone hour of my sor - row, through the dark - est

I have known pain.— But there's one thing, that I'll cling to;
night of my soul,— you sur - round me and sus - tain me;

you are faith - ful, Je - sus, you're true.
my de - fen - der, for - e - ver more.—

When hope is lost,

I'll call you Sa - viour.— When pain sur-rounds, I'll call you heal - er.—

(continued over...)

This song is recorded on the Spring Harvest 2005 New Songs Album and the Spring Harvest 2004 Live Worship Album

Copyright © 2003 Thankyou Music/Adm. by worshiptogether.com songs excl. UK & Europe, adm. by Kingsway Music
tym@kingsway.co.uk Used by permission.

I'll call you Sa - viour.___ When pain sur-rounds, I'll call you heal - er.___

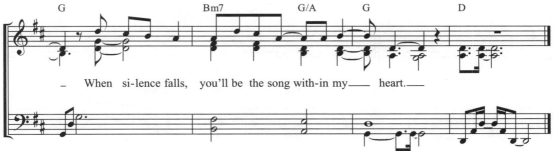

_ When si-lence falls, you'll be the song with-in my___ heart.___

58a The desert

Everywhere the emptiness stretches:
yet you fill all things.

The land is dry:
yet you give living water.

Bones lie bleached in the sun:
yet you promise life.

Death comes close and rattles in my throat:
breathe your song into my mouth, into my heart.

Copyright © 2005 Paul Sheppy

59 I've come to wash my soul
(I shall be clean again)

Capo 3 (D)

Graham Kendrick

1. I've come to wash my soul in the liv-ing wa-ter,
   bathe my eyes in your word, Lord Je-sus,
   I've been bought with the blood of Je-sus,

wash my heart in your cleans-ing stream. Here is mer-cy
cleanse my thoughts, my i-ma-gin-ings. May these eyes see
now my life is not my own; a tem-ple ho-ly,

and for-give-ness: I shall be clean a-gain, I shall be
as your love sees: light flood my be-ing, light flood my
for you on-ly where you are loved and known, where you are

clean a-gain. 2. I've come to -ing. O
be- known.
loved and

This song is recorded on the Spring Harvest 2005 New Songs Album

Copyright © 2005 Make Way Music, PO Box 263, Croydon, Surrey, CR9 5AP, UK.
International copyright secured. All rights reserved. Used by permission.

59a You have numbered our days

From Daniel 5: 24–28

O Lord, you have numbered our days,
you have weighed us in the scales of justice and found us wanting,
you have divided us and limited the damage we can do.
Help us to see with your eyes and to serve with your strength,
through Jesus Christ our Lord.
Amen

Copyright © 2005 Mark Earey

60 I will bless the Lord forever
(Made me glad)

Capo 3(D)

Miriam Webster

This song is recorded on the Spring Harvest 2004 Live Worship Album

Copyright © 2001 Miriam Webster/Hillsong Publishing/Kingsway Music. tym@kingsway.co.uk For the UK. Used by permission.

(continued over...)

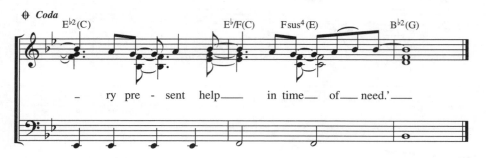

ry pre - sent help___ in time___ of___ need.'___

60a Faith

Lord give me faith, faith in my foreign land
Lord give me faith, faith for my future
Lord give me faith, faith in my fire
Lord give me faith, faith in your faithfulness.

Copyright © 2005 Nick Harding

I will return to you
(Open arms - Prodigal Song)

With intensity

Andy Flannagan

(continued over...)

This song is recorded on the Spring Harvest 2005 New Songs Album

Copyright © 2002 Daybreak Music Ltd, PO Box 2848, Eastbourne, East Sussex, BN20 7XP. All rights reserved. info@daybreakmusic.co.uk.
International copyright secured. Used by permission.

throw my-self._ Into your o-pen arms, in-to your o-pen arms,_

in-to your o-pen arms, your arms of sav - ing grace._

61a Always with God

From Hebrews 13: 5–6

God has said, 'Never will I leave you; never will I forsake you.'
So we say with confidence:
The Lord is my helper; I will not be afraid.
What can man do to me?

Jesus, hear my prayer
(Let it come)

62

Ryan Delmore

Copyright © 1999 Mercy/Vineyard Publishing admin. CopyCare, P.O. Box 77, Hailsham, East Sussex, BN27 3EF, UK
music@copycare.com Used by permission.

149

63

Jesus, I could sing
(If I have not love)

Matt Redman

1. Je-sus, I could sing in the tongues of men and an-gels, but
(2.) Je-sus, I could pray with a faith that moves a moun-tain, but
(3.) o-ver-flow of hearts, as we gaze up-on your beau-ty, a re-

1.

if I have not love I am just a clang-ing cym-bal, an emp-ty
if I have not love it is just a noise re-sound-ing, an emp-ty
flec-tion of your worth, for we've seen a glimpse of you in your glo-ry,

Repeat verse each time *2.*

sound. just a clang-ing cym-bal, an emp-ty
sound. 2. And just a noise re-sound-ing, an emp-ty
Lord. 3. It's the seen a glimpse of you in your glo-ry,

(Fine) *Chorus*

sound. This is a love song, this is a love
sound.
Lord.

Copyright © 2004 Thankyou Music/Adm. by worshiptogether.com songs excl. UK & Europe, adm. by Kingsway Music
tym@kingsway.co.uk Used by permission

song, Je-sus, a love___ song___ to__ you.___ A song of de-vo-

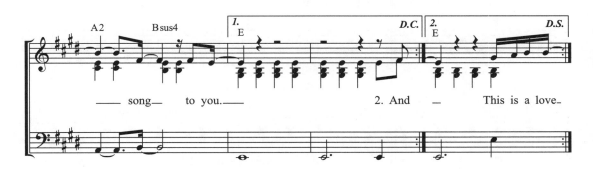

-tion,___ a re-ve-rent pas - sion,___ Sa-viour, a love

___ song___ to you.___ 2. And ___ This is a love__

3. It's the

64

Jesus, I stand for you
(I stand for you)

John Ellis

$\quad \mathbf{J} = 88$

1. Je - sus, I stand for you, no mat - ter what you lead me
   sus, I've stood my ground when un - be - lief was all a -

through,_____ they will chase me out____ and close me down,____ but Je - sus,____
round._____ I have felt the sting____ re - jec - tion brings,____ but Je - sus,____

_ I'll stand for you. I'll al - ways stand, I'll al - ways____ stand, I'll

Last time to Coda ⊕

al - ways stand for you. I'll al - ways stand, I'll al - ways____ stand, I'll

Copyright © 2003 Mouthfulofsongs/Birdwing Music/Near Bliss Music. All rights administered by EMI Christian Music Publishing.
For Europe: Unisong Music Publishers, Holland.

(continued over...)

65 Jesus is Lord

Stuart Townend
& Keith Getty

Majestically

1. 'Je-sus is Lord' – the cry that e-choes through cre-a-tion:
2. Je-sus is Lord – whose word su-stains the stars and pla-nets,
3. Je-sus is Lord – the tomb is glo-ri-ous-ly emp-ty!
4. 'Je-sus is Lord' – a shout of joy, a cry of an-guish,

re-splen-dent power, e-ter-nal word, our rock. The Son of
yet in his wis-dom, laid a-side his crown. Je-sus the
Not e-ven death could crush this King of love! The price is
as he re-turns, and e-very knee bows low. Then e-very

God, the King whose glo-ry fills the hea-vens, yet bids us
man, who washed our feet, who bore our suf-fering, be-came a
paid, the chains are loosed, and we're for-gi-ven, and we can
eye and e-very heart will see his glo-ry, the judge of

come to taste this liv-ing bread.
curse to bring sal-va-tion's plan.
run in-to the arms of God.
all will take his chil-dren home.

Fine

Copyright © 2003 Thankyou Music/Adm. by worshiptogether.com songs excl. UK & Europe, adm. by Kingsway Music
tym@kingsway.co.uk Used by permission.

66 Jesus, lead us to the Father
(Gathering song)

3 part round
Not too fast

Sam Hargreaves

*This is a cumulative round. Part 1 sings first,
then is joined by part 2. Finally all 3 parts sing together.*

Copyright © Sam Hargreaves/Jubilate Hymns, 4 Thorne Park Road, Torquay, TQ2 6RX www.jubilate.co.uk Used by permission

Using solo instruments in worship

Solo instruments bring new colour and life to our worship and often 'speak' in ways that is just not possible when everyone is playing and singing together. Often we don't use the ranges or expression or 'colours' available to us – like an artist who only uses limited colours from their palette!

Using specific instruments

Every instrument provides a new colour and can express worship in different ways.

- A brass instrument such as a french horn or trumpet is an obvious choice for 'proclamation' – for example in a song that speaks of the majesty of God.
- A string instrument such as a violin or cello could be perfect for enhancing a song that speaks of the beauty or love of God.
- A solo flute could express God's peace. An oboe has a plaintive quality to it, so could express 'longing for God' or his longing for us.
- Some 'band' instruments, such as electric guitar, could speak of the greatness of God, or expressing abandonment in worship.
- Drums or other percussion instruments could express conflict or strength.

Most instruments can express all sorts of emotions – we need to learn what they are capable of and are best used for!

What are the best contexts for using solo instruments?

- Introducing a song – setting the scene or mood. A nice gentle flute may not be the best instrument to use to introduce a song of proclamation, a loud electric guitar may not be the best for introducing a song which speaks of God's peace!
- A solo in the middle of a song, giving an opportunity to reflect on what has been sung or to 'colour' words. Learn to give way if someone else clearly has something to offer in terms of a solo!
- A solo without other instruments playing. God can often 'speak' to people in this way – reminding them of his love or sharing something on his heart.
- In the context of healing. Music often touches the heart and not just the mind. Playing over people can bring healing and relief (see 1 Sam 16:23)
- In intercession. Using solo instruments touches our hearts and helps us to identify more with the subject we're praying for.
- As a background to reading scripture or poetry – again adding life and expression to the words that are being spoken.

Richard Williamson, Wellspring

67 Jesus, you humbled yourself

Gareth Robinson

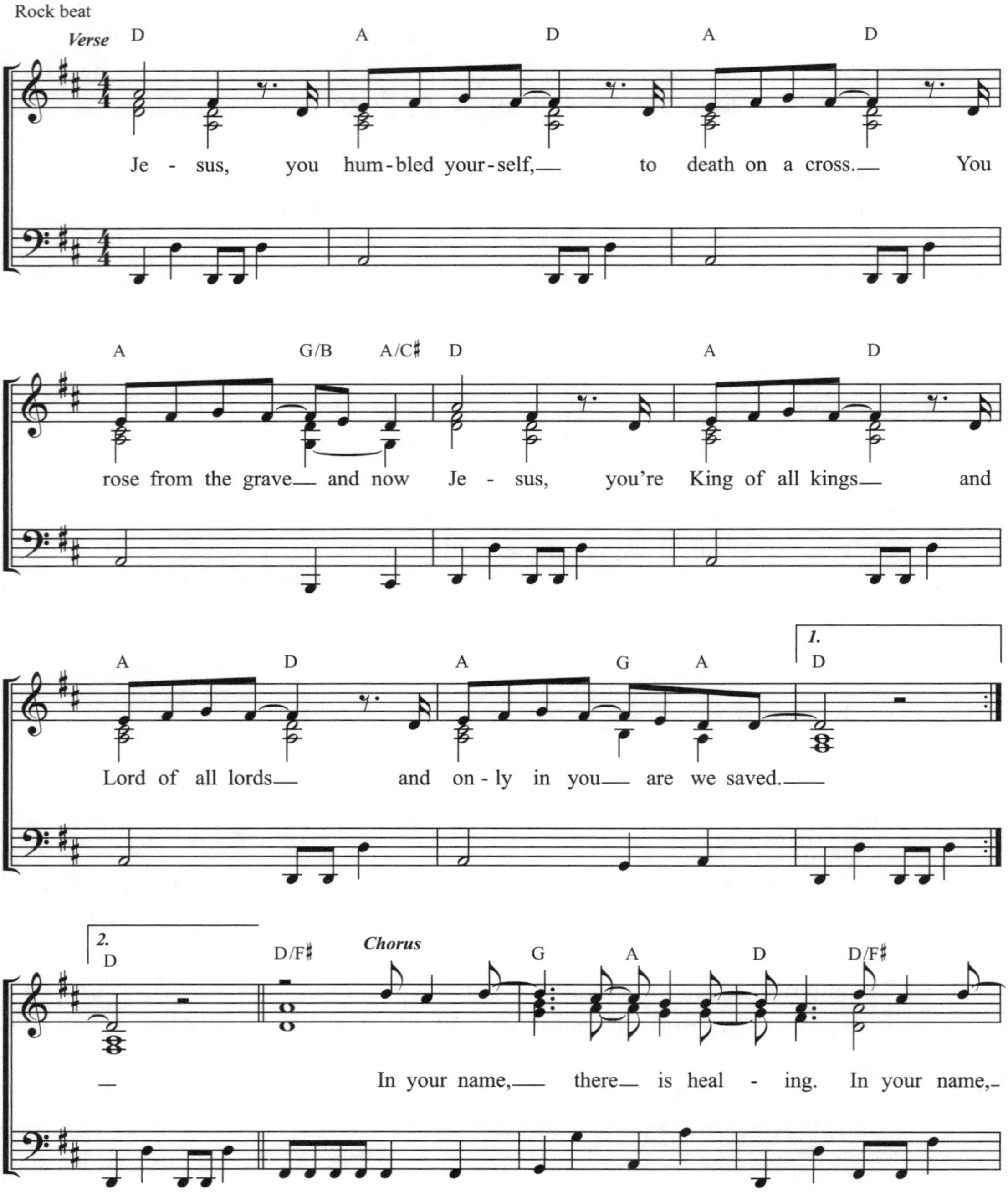
Rock beat
Verse
D A D A D
Je - sus, you hum-bled your-self, to death on a cross. You
A G/B A/C♯ D A D
rose from the grave and now Je - sus, you're King of all kings and
A D A G A 1. D
Lord of all lords and on - ly in you are we saved.
2. D D/F♯ Chorus G A D D/F♯
In your name, there is heal - ing. In your name,

Copyright © 2004 Thankyou Music/Adm. by worshiptogether.com songs excl. UK & Europe, adm. by Kingsway Music
tym@kingsway.co.uk Used by permission

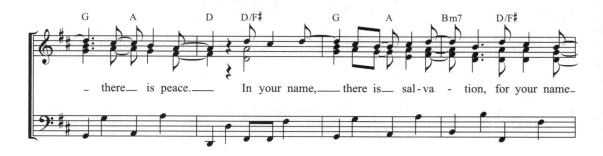

there— is peace.—— In your name,—— there is— sal-va - tion, for your name—

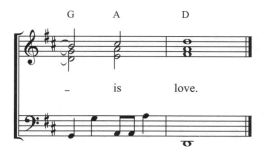

— is love.

67a The Lord's prayer

As our Saviour has taught us, so we pray

Our Father in heaven,
hallowed be your name,
your kingdom come,
your will be done,
on earth as in heaven.
Give us today our daily bread.
Forgive us our sins
as we forgive those who sin against us.
Lead us not into temptation
but deliver us from evil.
For the kingdom, the power,
and the glory are yours
now and for ever. Amen.

From Common Worship: Services and Prayers for the Church of England. Copyright © The Archbishops' Council 2000

Jesus, your name

Keith and Kristyn Getty
& Ian Hannah

Simple and powerful

1. Je - sus, your name, Prince of peace, qui - ets my soul, trea - sures the least. In per - fect rest____ you will keep all whose hope is in you. Je - sus, your name can si - lence the storms, the striv - ings that
2. Je - sus your name, Coun - sel - lor, won - der - ful way, life's com - for - ter. Spi - rit of truth de - fend - ing me though in me was the blame. Je - sus, your name has stood in my place and freed me from
3. Je - sus your name, migh - ty God, all pow'r - ful one rul - ing in love. There is a King up - on the throne earth can - not o - ver - throw. Je - sus, your name, great ban - ner of hope, stea - dies the

Copyright © 2004 Thankyou Music/Adm. by worshiptogether.com songs excl. UK & Europe, adm. by Kingsway Music
tym@kingsway.co.uk Used by permission

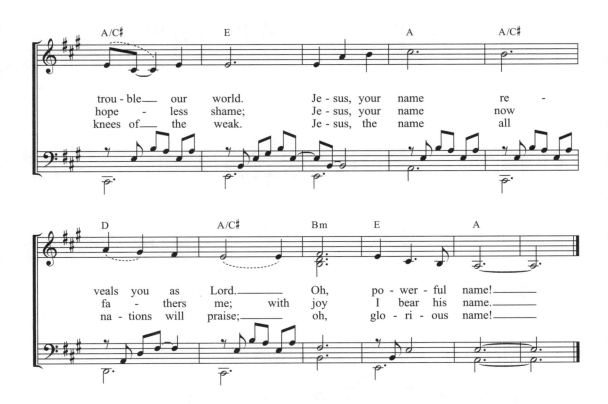

trou - ble___ our world. Je - sus, your name re -
hope - less shame; Je - sus, your name now
knees of___ the weak. Je - sus, the name all

veals you as Lord.___ Oh, po - wer - ful name!___
fa - thers me; with joy I bear his name.___
na - tions will praise;___ oh, glo - ri - ous name!___

68a Be still

Let your aching heart express itself.

Be still.
Do not fear what may be released.
In God's presence all is made safe.
Be still.

Be still.
Offer your heart to God –
he will receive you and shelter you,
until it is time for healing.

Be still.
Be with God.
Be whole.

Copyright © 2003 Ruth Sermon

69 Let love be found among us

NETTLETON

Celtic feel

Words: Martin Leckebusch
Tune: American trad.
Arr. David Peacock

1. Let love be found among us - the gift of God it is, the hall-mark of his chil-dren, the sign that we are his. We claim that God has called us; no idle boast or fraud, if

rea-son God has loved us is simply sov-'reign choice; our love is but an e-cho to his re-sound-ing voice: for God is love, and showed it by giving us his Son: through

deep-ly God has loved us, ac-cept-ing us as friends; so let us show each o-ther this love which ne-ver ends: for though we can-not find him with sight or touch or sound, yet

Words: Martin E Leckebusch. Copyright © Kevin Mayhew Ltd.
Music arrangement copyright © David Peacock/Jubilate Hymns, 4 Thorne Park Road, Torquay, TQ2 6RX www.jubilate.co.uk Used by permission

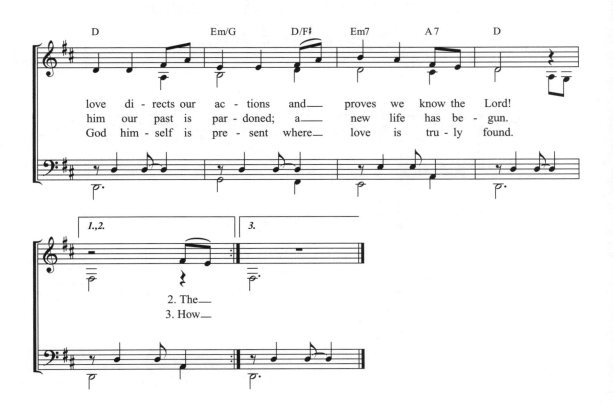

love di - rects our ac - tions and___ proves we know the Lord!
him our past is par - doned; a___ new life has be - gun.
God him - self is pre - sent where___ love is tru - ly found.

2. The___
3. How___

Copyright © 2005 Nick Harding

69a We have come together

We have come together as your children
We have come together as your children

We have come together as your church
We have come together as your church

We have come to be challenged
We have come to be challenged

We have come to be changed
We have come to be changed

70 Let our praises rise like incense
(Before the Lord)

Jo Boyce

Copyright © 2004 CJM Music Ltd www.cjmmusic.com

71 Lift up your heads

Words: James Montgomery (1771 - 1854) (Moravian hymn book)
Adpt. & music: Godfrey Birtill

1. Lift up your heads you gates of brass!
2. You ar - mies of the liv - ing God
3. O fear not, faint not, halt not now;
4. Up - lif - ted are the gates of brass,

You bars of i - ron yield!
stand in your Cap - tain's might.
don't quit, like men be strong.
the gates of i - ron yield.

And let the King of glo - ry pass; the cross is
Go where no hal - lowed feet have trod, a - rise my
To Christ shall e - v'ry na - tion bow and sing with
Be - hold the King of glo - ry pass: the cross has

in the field._____ Al - le - lu - ia, al - le - lu - ia,
war - rior bride!_____
you this song._____
won the field!_____

Music & words adpt. copyright © 2003 Thankyou Music/Adm. by worshiptogether.com songs excl. UK & Europe, adm. by Kingsway Music
tym@kingsway.co.uk Used by permission

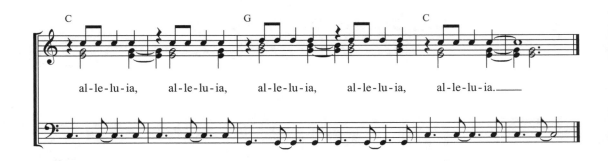

al-le-lu-ia, al-le-lu-ia, al-le-lu-ia, al-le-lu-ia, al-le-lu-ia.____

71a God of the whole world

God of the whole world, Lord of heaven and earth,
you made the whole human race. You have shown to us in Christ
the mystery of your purpose: you chose us all in Christ
to praise his glory.

You will bring all things together under Christ, all things in heaven,
all things on earth, under him as head: you chose us all in Christ
to praise his glory.

We have heard the word of truth, the good news of salvation,
you have stamped us with the seal of your Spirit of promise:
you chose us all in Christ
to praise his glory.

We who once were far away have been brought near
by the blood of Christ: you chose us all in Christ
to praise his glory.

He is the peace between us, and has broken down the barrier of
hostility. He has made us one new humanity and reconciled
us to you by the cross: you chose us all in Christ
to praise his glory.

He killed hostility and brought peace, peace to all near at hand,
peace to all far away: you chose us all in Christ
to praise his glory.

Through him we come, by the Spirit, to you, our Father in heaven,
saying:
Holy, holy, holy Lord, God of power and might,
heaven and earth are full of your glory. Hosanna in the highest.

From New Patterns for Worship (Church House Publishing 2002). Copyright © The Archbishops' Council 2002

72 Long before we were created
(The story of grace)

Geraldine Latty

1. Long be-fore we were cre-a-ted,
2. We're a part of his own fam-ily,
3. This is our Fa-ther's sto-ry,

at the dawn of space and time, God e-ter-nal, great and migh-ty
sim-ply through the love of Christ, what a per-fect, all em-brac-ing,
this is our Ma-ker's praise, and by the Spi-rit we're the

had us on his mind. He de-vised and set be-fore us,
self-less sa-cri-fice. God has thought of e-v'ry op-tion,
sto-ry of his grace. Us-ing or-di-na-ry peo-ple,

an a-ma-zing, per-fect plan, that would de-mon-strate to all the
he's pro-vi-ded all we need; that the weak, the strong, the rich, the
us-ing bro-ken jars of clay, he'll dis-play the grace that e-ven

Copyright © 2004 Thankyou Music/adm. by worshiptogether.com songs excl. UK & Europe, adm. by Kingsway Music
tym@kingsway.co.uk Used by permission

73 Looking for your presence

Copyright © 2000 Thankyou Music/Adm. by worshiptogether.com songs excl. UK & Europe, adm. by Kingsway Music
tym@kingsway.co.uk Used by permission.

Lyrics under the music:

-ty streets___ and homes.___ Car-ry-ing you,___ car-ry-ing you,___ _ we hear the foot - steps of_ the Lord.___ Can your hea - vy___ glo - ry,___ can your hea - vy___ glo - ry,___ can your hea - vy___ glo - ry___ rest on___ me?___

73a My daily prayer

Lord, make my mind sensitive to you
Lord, make my heart in tune with yours
Lord, make my lips willing to move for you
Lord make my ears sensitive to you
Lord, make my will in tune with yours
Lord, make my feet willing to move for you
Lord, make my hands open to you.

Copyright © 1998 Ruth Sermon

74 Lord, I come before your throne
(What a faithful God have I)

Capo 2 (A)

Robert & Dawn Critchley

Copyright © 1989 Thankyou Music/Adm. by worshiptogether.com songs excl. UK & Europe, adm. by Kingsway Music
tym@kingsway.co.uk Used by permission

God have I,— faith-ful— in ev-'ry way.

3. Lord all sov-'reign, grant-ing peace from heav'n, let me

com-fort those— who suf-fer with the com-fort you— have giv'n. I will

tell of your— great love for as long as I live, sing-ing

what a faith - ful God have I. What a faith - ful

Lord of all creation
(God of wonders)

75

Capo 1(G)

Marc Byrd
& Steve Hindalong

With praise

1. Lord of all cre-a-tion, of wa-ter, earth and sky, the hea-vens are your ta-ber-na-cle; glo-ry to the Lord on high.

2. Ear-ly in the morn-ing I will ce-le-brate the light, and as I stum-ble in the dark-ness I will call your name by night.

God of won-ders be-yond our ga-la-xy, you are ho-ly, ho-ly; the u-ni-verse de-clares your ma-je-sty. You are

Copyright © 2000 New Spring Publishing/Never Say Never Songs/Meaux Mercy/Storm Boy Music. For Europe: Unisong Music Publishers, Holland.

76 Lord, turn your footsteps

Copyright (c) 2002 Whitefield Music UK/Adm. by Copycare, P.O.Box 77, Hailsham, East Sussex, BN27 3EF, UK
music@copycare.com Used by permission.

177

Lord of the church

Words: Timothy Dudley-Smith
Music: Irish traditional melody
Arr. Christopher Norton

77

Lyrically ♩ = 108

Lyrics (verses):

1. Lord of the church, we pray for our re-new-ing: ___ Christ o-ver all, our un-di-vi-ded aim. ___ Fire of the Spi-rit, burn for our en-

Lord of the church, we seek a Fa-ther's bless-ing, ___ a true re-pen-tance and a faith re-stored, ___ a swift o-be-dience and a new pos-

Lord of the church, we long for our u-nit-ing, ___ true to one call-ing, by one vi-sion stirred; ___ one cross pro-claim-ing and one creed re-

Words copyright © Timothy Dudley-Smith, 9 Ashlands, Ford, Salisbury, Wilts., England SP4 6DY in the countries of Europe (including Great Britain and Ireland) and of Africa. Music: Irish Trad melody arr. Christopher Norton © HarperCollins Religious/Adm CopyCare P.O. Box 77, Hailsham, East Sussex, BN27 3EF, UK. music@copycare.com Used by permission

(continued over...)

78

Lord, you are good

Israel Houghton

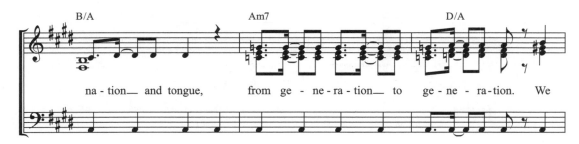

(continued over...)

This song is recorded on the Spring Harvest 2004 Live Worship Album

Copyright © 2001 Integrity's Praise! Music/Sovereign Music UK, P.O. Box 356, Leighton Buzzard, LU7 3WP, UK. sovereignmusic@aol.com &
Champions for Christ Publishing, published by Champions For Christ Publishing/Integrated Copyright Group, administered by Kobalt Music Group.

worship you,___ halleluja, halleluja. We

worship you,___ for who you___ are.___ We

worship you,___ halleluja, halleluja. We

worship you,___ for who you___ are.___

Repeat x 4 then D.C.

And you are___ good.___

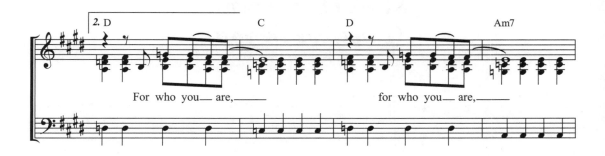

78a Opposites attract

Heavenly Father,
you are my strength in times of weakness,
you are my joy in times of sadness,
you are my comfort in times of distress,
you are my peace in times of unrest,
you are my rock when I feel insecure,
you are my river when I feel unclean,
you are my food when I cry of hunger,
you are my doctor when I feel sick,
you are my warmth when I feel cold,
you are my shelter in the storm.
You really are an awesome God.

Father, thank you for always being there when I need you,
I pray that you will make me aware of your presence more clearly
and help me to walk in the light of your love
today, tomorrow and always.
I thank you in the name of Jesus.
Amen

Copyright © 2004 Allister Walker

79

Most Holy Father
(*I believe in you*)

Chris Eaton
& John Hartley

Calmly

1. Most Ho-ly Fa-ther, I come to you, know-ing that
2. Thank-ful, so thank-ful, I come to you, know-ing that

you a-lone, you can make me whole.
you a-lone have made a way for me.

My pre-cious Je-sus, I long for you to make my heart a
Faith-ful, so faith-ful you are to me. Stead-fast and cer-

dwell-ing place for your love. For you a-lone are
tain is your love.

ho-ly, boun-ti-ful in mer-cy, for-e-ver you are wor-thy to re-ceive the glo-

Copyright © 2004 West Lodge Music & Here's to JO Music/Adm. by JO Music Services admin. SGO Music Publishing Ltd & Thankyou Music/Adm.
by worshiptogether.com songs excl. UK & Europe, adm. by Kingsway Music. tym@kingsway.co.uk Used by permission

80
My troubled soul
(Praise the mighty name of Jesus)

Capo 3 (G)

Robert Critchley

Gently

My— trou-bled soul, why so weighed down? You were— not made—

to bear— this hea-vy load.— Cast all your bur - dens up-on— the Lord;—

Je-sus cares, he cares— for you.— Je-sus cares,—

he cares for you.— And all your wor-ry-ing—won't help you make— it through..

Copyright © 2001 Thankyou Music/Adm. by worshiptogether.com songs excl. UK & Europe, adm. by Kingsway Music
tym@kingsway.co.uk Used by permission

(continued over...)

how you so ea-si-ly—for-get___ to cast—your bur - dens up-on— the Lord._

D.S. al Fine

Je-sus cares, he cares— for you.___ I will

80a God is with us

Isaiah 43:1–3

But now, this is what the Lord says – he who created you, O Jacob, he who formed you, O Israel:

Fear not, for I have redeemed you;
I have summoned you by name; you are mine.
When you pass through the waters, I will be with you;
and when you pass through the rivers, they will not sweep over you.
When you walk through the fire, you will not be burned;
the flames will not set you ablaze.
For I am the Lord your God, the Holy One of Israel, your Saviour.

Mysteriously

81

Mark Tedder

1. My - ste - ri - ous - ly, you came to earth___ and
2. Jea - lous - ly, you want our lives,___ for
3. lu - sive - ly, you___ speak,___ and

walked u - pon___ the soil___ of bro - ken men.___
you and you___ a - lone___ are my de - sire.___
all cre - a - tion waits___ at your com - mand.

In - ti - mate - ly, you em - braced___ our
Ten - der - ly, you sing a song,___ a
De - li - cate - ly, you take a - way___ the

hearts so we could live___ for - e - ver. We can
me - lo - dy_ of love_ that cap - tures me.___
sin that se - pa - rates___ us from your light.

(continued over...)

CCLI No: 4448529. Copyright © 2004 Mark Tedder

81a Post Communion prayer
for Palm Sunday

Lord Jesus Christ, you humbled yourself in taking the form of a
servant, and in obedience died on the cross for our salvation:
give us the mind to follow you and to proclaim you as Lord and King,
to the glory of God the Father.
Amen

From Common Worship: Services and Prayers for the Church of England. Copyright © The Archbishops' Council 2000

Name of all majesty

82

Capo 3 (G)

Building in strength

Words: Timothy Dudley-Smith
Music: Joel Payne

1. Name of all ma-je-sty,— fa-thom-less my-ste-ry,—
2. Child of our de-sti-ny,— God from e-ter-ni-ty,—
3. Sa-viour of Cal-va-ry,— cost-li-est vic-to-ry,—
4. Source of all sov-'reign-ty,— light, im-mor-ta-li-ty,—

King of the a-ges— by an-gels a-dored;
love of the Fa-ther— on sin-ners— out-poured;
dark-ness de-fea-ted— and E-den re-stored;
life e-ver-last-ing— and hea-ven— as-sured;

pow'r and au-tho-ri-ty,— splen-dour and dig-ni-ty,—
see now what God has done— send-ing his on-ly Son,—
born as a man to die,— nailed to a cross on high,—
so with the ran-somed, we— praise him e-ter-nal-ly,—

bow to his ma-ste-ry, Je-sus— is Lord! Je-sus— is
Christ the be-lo-ved—One, Je-sus— is Lord!
cold in the grave to— lie, Je-sus— is Lord!
Christ in his ma-je-sty, Je-sus— is Lord!

Words © copyright Timothy Dudley-Smith, 9 Ashlands, Ford, Salisbury, Wilts., England SP4 6DY in the countries of Europe (including Great Britain and Ireland) and of Africa. Music copyright © 2003 Joel Payne/Belfrey Music, 11/12 Minster Yard, York, YO1 7HH

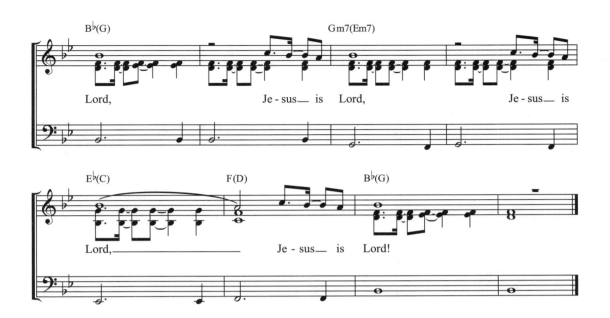

Lord, Je-sus— is Lord, Je-sus— is
Lord,_____ Je-sus— is Lord!

82a All knowing Lord

All knowing and ever present Lord,
who at various times has revealed your will through the prophets,
and who brought all things together for good
through your Son Jesus Christ.
Grant us wisdom to know the mysteries
that surround us in our current age, and turn our hearts
from disobedience to discernment.
Grant that we may be so fulfilled in doing your will
that we may withstand all temptation,
until you come again to reclaim the whole world.
By the power of Jesus Christ,
who is alive and reigns for ever.
Amen

Copyright © 2005 Marie Birkinshaw

None other

83

Steadily

Geraldine Latty

None o - ther is more wor - thy, none o - ther is more de - serv-

ing of— our praise.— None o - ther is so ho - ly, sov-'reign God—

_ we come— to you, we will give— the glo - ry due your name.—

None oth -

Copyright © 2002 Thankyou Music/Adm. by worshiptogether.com songs excl. UK & Europe, adm. by Kingsway Music
tym@kingsway.co.uk Used by permission.

On the shores of our doubt
(Riverwide)

Tré Sheppard

Simply

2. You are the one____ who un - der - stands,____ you lived down here,____

1. On the shores____ of____ our doubt,____ on the sands____

_ be - came a man,____ so we could hope____

_ of____ our pain____ we found____ a ri -

a - gain.____ Now take us to____ the ri - ver wide,____

- ver____ of grace,____ and it____ flows with____ your hope.____

(continued over...)

Copyright © 2004 Thankyou Music/Adm. by worshiptogether.com songs excl. UK & Europe, adm. by Kingsway Music
tym@kingsway.co.uk Used by permission

How can— it be— we found— such— love?—

Won't you come—— to the ri - ver?—

O come down——— and bring your—— pain.
O come down—— and find—— grace.

84a God go with us

God go with you
God go with us
Go with you into your comfortable places
God go with us
Go with you into your challenges
God go with us
Go with you into your futures
God go with us

Copyright © 2005 Nick Harding

85
O God, the God of blessing

Gareth Robinson

Driving rock style

1. O God, the God of bles - sing, the God of kind -
   sent your Son from glo - ry to be our Sa -
   sent your Ho - ly Spi - rit straight from hea -

- ness, the God of o - pen hear - ted love. God of grace
viour, to take on flesh and live like us. Now hea - ven's o -
ven, gua - ran - tee - ing what's to come: to be made whole

- and God of mer - cy, God of earth and heav'n a - bove.
pen, for - give - ness pur - chased on the al - tar of the cross;
- and be made ho - ly in the king - dom of your Son;

- God and Fa - ther of our Lord Je - sus Christ.
- now ex - al - ted as our Lord, Je - sus Christ.
- giv - ing glo - ry to our Lord, Je - sus Christ.

Copyright © 2004 Thankyou Music/Adm. by worshiptogether.com songs excl. UK & Europe, adm. by Kingsway Music
tym@kingsway.co.uk Used by permission

199

86

One day Lord

Capo 3 (D)

Tré Sheppard

1. One day, Lord,— I'll see— your face.—
2. One day, Lord,— I'll see— your face.—

One day, Lord,— I'll see— your face.—   And I'll
One day, Lord,— I'll see— your face.—   And I'll

(v.2)

sing of your glo - ry there.   in that ho - ly place,— in the
lay down my bur - dens,— I'm gon - na lay down these chains,— and my
(v.3) road is nar - row—   and the path is straight,— but the

ci - ty of peace,— there— with the sin - ners and saints.—
strug - gles all o - ver,— I'm gon - na walk through your gates.—
gates are wide o - pen— now by the hands— of grace.—   And I

Copyright © 2004 Thankyou Music/Adm. by worshiptogether.com songs excl. UK & Europe, adm. by Kingsway Music
tym@kingsway.co.uk Used by permission

201

87 Praise awaits you in this place today

Capo 2 (A)

Matt Redman

1. Praise a-waits you in this place to-day, O Lord.
2. Sea-sons come and sea-sons go but you re-main.

We are ga-thered, rea-dy, God, to sing your praise.
So un-chang-ing, all de-serv-ing of our praise.

Pre-chorus
Rea-dy to re-spond to the

glo-ries of your name, to the won-ders of your heart, to

Copyright © 2004 Thankyou Music/Adm. by worshiptogether.com songs excl. UK & Europe, adm. by Kingsway Music
tym@kingsway.co.uk Used by permission

won - ders— of your heart,   to

(to the won - ders— of your heart,)

your great love.——

your great love.——

87a A road back home

We are far from the village:
give us a road back home.
We are far from the friends we laughed with:
give us a road back home.
We are far from the well where we drew water:
give us a road back home.
We are far from the fire where we baked bread:
give us a road back home.
We are far from the house where we worshipped:
give us a road back home.
We are far, far away:
be our village, be our friend;
give us water, give us bread:
dwell among us and be our home – here in exile.

Copyright 2005 © Paul Sheppy

'Let them praise his name with dancing' (Psalm 149 v 3)

Tips for dancing in congregational worship

The primary purpose of dance in worship is to bring glory to God, to draw attention to his character and attributes; it can also be a personal expression of love and praise that others can share in. Dancers should first and foremost be worshippers, drawing attention away from themselves (and ourselves) and onto God. They are offering an abandoned sacrifice of praise which is pleasing in God's eyes.

Dance should bring members of the congregation into a deeper sense of worship, awe and wonder at God. It will visually lift and enhance the worship experience. Dancers need to have a close personal relationship with God and be open to the guidance of the Holy Spirit. Technique is not as important as humbleness and a heart to worship, glorify and please God.

It is helpful for dancers to meet, pray and plan with the worship leader and others responsible for planning the service. They should be encouraged to be open to dancing spontaneously and prophetically if the Holy Spirit should lead. Choreography can be prepared in advance as long as it is suitable for the moment. Dancers can move between prepared and spontaneous dance. Dancers can also experiment using flags, banners and ribbons.

Dance should be an encouragement and an aid to worship; not a distraction. Don't allow your movements to become too small or contained. Focus on thinking outwards and use the full space provided. It is not necessary to dance during every song. Be open to the Holy Spirit and to the direction of the leadership. Be sensitive and careful when waving banners or ribbons in close proximity to people!

88 Praise the Lord from the heavens
(Psalm 148)

Capo 3 (D)
Steady 3

Graham Kendrick

1. Praise the Lord, from the heavens, praise him from the skies. Praise the Lord, hosts of
   angels, sing celestial choirs. Praise him sun and moon, praise him shining stars, clouds that ride on the wind: let everything with

Lord, earth and oceans, creatures of the deep. Fire and hail, ice and hurricane, let the thunder speak. Beasts of forest, field and desert, every bird in the sky: from least of all to

all praise the one name worthy of all praise. Only God, our Creator from eternal days. All his excellence far outshining, all the worlds he has made: yet comes to us, de-

This song is recorded on the Spring Harvest 2004 Live Worship Album

Copyright © 2004 Make Way Music, P.O. Box 263, Croydon, CR9 5AP, UK. International copyright secured. All rights reserved. Used by permission.

88a Lord of the universe
Ephesians 4:10

He who descended is the very one who ascended higher
than all the heavens, in order to fill the whole universe.

89
Praises to the Holy One
(Let every voice)

With energy

Paul Oakley

Copyright © 2003 Thankyou Music/Adm. by worshiptogether.com songs excl. UK & Europe, adm. by Kingsway Music
tym@kingsway.co.uk Used by permission.

(continued over...)

Let e-vr'y heart___ burst in - to song,___ let e-v'ry word___ up-on___ my tongue___ de-clare___ the praise___ of who___ you___ are.___

89a I come before God

I come before God and realise how empty I am.
I come before God and realise how little I understand of him.
I come before God and realise how I rely on him for everything.
I come before God and know my need of him.

I come before God and smile as he gives me everything;
as he gives me himself!
God gives with joy and generosity!
God gives with abundance and eagerness that takes my breath away!
God gives; I receive.
I am truly blessed and eager to share this most holy and devoted God
with others who are empty.

Copyright © 2004 Ruth Sermon

Saviour I must sing

Kate Simmonds
& Mark Edwards

With strength

90

Verse

1. Sa - viour, I __ must sing __ of love that bore __ my sin __
2. I have seen __ the King, __ crowned with pow'r and ma -

__ for me. __ Free - ly wel - comed in __ with
- je - sty. __ My hope is set __ on him __ who

gifts of life __ and li - ber - ty, __ you let me rise __ with dig -
reigns with all __ au - tho - ri - ty. __ Now saved for all __ e - ter -

(v.2)

- ni - ty, __ and turn my shame __ in - to __ a shout __ of __ praise!
- ni - ty, __ let all who know his mer - cy give __ him __ praise!

(continued over...)

Copyright © 2004 Thankyou Music/Adm. by worshiptogether.com songs excl. UK & Europe, adm. by Kingsway Music
tym@kingsway.co.uk Used by permission

wrath of God___ is turned___ a - way.___ E - mul - ti -
all who call___ up - on___ your name.___ And

tudes will bow be-fore___ your throne___ and praise.___ Your righ-teous -

ness brings ma - ny sons___ to glo - ry.

D.S. al Coda ⊕ *Coda*

90a He can get no closer

God is within you –
he can get no closer.
We cannot distance ourselves from God physically,
the distance between us
is created by our attitude and our awareness.

God is surrounding our lives –
he can get no closer.
He touches all we touch,
he hears and sees all that happens to us,
he weeps and rejoices alongside us.

And so, be aware of God's presence each moment –
he can get no closer.

Copyright © 2002 Ruth Sermon

91

See, what a morning
(Resurrection hymn)

Stuart Townend
& Keith Getty

Victoriously

1. See,——— what a mor - ning, glo - rious-ly bright, with the
2. See——— Ma-ry weep-ing, 'Where——— is he laid?' As in
3. One——— with the Fa - ther, An - cient of Days, through the

dawn - ing of hope in Je - ru - sa - lem;
sor - row she turns from the emp - ty tomb;
Spi - rit who clothes faith with cer - tain-ty,

fold - ed the grave - clothes, tomb——— filled with light, as the
hears——— a voice speak - ing, call - ing her name; it's the
ho - nour and bles - sing, glo - ry and praise to the

an - gels an - nounce Christ is ris - en!
Ma - ster, the Lord raised to life a - gain!
King crowned with pow'r and au - tho - ri - ty!

This song is recorded on the Spring Harvest 2004 Live Worship Album

Copyright © 2003 Thankyou Music/Adm. by worshiptogether.com songs excl. UK & Europe, adm. by Kingsway Music
tym@kingsway.co.uk Used by permission.

See God's sal - va - tion— plan, wrought in love, borne in pain,— paid in
The voice that spans the— years, speak - ing life, stir - ring hope,— bring-ing
And we are raised with— him, death is dead, love has won,— Christ has

sa - cri - fice,____ ful - filled in Christ, the— man, for he
peace— to us,____ will sound till he ap - pears, for he
con - quered;____ and we shall reign with— him, for he

lives: Christ is ri - sen from the dead!____
lives, Christ is ri - sen from the dead!____
lives, Christ is ri - sen from the dead!____

1.,2.   *3.*

92 Spirit of the living God

Jo Puleston

♩ = 90

Chorus

Spi - rit of— the liv - ing God,— Spi - rit of— the liv - ing God,—

Spi - rit of— the liv - ing God,— fall a - fresh— on us,— we pray.—

fall a - fresh— on us,— we pray.— With con - fi - dence— we come— to— you, ap -

proach your throne, know - ing that— we're loved— by— you we draw near. With hu -

Copyright © 2004 Thankyou Music/Adm. by worshiptogether.com songs excl. UK & Europe, adm. by Kingsway Music
tym@kingsway.co.uk Used by permission

216

mi - li - ty— we come— to— you and seek your face, know-ing that— we're loved— by— you

we draw near to you._____

fall a - fresh— on us,— we pray.—

92a His glorious riches

Ephesians 3: 16–19

I pray that out of his glorious riches he may strengthen you with power through his Spirit in your inner being, so that Christ may dwell in your hearts through faith. And I pray that you, being rooted and established in love, may have power, together with all the saints, to grasp how wide and long and high and deep is the love of Christ, and to know this love that surpasses knowledge – that you may be filled to the measure of all the fulness of God.

93

Surely our God
(Revealer of mysteries)

David Lyle Morris
& Liz Morris

Moderately

Chorus

Sure - ly our— God is the God of— gods, and the Lord of— kings, the re-

veal - er of mys - te - ries. Sure - ly our— God is the God of— gods, and the

Lord of— kings, the re - veal-er of mys - ter - ies. *(Fine)*

1. He
2. I'll
3. Thank

Verse

chan - ges the times and the sea - sons, he gives rhy - thm to— the
praise— you al - ways my Fa - ther, you are Lord of hea - ven and
you— for send - ing your on - ly Son, we may know the my - st'ry of

Copyright © 2000 Thankyou Music/Adm. by worshiptogether.com songs excl. UK & Europe, adm. by Kingsway Music
tym@kingsway.co.uk Used by permission.

tides,   he   knows what is hid - den   in the   dark - est of pla - ces, brings the
earth.   You   hide——— your se - crets from the 'wise' and the lear - ned, and re-
God;   he o - pens the trea-sures of—— wis - dom and know - ledge to the

sha - dows   in - to his—— light.
veal them   to   this, your—— child.
hum - ble,   not   to   the—— proud.

93a Let us sing to the Lord

Let us come together to sing out to the Lord.
**We'll let our joy for him spill out in songs and shouts to our
mighty Saviour.**

We will thank him and lift up his name.
With songs, music and prayers we'll praise our wonderful Lord.

For our God is amazing, awesome and glorious.
He is the unrivalled King!

He holds planet earth in his palm and his name is stamped on
mountain peaks.
**The ocean depths are his; he called them into being and the land
he raised up.**

So, let us get on our knees in worship before him
**Let us put ourselves in our proper place,
kneeling at the feet of our Maker.**

For he is our God, our Lord
**And we are his precious children, those he gave his life to save.
Amen.**

Copyright © 2005 Mel Holden

94

Take us and break us
(I am not my own)

Russ Hughes

Copyright © 2001 Joshua Music Ltd/Admin by Daybreak Music Ltd, P.O. Box 2848, Eastbourne, BN20 7XP. All rights reserved. info@daybreakmusic.
co.uk International copyright secured. Used by permission

own,_____ but I am yours, O___ Lord.___ I am not__ my___

own,_____ but I am yours,_ O Lord:___ take me, O Lord.___

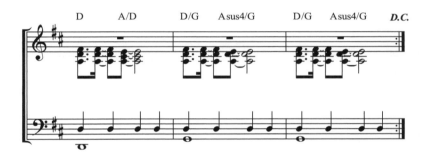

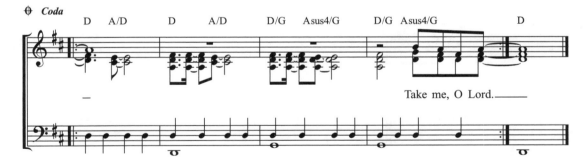

Take me, O Lord.___

95 The cross before me
(Not to us)

With a strong rock beat

Chris Tomlin
& Jesse Reeves

1. The cross be-fore me, the world be-hind; no turn-ing back, raise the ban-ner high: it's not for me, it's all for you.

2. Our hearts un-fold be-fore your throne, the on-ly place for those who know: it's not for us, it's all for you.

Let the hea-vens shake and split the sky, let the peo-ple clap their hands and cry: it's not for us, it's all for you.

Send your ho-ly fire on this of-fer-ing, let our wor-ship burn for the world to see: it's not for us, it's all for you.

Not to us,

Copyright © 2002 worshiptogether.com songs/Six Steps Music/Adm. Kingsway Music. tym@kingsway.co.uk
For the UK & Europe. Used by permission.

but to your name be the glo - ry. Not to us,

but to your name be the glo - ry.

- ry. The

earth is shak - ing, the moun - tains shout - ing: it's all for you.

The waves are crash - ing, the sun is ra - ging:

(continued over...)

96

The wonder of your cross

Robin Mark

♩ = 85

1. The won- der of your cross shall be our me- di- ta- tion,
2. To steal a- way at night, when they took down your bo- dy,
3. 4. Were hea- ven's prai- ses si- lent in those hours of dark- ness?

to ga- ther in that sha- dow as the sun went down,
with love and tears to leave you in a bor- rowed grave,
Your Ho- ly Spi- rit brood- ing 'round that emp- ty throne?

to weep with those who thought that you were leav-
to go with Ma- ry to that place they laid
Un- til the de- cla- ra- tion: 'he is ri-

(continued over...)

Copyright © 2004 Integrity's Hosanna! Music/Sovereign Music UK, PO Box 356, Leighton Buzzard, LU7 3WP, UK. sovereignmusic@aol.com

vic - t'ry— I've found.
(vic - t'ry— I've found;)

I'll come— to— the

won - der - ful cross,—
(won - der - ful cross,)

and my—

whole— life I— lay down.

227

97

The splendour of the King
(How great is our God)

Capo 3 (G)

Chris Tomlin, Jesse Reeves
& Ed Cash

This song is recorded on the Spring Harvest 2005 New Songs Album

Copyright © 2004 worshiptogether.com songs/Six Steps Music/Adm. by Kingsway Music. tym@kingsway.co.uk For the UK & Europe
and Alletrope Music/Music Services Adm. by CopyCare, P.O. Box 77, Hailsham, BN27 3EF, UK. Used by permission.

229

98
The world's shaking
(My glorious)

Martin Smith
& Stuart Garrard

1. The world's shak-ing with the love of God,
2. Clouds are break-ing, hea-ven's come to earth.

great and glo-rious, let the whole earth sing. And all
Hearts a-wake-ning, let the church bells ring.

_ you e-ver do_ is change_ the old_ for new._ Peo-ple,

we be-lieve that God_ is big-ger than_ the air_ I breathe,_ the world_ we'll

Copyright © 2000 Curious? Music UK. P.O. Box 40, Arundel, BN18 0UQ, UK. Rights administered by Bucks Music Group Ltd.

leave. God___ will save the day,___ and all___ will say:___ my glo-ri-

1. ous. ous. My glo-ri-

ous,___ my glo-ri-ous, my glo-ri-ous,___ my glo-ri-ous, my glo-ri-

ous,___ my glo-ri-ous, my glo-ri-ous,___ my glo-ri-ous. My glo-ri-

2. ous. *Last time* ous.

99

There is a higher throne

Keith & Kristyn Getty

1. There is a high-er throne than all this world has known, where
2. And there we'll find our home, our life be-fore the throne; we'll

faith-ful ones from e-very tongue will one day come.
ho-nour him in per-fect song, where we be-long.

Be-fore the Son we'll stand, made fault-less through the Lamb; be-
He'll wipe each tear-stained eye, as thirst and hun-ger die; the

liev-ing hearts find pro-mised grace, sal-va-tion comes.
Lamb be-comes our Shep-herd King, we'll reign with him.

Copyright © 2002 Thankyou Music/Adm. by worshiptogether.com songs excl. UK & Europe, adm. by Kingsway Music
tym@kingsway.co.uk Used by permission.

Hear hea-ven's voi-ces—sing, their thun-derous an-them—rings; through
em - erald courts and sap - phire skies their prai - ses rise.
All glo - ry, wis - dom,—power, strength, thanks and ho - nour— are to
God, our King who reigns on high for e - ver - more.

99a Refuge in the Lord
Psalm 118: 7–9

The Lord is with me; he is my helper.
I will look in triumph on my enemies.
It is better to take refuge in the Lord than to trust in humanity.
It is better to take refuge in the Lord than to trust in princes.

100

There's a lot of pain
(Outrageous grace)

Slowly

Godfrey Birtill

1. There's a lot of pain,— but a lot more heal - ing,—
   lot of fear,— but a lot more free - dom;—

- there's a lot of trou - ble,— but a lot more peace.
- there's a lot of dark - ness,— but a lot more light.

There's a lot of hate,— but a lot more lov - ing,—
There's a lot of cloud,— but a lot more vi - sion;—

- there's a lot of sin,— but a lot more grace.—
- there's a lot of pe - rish-ing,— but a lot more life.—

Chorus

- Oh, out - ra - geous grace!— Oh, out - ra - geous grace!— Love un-
-   Through my

Copyright © 2000 Thankyou Music/Adm. by worshiptogether.com songs excl. UK & Europe, adm. by Kingsway Music
tym@kingsway.co.uk Used by permission.

235

101 Though I've seen troubles

Verse

1. Though I've seen trou - bles, you will re - store my life a - gain. Though I've been woun - ded, and tas - ted bit - ter - ness from the depths of the earth, you al - ways bring me up a - gain, in - crease my ho - nour, and com - fort me. Thank

- ments you breathe en - cou - rage - ment and hope. My lack of wis - dom you've of - ten o - ver - looked. Blown a - way by your grace and by the po - wer in the blood I grow in free -

Verse 1.

Copyright © 2003 Whitefield Music UK/Adm. by Copycare, P.O.Box 77, Hailsham, East Sussex, BN27 3EF, UK
music@copycare.com Used by permission.

101a High Priestly prayer
Numbers 6:24–26

The Lord bless you and keep you;
the Lord make his face shine upon you and be gracious to you;
the Lord turn his face towards you and give you peace.

102 There is no god above you
(Most holy)

Miriam Webster

Capo 3 (G)

Slow ♩ = 75

1. There is no god above you, there is no other like you; Jesus, in you alone is righteousness and strength.

2. Faithful in all your ways, exalted above all names, desire of e-

3. All nations shall come worship, for you alone are holy. Who would not fear

This song is recorded on the Spring Harvest 2005 New Songs Album

Copyright © 2003 Miriam Webster/Hillsong Publishing/Kingsway Music. tym@kingsway.co.uk For the UK. Used by permission

(continued over...)

240

103

We are a shining light
(Do something beautiful)

Graham Kendrick

1. We are a shin-ing light, ci-ty on a hill that can't be hid-den,
2. We are the salt of the earth, here to pu-ri-fy and fla-vour,

a shin-ing light. And this shin-ing light
salt of the earth. Sent through all the earth

is the life of Je-sus in us, oh what a light! The fire of his
to love God and love our neigh-bour, salt of the earth. As free-ly as

Spi-rit burns with jus-tice, joy and peace
we re-ceived so free-ly we must give,

(continued over...)

Copyright © 2003 Make Way Music, P.O Box 263, Croydon, CR9 5AP, UK International copyright secured. All rights reserved. Used by permission.

and works through our hands and feet.
and we are his hands and feet.

Chorus

Go do some-thing beau-ti-ful, in the name of Je-sus

do some-thing beau-ti-ful. Go do some-thing Je-sus would,

do some-thing beau-ti-ful, do some-thing

beau-ti-ful. do some-thing beau-ti-ful.

103a Body of Christ
From 1 Corinthians 12:27

Now you are the body of Christ, and each one of you is a part of it.
We are the body of Christ

104 We come to be with you today

Gareth Robinson

Copyright © 2004 Thankyou Music/adm. by worshiptogether.com songs excl. UK & Europe, adm. by Kingsway Music
tym@kingsway.co.uk Used by permission

105

We have come into this place
(King of kings)

Capo 3 (D)

Russ Hughes
& Simon Goodall

Verse

1. We have come into this place to lift our hearts to worship Jesus, he alone deserves the praise, an anthem of our love that pleases. May our praise be the sweetest sound, rising up let the earth re-

2. We have come into this place to shout aloud the name of Jesus. Ev'ry pow'r and authority surrender to the name of Jesus. May our praise be a battle sound, rising up let the earth re-

This song is recorded on the Spring Harvest 2005 New Songs Album

Copyright © 2004 Joshua Music Ltd/Admin. by Daybreak Music Ltd. PO Box 2848, Eastbourne, BN20 7XP. All rights reserved.
info@daybreakmusic.co.uk International copyright secured. Used by permission.

(continued over...)

106
We have heard the thunder
(King)

Capo 3 (G)

John Ellis

♩ = 144

Verse

1. We have heard— the thun - der, and we have seen— the storm,—
(2.) now we walk— in dark - ness, though now we see— in part,—

_ e - choes of— your king - dom come, and—
_ right now we're warmed— by the burn - ing flames— of the

ru - mours of— our home,— where one day we— will stand
fi - re in— our hearts.— You've pro - mised you— will lead

_ be - fore— you, Lord;— our al - to - ge - ther beau-
_ us to— your throne— where we will wor - ship you—

(continued over...)

Copyright © 2003 Mouthfulofsongs/Birdwing Music/Near Bliss Music. All rights administered by EMI Christian Music Publishing.
For Europe: Unisong Music Publishers, Holland.

250

107 We have sung our songs of victory
(How long?)

Stuart Townend

Thoughtfully

Verse

1. We have sung our songs of vic - tory, we have
2. Lord, we know your heart is bro - ken by the
3. But I know a day is com - ing when the

prayed to you for rain; we have cried for your com - pas - sion to re -
e - vil that you see, and you've stayed your hand of judge - ment for you
deaf will hear his voice, when the blind will see their Sa - viour, and the

new the land a - gain. Now we're stand - ing in your pre - sence, more
plan to set men free. But the land is still in dark - ness, and we've
lame will leap for joy. When the wi - dow finds a hus - band who will

hun - gry than be - fore; now we're on your steps of mer - cy, and we're
fled from what is right; we have failed the si - lent chil - dren who will
al - ways love his bride, and the or - phan finds a fa - ther who will

Copyright © 1997 Thankyou Music/Adm. by worshiptogether.com songs excl. UK & Europe, adm. by Kingsway Music
tym@kingsway.co.uk Used by permission.

knock - ing at__ your door.__ How long_____ be - fore__ you
ne - ver see__ the light.__ *(Final chorus)*
ne - ver leave__ her side.__ *How long_____ be - fore__ your*

drench the bar - ren land?__ How long_____ be - fore__ we
glo - ry lights__ the skies?__ How long_____ be - fore__ your

see your right - eous hand?__ How long_____ be - fore__ your
ra - diance lifts__ our eyes?__ How long_____ be - fore__ your

name is lift - ed high?__ How long_____ be - fore__ the
fra - grance fills__ the air?__ How long_____ be - fore__ the

weep - ing turns__ to songs__ of joy?
earth re - sounds__ with songs__ of joy?

We have nothing to give
(Breathing the breath)

108

Matt Redman

1. We have no-thing to give that did-n't first come from your hand,
2. Who has gi-ven to you that it should be paid back to him?

we have no-thing to of-fer you which you did not pro-vide.
Who has gi-ven to you as if you need-ed a-ny-thing?

E-v'ry good, per-fect gift comes from your kind and gra-cious heart, and all_
From you and to you and through you come all things, O Lord, and all_

_ we do_ is give back_ to you_ what al - ways has_ been yours._
_ we do_ is give back_ to you_ what al - ways has_ been yours._

Copyright © 2004 Thankyou Music/Adm. by worshiptogether.com songs excl. UK & Europe, adm. by Kingsway Music
tym@kingsway.co.uk Used by permission

(continued over...)

breath - ing— the breath— that you gave us— to breathe,— we are

breath - ing— the breath— that you gave us— to breathe.—

Lord, we're

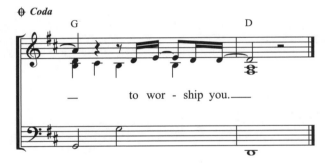

— to wor - ship you.—

108a God, you transform your people

God, you transform your people
God, you transform your people

God, you transform your church
God, you transform your church

God, transform us
God, transform us

God, transform me
God, transform me

Copyright © 2005 Nick Harding

109 Welcomed in to the courts of the King
(Facedown)

Capo 5 (Am)

Matt & Beth Redman

Steadily, with reverence

1. Wel - comed in ___ to the courts of the King, ___ I've been
2. There is none ___ in the hea - vens like you, ___ and up -

u - shered in ___ to your pre - sence. ___ Lord, I stand ___ on your
on the earth, who's your e - qual? You are far a - bove, ___ you're the

mer - ci - ful ground, ___ yet with e - v'ry step ___ tread with
high - est of heights, ___ I am bow - ing down ___ to ex -

re - v'rence. ___

(continued over...)

This song is recorded on the Spring Harvest 2005 New Songs Album

Copyright © 2003 Thankyou Music/Adm. by worshiptogether.com songs excl. UK & Europe, adm. by Kingsway Music
tym@kingsway.co.uk Used by permission.

110

We sing your song
(*We are the people of God*)

Mark Tedder

1. We sing your song— when the pas - sion is fad - ing,
2. We sing your song— when the world— is chang - ing,
3. We sing your song— in the still - ness of night,—

we sing your song— in a thir - sty land,— and
we sing your song when we don't un - der-stand.—
we sing your song when the fu - ture's un - cer - tain,

we sing your song— when— dark - ness sur-rounds,— we sing your song
We sing your song— when the bat - tle is rag - ing, we sing your song
we sing your song— with a cry and a whis - per, we sing your song

o - ver and o - ver. And we are the peo - ple of God, hum - bled— and in

CCLI No: 4442233. Copyright © 2004 Mark Tedder

261

111 We stand and lift up our hands
(Holy is the Lord)

Chris Tomlin & Louie Giglio

With praise ♩ = 84

We stand and lift up our hands,_____ for the joy___ of the Lord___ is our strength._

_ We bow down___ and wor - ship him now;___ how great,_

_ how awe - some is he.____ And to-ge-ther we___ sing,_____

e - v'ry - one____ sing:_____ ho - ly is___ the Lord_

Copyright © 2003 worshiptogether.com songs/Sixsteps music adm. by Kingsway Music
tym@kingsway.co.uk For the UK & Europe. Used by permission

-ing up—— all—— a-round;— it's the an - them of—— the Lord's—

1. D **2.** D *D.S. al Coda*

—— re-nown.— It is ris - —— re-nown.— And to-ge-ther we— sing—

Coda Esus4 F#m7 D2 Esus4

— ry,—— the earth—— is filled— with his glo - ry.——

111a   Give hope to us

God who gave hope to your people
Give hope to your church

God who gave hope to your exiles
Give hope to your servants

God who gave hope to your leaders
Give hope to us

Copyright © 2005 Nick Harding

112 What shall I bring
(Love mercy)

Capo 2 (A)

Andy Bromley

With energy

1. What shall I bring be-fore the Lord, and bow my
   Can I give you a thou-sand words, or please you
2. My life I bring be-fore the Lord, and bow my
   My love, more than a thou-sand words, my praise, more

knee be-fore my God?
with ten thou-sand songs?
knee be-fore my God;
than ten thou-sand songs:

Ex-tra-va-gant sa-cri-fice.

You have shown us what is good through the mes-sage of your Son.

Show jus-tice,

(continued over...)

This song is recorded on the Spring Harvest 2005 New Songs Album

Copyright © 2004 Thankyou Music/Adm. by worshiptogether.com songs excl. UK & Europe, adm. by Kingsway Music
tym@kingsway.co.uk Used by permission

266

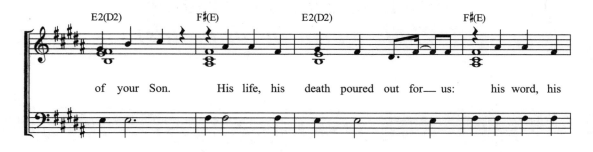

of your Son.   His life, his   death poured out for— us: his word, his

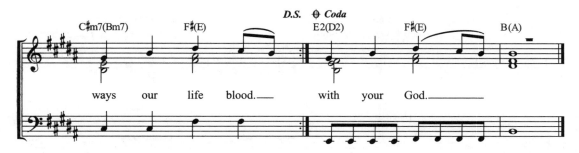

ways   our   life   blood.—   with   your   God.———

112a   Brought to perfection

Gracious and ever faithful God,
who, in Jesus, repeated the great commandments to love you
and to love our neighbour,
help us to obey your calling in a world
of continual change and uncertainty.
Keep us holy and renew our minds.
Enrich our hearts so that we may be brought to perfection
through Jesus Christ our Lord,
who is alive and reigns with you,
in the unity of the Holy Spirit, one God,
now and for ever.
Amen

Copyright © 2005 Marie Birkinshaw

113 When all around is fading
(Whole world in his hands)

Tim Hughes

1. When all a-round is fad - ing, and no-thing seems to last,
2. When I walk through fi - re, I will not be burned:

when each day is filled with sor - row, still I
when the waves come crash - ing round me, still I

know with all my heart: He's got the whole world in his hands,

he's got the whole world in his hands, I'll fear no e-

Copyright © 2004 Thankyou Music/Adm. by worshiptogether.com songs excl. UK & Europe, adm. by Kingsway Music
tym@kingsway.co.uk Used by permission

-vil, for you are with___ me, strong to de-li - ver, migh-ty to save.___

He's got the whole world in his hands.___

Tag

He's got the whole world in his hands.___

113a Living by faith
From Hebrews 11: 13–16

All these people were still living by faith when they died.
Lord help me to live by faith
They did not receive the things promised;
they only saw them and welcomed them from a distance.
Give me eyes of faith
If they had been thinking of the country they had left,
they would have had opportunity to return.
Instead, they were longing for a better country – a heavenly one.
Give me a heart of faith
Therefore God is not ashamed to be called their God,
for he has prepared a city for them.
May I, at the end, receive the goal of faith

114 When I look at the blood

Godfrey Birtill

Copyright © 2004 Thankyou Music/Adm. by worshiptogether.com songs excl. UK & Europe, adm. by Kingsway Music
tym@kingsway.co.uk Used by permission

115

When the sun's brightly shining
(Rest in his promise)

David Ruis

1. When the sun's bright-ly shin-ing, and it's
(2.) sun - light has fa - ded, and the
(3.) wars and the ru - mours are en -
(4.) hea - vens are o - pened, and you

touch - ing my face, and your fa - vour is
dark - ness' my friend, and the sor - rows are
cir - cling the earth, and your judge - ments are
ride like the wind, and your king - dom of

rest - ing, and it seems all is grace; I will
roll - ing, and the suf - f'ring just won't end.
fall - ing, and there's no - where to turn.
jus - tice, it will come with - out end.

lift up my eyes and give glo - ry to your name and I'll

Copyright © 2003 Vineyard Songs Canada/Adm. CopyCare, P.O. Box 77, Hailsham, East Sussex, BN27 3EF, UK
music@copycare.com Used by permission

273

116

Where do I go
(My help)

Mark Beswick
& Howard Francis

Capo 3 (D)

Copyright © 2003 Thankyou Music/Adm. by worshiptogether.com songs excl. UK & Europe, adm. by Kingsway Music
tym@kingsway.co.uk Used by permission.

whence com - eth my strength,_____ my help com - eth from the

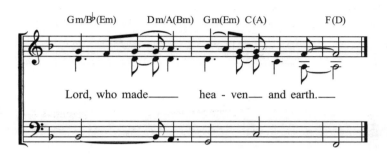

Lord, who made_____ hea - ven_ and earth._

116a On making time for prayer

Take no care what folk may say.
Put aside some time to pray.
Gently knock on heavens door.
There you'll find what living's for.

Look for peace and true content.
Let yourself an offering be,
giving praise eternally.

Know Christ's power at work in you,
may his Spirit fill you through.
Show God's glory and his worth,
be his image here on earth.

Copyright © 2005 Marie Birkinshaw

Where O where's your presence O God?

117

Steady 4

Godfrey & Gill Birtill,
Geraldine Latty & Tim Lomax

1. Where, oh where's your pre-sence, O God,— in this dry and wea-ry land?_____ So ma-ny peo-ple drift-ing a-way;— how we need to un-der-stand_____ you're still God, e-ven when— we're un-be-liev-ing, still— God, when we're

2. Where, oh where's your king-dom, O God?_ We have let ho-li-ness go._____ So ma-ny i-dols lit-ter our land.__ We've got to let this na-tion know_____ you're still God, when the go-vern-ment have— no an-swers, still— God, when the

3. When will Je-sus real-ly be seen— through the church that bears his name?_____ A-gents of his king-dom, his peace,— in the world for which he came,_____ you're still God. E-ven though— you were— re-jec-ted, still— God. Though you

Copyright © 2004 Thankyou Music/Adm. by worshiptogether.com songs excl. UK & Europe, adm. by Kingsway Music
tym@kingsway.co.uk Used by permission

des-p'rate for___ our___ heal - ing; still___ God, still___ God, still___ God,_____
me - dia lo - wers the stan - dard, still___ God, still___ God, still___ God,_____
were ri - di - culed, de - ser - ted, still___ God, still___ God, still___ God,_____

___ you're still God, e - ven when our friends___ de - sert___ us, still___
___ you're still God, when the plans we make___ are worth - less, still___
___ you're still God. Though you suf - fered e - xe - cu - tion, still___

God, e - ven through the things___ that hurt___ us, still___ God, still___
God, when we lose our sense___ of pur - pose, still___ God, still___
God. You're a - live and Christ___ our cham - pion, still___ God, still___

God. So I will_____ be still_____ and know you are God._____
God, so I will_____ be still_____ and know you are God._____
God, so I will_____ be still_____ and know you are God._____

118 Who can I trust but you alone?
(Countless are the mercies)

Leigh Barnard

This song is recorded on the Spring Harvest 2005 New Songs Album

Copyright © 2005 Daybreak Music Ltd, P.O. Box 2848, Eastbourne, BN20 7XP. All rights reserved. info@daybreakmusic.co.uk
International copyright secured. Used by permission.

You lead me by your cords of lov-ing kind - ness: Fa-ther, I will
trust in you a-lone. (Count-less are the)

Last time to Coda 𝄉

D.S. to repeat last chorus

rit. . .

𝄌 *Coda*

Fa - ther, I will trust in you a - lone.

118a Shepherd
From Psalm 23

All: **The Lord is my shepherd I shall not be in want.**

Leader: May the Lord lead you; spirit, soul and body, into peace

119 Worthy, you are worthy

Matt Redman

With a 'half time' feel

1. Wor-thy, you are wor-thy, much more wor-thy than I've known,—
2. Glo-ry, I give glo-ry to the one who saved my soul.— You

I can-not i-ma-gine just how glo-ri-ous you are.
found me and you freed me from the shame that was my own.

I can-not be-gin— to tell— how deep a love— you bring,—
I can-not be-gin— to tell— how mer-ci-ful— you've been,—

Lord, my ears have heard— of you— but now my eyes have seen.
Lord, my ears have heard— of you,— but now my eyes have seen.

2nd time to Chorus 2   Chorus 1

You're wor-thy, you're wor-thy, you're

Copyright © 1999 Thankyou Music/Adm. by worshiptogether.com songs excl. UK & Europe, adm. by Kingsway Music
tym@kingsway.co.uk Used by permission.

worthy, you're worthy to be praised, for - e - ver and a day. You're

e - ver and a day. You're worthy, you're worthy, you're
glory, your glory, your

worthy you're worthy to be praised, for - e - ver and a day. You're
glory, your glory reaches high, so high above the heav'ns. Your

worthy, you're worthy, you're worthy. You're worthy to be praised, for
glory, your glory, your glory, your glory reaches high, so

e - ver and a day. Your high a - bove the heav'ns.

120

Yet will I praise him

From Habakkuk 3

Geraldine Latty

Flowing celtic style

Chorus

Yet will I praise—him, I will lift my hands to my Re-deem-er. Yet will I
(Last chorus) Yes, I will praise—you, I will lift my hands to my Re-deem-er; yes, I will

praise—him, my Cre - a-tor and my Lord. Yet will I praise—him, I will
praise—you, my Cre - a-tor and my Lord. Yes, I will praise—you, I will

put my trust in my Pro-vi - der. Yet will I praise—him,——— my———
put my trust in my Pro-vi - der. Lord, I will praise—you,——— my———

Last time to Coda

Sa-viour and my God. 1. 'Tho the fruit tree does-n't
Sa-viour and my 2. When the night is o - ver -
3. Be the strength, Lord, in my

Copyright © 2001 Thankyou Music/Adm. by worshiptogether.com songs excl. UK & Europe, adm. by Kingsway Music
tym@kingsway.co.uk Used by permission.

282

blos - som 'tho no ri - pened grapes ap - pear, when the har - vest fails and
whelm - ing and the day is far from clear, when my heart is rest - less
weak - ness, let your song be in my night; be my rock when all a -

fields pro - vide no food;_____ I'll be joy - ful in my
for the peace of God;_____ let your word, Lord, through the
round is sink - ing sand._____ Be the light, Lord, in my

Sa - viour, the___ Lord who is my strength; he will keep my ways and
a - ges, be the word that now I hear; come, re - mind me once a -
dark - ness, be the vi - sion of my eyes: in my pas - sing days you

D.C. ⊕ Coda

lead me in his truth._____ God._____
gain to trust you, Lord._____
are the great 'I Am'._____

This is the Second Tune with slightly revised words December 2004

Original version December 14 2000

The phrase 'Yet will I praise him' and the lyrics for Verse 1 are
from Habakkuk 3 verses 17 - 19 NIV

121 You are the name
(Invocation)

Capo 3 (C)

♩ = 75

Chris O'Hara
Based on the prayer of St Simeon

1. You are the name—— that fills the soul with long-ing,
2. You are a love—— be-yond our un-der-stand-ing,
3. You are the hope—— that gives a sure foun-da-tion,
4. You are the my-ste-ry that walks be-side us,

you are the lan-guage be-yond all words: you are the wis-dom be-
you are the rais-ing of all who fall: you are the still-ness, who
you are the pro-mise of life be-yond: you are the one—— light, shine
you are as near—— as the air we breathe: you are Mes-si-ah, the

yond all know-ing;
moves with-in us;   come,   Je-sus, come!——
in our dark-ness;
one true Sa-viour;

Copyright © 2002 Chris O'Hara. Published by Viewpoint Resources Direct, Ltd. All rights reserved.

121a Post Communion prayer for Easter Day

God of Life, who for our redemption gave your only-begotten Son to the death of the cross, and by his glorious resurrection have delivered us from the power of our enemy: grant us so to die daily to sin, that we may evermore live with him in the joy of his risen life; through Jesus Christ our Lord.

From Common Worship: Services and Prayers for the Church of England. Copyright © The Archbishops' Council 2000

You are there

Capo 3 (D)

Lara Martin

Lara Martin (Abundant Life Ministries, Bradford, England). Copyright © 2003 Thankyou Music/Adm. by worshiptogether.com songs excl. UK & Europe, adm. by Kingsway Music. tym@kingsway.co.uk Used by permission.

123 You are the Lord, the famous one
(Famous one)

With excitement

Chris Tomlin
& Jesse Reeves

Lyrics:
You___ are the Lord,___ the fa-mous___ one, fa-mous___ one; great___ is your name in all___ the earth. The hea-vens de-clare___ you're glo-ri-ous,___ glo-ri-ous; great___ is your fame be-yond___ the earth.

Copyright © 2002 worshiptogether.com songs/Six Steps Music/admin. by Kingsway Music. tym@kingsway.co.uk
For the UK & Europe. Used by permission.

yet to do,___ with ev - 'ry breath,___ I'm
shin - ing through,___ and ev - 'ry eye___ is

_ prais - ing you. De - sire___ of na - tions___ and___
_ watch - ing you. Re - vealed___ by na - ture___ and___

_ ev - 'ry heart, you a - lone are God, you a -
_ mi - ra - cles you are___ beau - ti - ful, you are

1. And for all___ you've done___ and
2. The Morn - ing Star___ is

(continued over...)

289

lone are God.
beau - ti - ful.

Coda

the earth.

123a An Easter psalm of praise

Jesus Christ is risen!
Sound out his praise on this Easter Day.
Jesus Christ is risen!
He's the Saviour of the world.

Jesus Christ is risen!
Death holds no sting for our risen King.
Jesus Christ is risen!
He's the Saviour of the world.

Shout, 'Allelluia!
Alleluia to the Son of God!'
He's the King of kings, Lord of lords!
He's the Saviour of the world!

Shout, 'Alleluia!
Alleluia to the Son of God!'
He's the King of kings, Lord of lords!
He's the Saviour of the world!

Copyright © 2005 Marie Birkinshaw

You broke the night
(Take all of me)

Marty Sampson

(continued over...)

Copyright © 2003 Marty Sampson/Hillsong Publishing/Kingsway Music. tym@kingsway.co.uk For the UK. Used by permission.

292

love you___ so,___ and I give___ up my life___ to say___ I need___ you so,___ my e - v'ry - thing.___

124a Living with God
Psalm 84:10–12

Better is one day in your courts than a thousand elsewhere; I would rather be a doorkeeper in the house of my God than dwell in the tents of the wicked. For the Lord God is a sun and shield; the Lord bestows favour and honour; no good thing does he withhold from those whose walk is blameless.
O Lord Almighty, blessed is the man who trusts in you.

125 Your blood speaks a better word
(Nothing but the blood)

Matt Redman
Chorus inspiration: Nothing but the blood
by Robert Lowry (1876-1899)

This song is recorded on the Spring Harvest 2005 New Songs Album

Copyright © 2004 Thankyou Music/Adm. by worshiptogether.com songs excl. UK & Europe, adm. by Kingsway Music
tym@kingsway.co.uk Used by permission

What can make us whole again? Nothing but the blood,
Welcomed as the friends of God? Nothing but your blood,

nothing but the blood of Jesus. Jesus.
nothing but your blood King

2. Your Jesus.

125a Absolution

Almighty God, our heavenly Father, who in his great mercy
has promised forgiveness of sins to all those who with heartfelt
repentance and true faith turn to him:
have mercy on you, pardon and deliver you from all your sins,
confirm and strengthen you in all goodness, and bring you to
everlasting life, through Jesus Christ our Lord.
Amen

From Common Worship: Services and Prayers for the Church of England. Copyright © The Archbishops' Council 2000

126 Your love, O Lord, is like the oceans
(Highest)

Reuben Morgan

With a driving rhythm

Your love, O Lord, is like the oceans, dee-per
Your faith-ful-ness is like the moun - tains, and your

than end-less seas. Glo - ry to God,
word nev-er fails.

let e-v'ry heart sing; glo-ry to God in the high-

- est. Let us a-dore,

Copyright © 2002 Reuben Morgan/Hillsong Publishing/Kingsway Music. tym@kingsway.co.uk. For the UK. Used by permission.

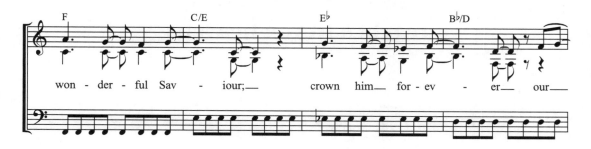

won - der - ful Sav - iour;— crown him— for - ev - er— our—

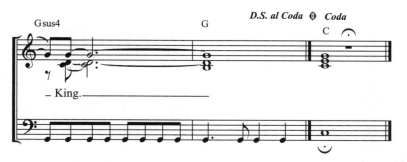

— King.

126a Confession

Father eternal, giver of light and grace, we have sinned against you
and against our neighbour, in what we have thought, in what we
have said and done, through ignorance, through weakness, through
our own deliberate fault.
We have wounded your love, and marred your image in us.
We are sorry and ashamed, and repent of all our sins.
For the sake of your Son Jesus Christ, who died for us, forgive us
all that is past; and lead us out from darkness to walk as children of
light.
Amen

From Common Worship: Services and Prayers for the Church of England. Copyright © The Archbishops' Council 2000

127

Your love, oh Lord, reaches to the heavens

Tim Burnage

Copyright © 2003 Tim Burnage/Belfrey Music, 11/12 Minster Yard, York, YO1 7HH

128 Your mind is so much higher
(Your love)

Dan Wheeler

1. Your mind is so much high-er than mine, you
2. Your words are so much wi-ser than mine, they

think in ways that I can't com - pre-hend.
ne - ver fail to light the road a - head.

My life is safe with the Lord of all time, so
My hope is safe cos I know you don't lie,

I don't have to fear the fu - ture. Your love

rea-ches to the hea - vens, your love ne - ver ends and

This song is recorded on the Spring Harvest Distinctive Sounds – Glory Album

Copyright © Dan Wheeler 2002 Authentic Publishing/Admin by CopyCare, P.O. Box 77, Hailsham, East Sussex, BN27 3EF, UK. music@copycare. com Used by permission

I close — my eyes — and hear — you sing-ing o - ver me; —

so I sing with you, I sing for you, I sing

with you, I sing for you.

℗ Coda

Your love rea - ches me. —

302

129 Your name is highly exalted
(Name above all names)

Tim Hughes

1. Your name is high-ly ex-al-ted, Jesus, for-ever be glo-ri-fied, for-ever be glo-ri-fied. Your name has pow-er to con-quer, your fame re-sounds through-out hea-ven and earth, re-

2. Ru-lers will one day be si-lent, lost in the won-der and awe of your name, the won-der and awe of your name. E-ter-nal, none is your e-qual. We cry: 'no o-ther God but you,

(continued over...)

This song is recorded on the Spring Harvest 2004 Live Worship Album

Copyright © 2003 Thankyou Music/Adm. by worshiptogether.com songs excl. UK & Europe, adm. by Kingsway Music
tym@kingsway.co.uk Used by permission.

130 Your voice has stilled the raging storms
(Beauty of your peace)

Tim Hughes
Chorus words: John Greenleaf Whittier (d. 1892)

Copyright © 2004 Thankyou Music/Adm. by worshiptogether.com songs excl. UK & Europe, adm. by Kingsway Music
tym@kingsway.co.uk Used by permission

store our— souls,— and all our earth - ly striv - ings come to cease. Take
store our— souls,— and all our earth - ly striv - ings come to cease.

Chorus

from our souls the strain and stress, and let our or-dered lives con - fess the

beau - ty of your peace, the beau - ty of your peace.

130a Deep peace

Deep peace of the running wave to you.
Deep peace of the flowing air to you.
Deep peace of the quiet earth to you.
Deep peace of the shining stars to you.
Deep peace of the Son of peace to you.

Fiona Macleod
Copyright © Northumbria Community Trust Ltd, Hetton Hall, Chatton, Northumberland, NE66 5SD.

Guitar Chords

Introduction

A good chord vocabulary is essential for a guitarist to feel confident when playing in worship, especially when the situation may involve reading a previously unseen piece of music or picking up a song quickly by ear. The chords on these pages are arranged in 'families' according to key. This is a beneficial way of remembering chords as most songs stick to these groupings. For each key, the first row shows the simplest form of each chord and the second line gives a more interesting substitution. The third line shows the chords most commonly used by guitarists derived by keeping some sort of pedal tone ringing in each chord and the fourth line shows inverted chords with an alternate bass note.

Also included are the Roman Numerals and Nashville Numbers associated with each chord. If you've not come across these before, they are simply an easy way of numbering each chord within a key. This is useful as it means you can take any chord progression in one key and instantly transpose it to another. Furthermore you can try out any of the chords in each column that corresponds to the relevant Roman Numeral and see if there is chord type or inversion which still fits but adds a different flavour. Experimentation like this may open up creative chord progressions that serve as a catalyst to help you to worship in fresh ways or to write new songs.

Please see the CD-ROM section of Spring Harvest Distinctive Sounds – More than a Song album and the Academy of Music Ministry's website at www.nexustrust.co.uk for details of more material relating to developing these skills.

Roman	I	II	III	IV	V	VI	VII
Nashville	1	2	3	4	5	6	7
3-note chord (triad)	C	Dm	Em	F	G	Am	Bdim
4-note chord	C maj7	D m7	E m7	F maj7	G7	A m7	B m7♭5
Alternative substitute	C	D7sus4	E m7	F sus2	G5	A m7	Dsus4/B
Alternative bass note	C/E	Dm/F	Em/G	F/A	F/G	Am/E	

Key of C

For all chords in the key of C♯ or D♭, use the chords from the key of C with capo 1

Guitar Chords

Roman	I	II	III	IV	V	VI	VII
Nashville	1	2	3	4	5	6	7

Key of D

	I	II	III	IV	V	VI	VII
3-note chord (triad)	D	Em	F#m	G	A	Bm	C#dim
4-note chord	Dmaj7	Em7	F#m7	Gmaj7	A7	Bm7	C#m7♭5
Alternative substitute	Dsus2	Em9	F#m7	G6sus2	A7sus4	Bm11	Aadd9/C#
Alternative bass note	D/F#	Em/B	F#m/A	G/B	G/A	Bm/F#	

For all chords in the key of D# or E♭, use the chords from the key of D with capo 1

Key of E

	I	II	III	IV	V	VI	VII
3-note chord (triad)	E	F#m	G#m	A	B	C#m	D#dim
4-note chord	Emaj7	F#m7	G#m7	Amaj7	B7	C#m7	D#m7♭5
Alternative substitute	E5	F#m11	G#madd♭6	Aadd9	Badd4	C#m7	D#alt
Alternative bass note	E/G#	F#m/C#	G#m/D#	A/C#	A/B	C#m/G#	

For all chords in the key of F, use the chords from the key of E with capo 1

For all chords in the key of F# or G♭, use the chords from the key of E with capo 2

Guitar Chords

Roman	I	II	III	IV	V	VI	VII
Nashville	1	2	3	4	5	6	7

Key of G

	I	II	III	IV	V	VI	VII
3-note chord (triad)	G	Am	Bm	C	D	Em	F#dim
4-note chord	Gmaj7	Am7	Bm7	Cmaj7	D7	Em7	F#m7♭5
Alternative substitute	G	A7sus4	Dsus4/B	Cadd9	Dsus4	Em7	G/F#
Alternative bass note	G/D	Am/C	Bm/D	C/G	C/D	Em/G	

For all chords in the key of G# or A♭, use the chords from the key of G with capo 1

Key of A

	I	II	III	IV	V	VI	VII
3-note chord (Triad)	A	Bm	C#m	D	E	F#m	G#dim
4-note chord	Amaj7	Bm7	C#m7	Dmaj7	E7	F#m7	G#m7♭5
Alternative substitute	Asus2	Bsus4	C#m7	D6sus2	Eadd9	F#m11	Eadd9/G#
Alternative bass note	A/E	Bm/F#	C#m/E	D/A	D/E	F#m/A	

For all chords in the key of A# or B♭, use the chords from the key of A with capo 1

For all chords in the key of B, use the chords from the key of A with capo 2

Richard Stephenson & Andy Flannagan

310

Scripture Index

Scripture Index cont'd

Philippians cont'd

Colossians

1 Thessalonians

2 Thessalonians

1 Timothy

2 Timothy

Titus

Hebrews

James

1 Peter

1 John

Revelation

Thematic Index

Thematic Index cont'd

Thematic Index cont'd

Unity

Spoken worship Index

TWENTY songs from this book
TWO top quality CDs

Spring Harvest's New Songs album for 2005/06 is a
double CD, featuring twenty songs. One CD gives the
familiar full treatment – rich arrangements of new worship
songs. On the second CD, the same production team
offers simple acoustic arrangements of more new songs.

It's an album that shows how the songs we fall in love with
at major events can be successfully translated into a smaller
setting. Home groups will be able to use the acoustic tracks
to sing along to, as they use simple vocals and guitar or
piano accompaniment. Local church bands will be able
to better interpret today's most powerful worship songs.

Available from your local Christian bookshop
or direct from Spring Harvest.

www.springharvest.org/resources